SABTAGE

THE MISSION TO DESTROY HITLER'S ATOMIC BOMB

NEAL BASCOMB

ARTHUR A. LEVINE BOOKS
AN IMPRINT OF SCHOLASTIC INC.

Library of Congress Cataloging-in-Publication Data

Names: Bascomb, Neal, author.
Title: Sabotage : the mission to destroy Hitler's atomic bomb / Neal Bascomb.
Description: First edition. | New York : Arthur A. Levine Books, an imprint
   of Scholastic Inc., 2016. | Includes bibliographical references and index.
Identifiers: LCCN 2015043455 | ISBN 9780545732437 (hardcover : alk. paper)
Subjects: LCSH: World War, 1939-1945—Commando operations—Norway—
   Juvenile literature. | World War, 1939-1945—Underground
   movements—Norway—Juvenile literature. | Sabotage—Norway—History—20th
   century—Juvenile literature. | Atomic bomb—Germany—History—Juvenile
   literature. | World War, 1939-1945—Germany—Technology—Juvenile
   literature.
Classification: LCC D794.5 .B37 2016 | DDC 940.54/864109481--dc23 LC record
available at http://lccn.loc.gov/2015043455

10 9 8 7 6 5 4 3 2 1   16 17 18 19 20

Printed in the U.S.A.   23

First edition, June 2016

To those who brave the fight
—N.B.

TABLE OF CONTENTS

LIST OF PARTICIPANTS

OPERATION GROUSE

Einar Skinnarland

Jens-Anton Poulsson, leader of Grouse

Claus Helberg

Knut Haugland, radio operator

Arne Kjelstrup

OPERATION GUNNERSIDE

Joachim Rønneberg, leader of Gunnerside

Knut Haukelid

Birger Strømsheim

Fredrik Kayser

Kasper Idland

Hans Storhaug

D/F *HYDRO* SINKING

Rolf Sørlie, construction engineer at Vemork

Knut Lier-Hansen, Milorg resistance fighter

Alf Larsen, engineer at Vemork

Gunnar Syverstad, laboratory assistant at Vemork

Kjell Nielsen, transport manager at Vemork

Ditlev Diseth, Norsk Hydro pensioner

NORWEGIANS

Leif Tronstad, scientist and Kompani Linge leader

Haakon VII, king of Norway

Jomar Brun, chief engineer at Vemork

Odd Starheim, member of the resistance

Oscar Torp, defense minister

Torstein Skinnarland, brother of Einar

Olav Skogen, leader of local Rjukan Milorg

ALLIES

Winston Churchill, prime minister of Great Britain

Franklin D. Roosevelt, president of the United States

Eric Welsh, head of the Norwegian branch of the British Secret
Intelligence Service (SIS)

Colin Gubbins, major general who served as second-in-command of the
British Special Operations Executive (SOE)

John Wilson, chief of the Norwegian section of the SOE

Wallace Akers, head of the British Directorate of Tube Alloys

Mark Henniker, British lieutenant colonel in charge of Operation
Freshman

Owen Roane, American Air Force pilot

NAZIS IN NORWAY

Josef Terboven, Reichskommissar in Norway

General Nikolaus von Falkenhorst, head of German military forces in
Norway

SS Lieutenant Colonel Heinrich Fehlis, head of the Gestapo and security
forces in Norway

GERMAN SCIENTISTS

Kurt Diebner

Werner Heisenberg

Otto Hahn

Walther Gerlach

Paul Harteck

Abraham Esau

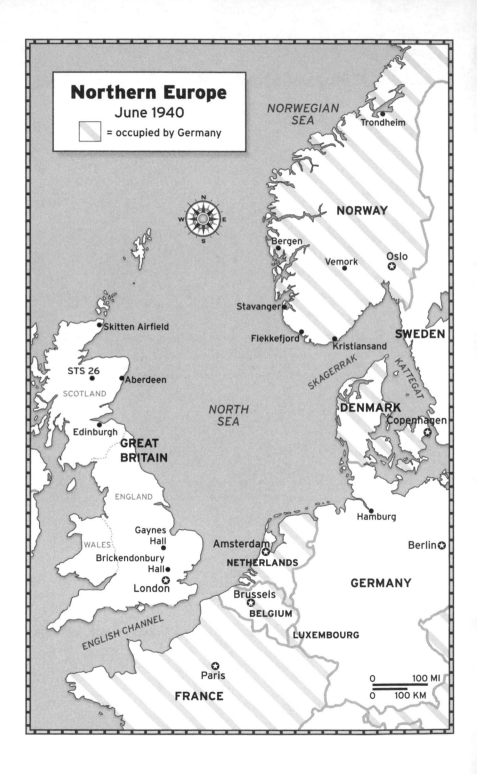

Northern Europe
June 1940

☐ = occupied by Germany

NORWEGIAN SEA

Trondheim

NORWAY

Bergen

Vemork

Oslo ✪

Stavanger

Flekkefjord

Kristiansand

SWEDEN

SKAGERRAK

KATTEGAT

Skitten Airfield

STS 26

Aberdeen

SCOTLAND

NORTH SEA

DENMARK

Copenhagen ✪

Edinburgh

GREAT BRITAIN

ENGLAND

Hamburg

Berlin ✪

Gaynes Hall

Amsterdam ✪

NETHERLANDS

GERMANY

Brickendonbury Hall

WALES

London ✪

Brussels ✪

BELGIUM

LUXEMBOURG

ENGLISH CHANNEL

Paris ✪

FRANCE

0   100 MI

0   100 KM

A NOTE ON THE PRONUNCIATION
OF NORWEGIAN VOWELS

The ø is pronounced "uh," like the "u" in "burn." "Rønneberg" would thus be pronounced "Runneberg."

The å is pronounced "oh," in short or long forms. "Måna" would thus be pronounced "Mona."

The æ is pronounced "ah," like the "a" in "cat" (short form) or in "bad" (long form). "Mæl" would thus be pronounced "Mahle."

In a staggered line, they cut across the mountain on their skis. Dressed in white camouflage suits over British Army uniforms, the young men threaded through the stands of pine and moved down the sharp, uneven ground. The silence was broken only by the swoosh of skis and the occasional slap of a pole against a branch. The warm, steady wind that blew through Vestfjord Valley dampened even these sounds. This was the same wind that would eventually, hopefully, blow their tracks away.

A mile into their trek, the woods became too dense and steep to descend by any means other than by foot. The nine Norwegian commandos took off their skis and balanced them on their shoulders. Then they slid and trudged down through the wet and heavy snow. They carried thirty-five-pound backpacks filled with survival gear, submachine guns, grenades, pistols, explosives, and knives. Each one also had a cyanide pill in case of capture by the enemy. Often the weight of their equipment made them sink to their waists in the snow.

Suddenly, the forest cleared, and they came upon the road. Ahead of them, on the other side of a terrifying gorge, stood Vemork, their target. The enormous power station, and the eight-story hydrogen plant in front of it, were built on a rocky shelf that extended over the gorge. Below it, the Måna River snaked through a valley so deep that the sun rarely reached its base.

Despite the distance across the gorge, and the wind singing in their ears, the commandos could hear the station's low hum.

Before Hitler invaded Norway and the Germans seized control of the plant, Vemork would have been lit up like a beacon. But now its windows were blacked out to discourage nighttime raids from Allied bombers. High on the icy crag, its dark silhouette looked like a winter fortress. A single-lane suspension bridge provided the only point of entry for workers and vehicles, and it was closely guarded by the Nazis. Mines littered the surrounding hillsides. Patrols swept the grounds. Searchlights, sirens, machine-gun nests, and a barrack of troops were also at the ready.

And now the commandos were going to break into it.

The young men stood mesmerized. They had been told the plant produced something called "heavy water," and with this mysterious substance, the Nazis would be able "to blow up a good part of London." But none of the saboteurs were there for heavy water, or for London. They had seen their country invaded by the Germans, their friends killed and humiliated, their families starved, their rights curtailed. They were there for Norway, for the freedom of its lands and people from Nazi rule.

They refastened their skis and started down the road to their mission.

German forces attack Norway in April 1940.

In the dark early hours of April 9, 1940, a fierce wind swept across the decks of the German cruiser *Hipper* and the four destroyers at its stern as they cut into the fjord toward Trondheim, Norway. The ships approached the three forts guarding the entrance to the city, all crews at the ready. A Norwegian patrol signaled for the boats to identify themselves. In English, the *Hipper*'s captain returned that they were a British ship with orders to "go towards Trondheim. No unfriendly intentions." As the patrol shone a spotlight across the water, it was blinded by searchlights from the *Hipper*, which suddenly sped up and blew smoke to hide its whereabouts.

Signals and warning rockets lit up the night. Inside the Norwegian forts, alarms rang and orders were given to fire on the invading ships. But the inexperienced Norwegian soldiers struggled to shoot their guns. By the time they were prepared, the *Hipper* was already steaming past the first fort. At the second fort, the bugler who should have sounded the alarm had fallen asleep at his post. The moment the gunners there opened fire, their searchlights malfunctioned, so they could not see their targets.

At 4:25 A.M., the German force set anchor in Trondheim's harbor. Cutters began bringing hundreds of soldiers from the warships to the shore. The soldiers spread out from the port into the defenseless streets. The Nazi invasion of Norway had begun.

•••

In a large hall at the Norwegian Institute of Technology (NTH), twenty minutes away from Trondheim's harbor, Leif Tronstad gathered his fellow teachers, their students, and a handful of others. Word of the invasion had reached him before the break of day, and while his wife and children slept, he had rushed to the Institute. From the few reports he and others had received, all of Norway looked to be under attack. Most major cities had fallen alongside Trondheim, but the capital, Oslo, was rumored to be holding out.

The group debated what they should do. One among them, a firebrand named Knut Haukelid, who was visiting friends in the city, wanted to fight with whatever weapons they could find. The Germans were invading their country, and they must resist. Others preached caution. They did not know exactly what Hitler intended for Norway, and their small country, with its limited military, stood little chance against German might.

When Tronstad spoke, he held everyone's attention. At thirty-seven years of age, he was the university's youngest full professor, and a favorite in its classrooms. Of medium height, he had blue eyes and ash-blond hair parted neatly on the side, with a light dance of crow's feet around his eyes.

He told those assembled that he would travel to Oslo, where, as a reserve officer in the Army, he had standing orders to go once war broke out. He suggested those with military experience should do the same. As for the others, he said, each man needed to follow his own conscience on what action he should take, but all must remember their country was in desperate need. "Whatever you do," he said, "your actions will be history in a hundred years." With that, he said his goodbyes.

Tronstad had feared this would happen — that Norway would be attacked and its "sleeping government" would leave the country unprepared to mount a defense. Since the day Adolf Hitler had invaded Poland in September 1939, and Britain's soon-to-be prime minister Winston Churchill had announced, "We are fighting to save the whole world from the pestilence of Nazi tyranny," it was clear to Tronstad that Norway would not be allowed to maintain the neutral stand it had held in the First World War. The fight between the Allies and the Nazis in mainland Europe had stalled, and the two sides had circled around Norway for months. With its rich natural resources and strategic position in the North Sea, Tronstad's homeland was too good a prize to leave unclaimed.

As Tronstad hurried home, German soldiers occupied the city around him, marching in columns through the streets. They established machine-gun nests and mortar positions at key spots throughout the city, and called out warnings in German not to resist. Tronstad ignored them. When he reached his two-story house on the city's outskirts, he told his wife, Bassa, that they were not safe in Trondheim. He would take her and the children to a mountain tourist lodge 100 miles to the south, then he would go to Oslo to join the Army.

Together, they woke up their young children, Sidsel and Leif, and helped them dress and pack. Fifteen minutes later, they piled into their car. As they headed south over a river bridge, two ash-colored bombers flew overhead.

"What kind of plane is that?" Sidsel asked.

"It is a German plane," Tronstad said, his first explanation of their hurried departure. "I'm afraid the war's come to our country."

German police troops march into Oslo in May 1940.

Twenty-eight-year-old Knut Haukelid chose a different path out of Trondheim. He and a few NTH students took control of a freight train in the city and drove it almost halfway to Oslo, until they found the tracks closed. They abandoned the train and took a bus to the nearest Army headquarters. There, they learned the heartbreaking news that the Nazis had taken Oslo, and King Haakon VII and the Norwegian government had fled the capital.

In fighting to free his country, Haukelid found his purpose. He tracked down a regiment battling the Germans and received a Krag rifle and thirty rounds of ammunition. At first glance, Haukelid probably looked similar to all the other soldiers the commander was sending into war, with nothing particularly notable about him. He had fair hair, blue eyes, and a medium build that hunched slightly at the shoulders, and at five foot ten, he was just above average height.

Yet over the next three weeks, despite having no military experience, Haukelid fought ferociously for his country and king, refusing to surrender as their invaders demanded. His battalion ambushed a line of German tanks at a mountain pass, wiping them out with homemade bombs and a single cannon, but apart from that one success, they were pushed back again and again. The German *Blitzkrieg*, with its armored vehicles, fast bombers, and well-trained troops, were simply too overwhelming a force to resist.

His regiment surrendered, but Haukelid did not. He tried to reach the fighting in the two strategic valleys that ran between Oslo and Trondheim, but his countrymen were already in retreat. Finally, he traveled into the capital and went to his parents'

Knut Haukelid.

home, a spacious apartment in the city center. His father was away, so only his mother was there to welcome him. Haukelid went into the room where he still kept a few possessions and closed the door. "What are you doing?" his mother asked.

"Getting some things," Haukelid said, grabbing his cross-country skis and boots from the closet.

"You need to get out and fight," she told him.

That was exactly his plan.

Before the war came, Knut Haukelid was a bit of a lost soul. He was born in Brooklyn, New York, to Norwegian immigrants, but his family returned to Oslo when he and his twin sister, Sigrid, were only toddlers. Dyslexic and restless, he hated school. Sitting still in those hard chairs all day, listening to the drone of teachers, was torture for him. Talking in class only turned the screws, thanks to a slight stutter. He entertained himself by pulling pranks. Once, he released a snake in the middle of class, earning one of his many suspensions.

The lone place Haukelid was able to run free was the family's country lodge. On weekends and in summertime, he skied, fished, camped, and hunted with his grandfather in the mountains and lakes of Telemark, west of Oslo. Haukelid was told the old tales of trolls inhabiting and protecting the lands of Norway, and he believed them. His faith in these creatures lent even more magic to the woods he loved.

After high school, Haukelid left for the United States to attend college. He traveled the country, working at farms for spare cash. A few years later, he came back to Norway. His father found him a well-paid job at Oslo's biggest bank, but Haukelid turned it down. He could earn more money, he told his father, fishing for trout — and off he went. After several months of fishing, he moved again, this time to Berlin. (His sister, Sigrid, left the country as well; she went to Hollywood and became a movie star known as the "siren of the fjords.") Haukelid studied engineering, learned German, and questioned his future. In 1936, he saw Hitler's propaganda parade at the Olympics. One night, when he ran into a drunk Nazi Party member who was spouting one nasty statement after another, he dropped him with a punch.

At last, he returned again to Oslo, and finally gave in to his father's wish for him to get serious with his career and his life. He took a job with his father's firm, importing engineering equipment from the United States, and he fell in love with a young woman named Bodil, a physical therapist who treated him for some back pain from all his outdoor adventures. Still, Haukelid was restless, not quite at peace with himself, until he found his purpose in defending his country.

•••

Despite the heroic efforts of many Norwegians like Haukelid, by early June 1940, Hitler controlled the entire country. King Haakon and the government fled to England by ship, and the nation's top general pleaded to his former soldiers, "Remain true and prepared" for the future fight.

Haukelid got straight to it. In Oslo, he and a friend who had received wireless training in Britain launched their own spy network for the Allies. For months, the two moved from hut to hut in the woods outside Oslo, sending radio signals to Allied forces but hearing nothing in return. Through a range of contacts in the city, they collected intelligence on the German command in the capital — everyone from Reichskommissar Josef Terboven, who served as Hitler's right hand in Norway, to General Nikolaus von Falkenhorst, who oversaw the German military forces, to SS Lieutenant Colonel Heinrich Fehlis, who ran the security services. Unable to make contact with British or Norwegian allies in London, they continued their efforts nevertheless, and even hatched a plot to kidnap Vidkun Quisling, the Norwegian fascist whose political party served as a puppet government for Terboven. Haukelid and his friend were daring and brave; they were also amateurish and terribly ineffective. But they had joined a growing resistance movement that hoped to drive the Nazis from their land. They all felt they had to do *something*.

Reichskommissar Terboven moved quickly to consolidate Nazi rule. He removed any Norwegians not loyal to the "New Order" from positions of influence: judges, clergy, journalists, business heads, policemen, mayors, and teachers alike. The

SS Lieutenant Colonel Heinrich Fehlis and Reichskommissar Josef Terboven.

Norwegian parliament was closed permanently, its members sent home. The main government buildings in the heart of Oslo flew Nazi flags.

The Nazis' presence extended well beyond Oslo. Travel after curfew or beyond a certain place without an identity card or pass was made illegal. Radios were banned. Anyone breaking the rules was subject to arrest — or whatever punishment the Nazis chose, since it was the Nazis, not the police, who enforced the law. Nothing was published in Norway without the censor's stamp of approval. New schoolbooks were printed to teach students that Hitler was Norway's savior. Strict rationing of coal, gas, food, milk, and clothing left families scraping by. People found themselves making shoes from fish skins and clothes from old newspaper. All the while, the Germans took whatever they

Nazi flags hang in the central Oslo train station.

wanted for themselves, from the finest cuts of meat to the best houses.

Some Norwegians supported the new German order. Many others merely did what they were told. But there were others still who pushed back against the Nazis. In September 1941, workers throughout Oslo went on strike against the strict rationing of milk. Terboven put martial law into effect. Hundreds were arrested, and the security chief, Fehlis, ordered the execution of the two strike leaders. Following this, the Nazi secret police, the Gestapo, intensified their hunt for underground resistance cells.

Soon they came for Haukelid, storming his family's apartment. He was not home, but the Gestapo arrested his mother, Sigrid, and his new wife, Bodil. When asked where her son was, Sigrid slapped the Gestapo officer in the face and said, "He's in the mountains."

"No," the Nazi said. "He's in England. Our contact tells us he's already been taken across the North Sea. And what do you think he is doing there?"

"You will find out when he comes back!" she promised.

●●●

Leif Tronstad would not stand for the Nazis living in his country and lording power over its people. Their presence was a violation of everything he held dear, and their occupation robbed him of the life he'd built from nothing.

Three months before Tronstad was born, his father died of a heart attack. His mother supported her four sons by serving as a maid at private dinner parties hosted by the wealthier families in their neighborhood outside Oslo. Growing up, Leif was either studying, running, or working. He excelled at all three activities, setting new track records and making the highest marks at school. His favorite subject was always science. He simply liked to understand how the world worked. He graduated college with top honors, married his childhood sweetheart, Bassa, and won scholarships to focus on chemistry at some of the best institutes in the world, including Cambridge University in England and the Kaiser Wilhelm Institute of Chemistry in Berlin.

Talented not just in the lab but also in theoretical work, Tronstad found many opportunities open to him. Since his first student days, he had wondered whether he should work in industry or teach. In the end, he told Bassa that, while he wanted to be a professor, he would leave the decision to her. "If you like, I can make as much money as you want," he said. She gave him her blessing to teach. He was soon a professor at NTH. He bought a nice house a ten-minute walk from the university and a car to drive out to his mountain cabin, where he, Bassa, and their two children skied and hiked. During these prewar years, Tronstad also worked as a consultant to several Norwegian companies, advising them on the manufacture of steel, rubber, nitrogen, aluminum, and other industrial products.

After his government surrendered to the Germans, Tronstad returned to Trondheim with his family. He kept his job, but NTH was now under German control. Professors who pledged their allegiance to the Nazis quickly gained power within the university, not to mention board seats on many of the companies where Tronstad consulted. The Nazis intended to use every sector of Norwegian industry to supply its war machine.

Tronstad wanted nothing to do with such efforts. Instead, like Haukelid, he became deeply involved in the underground —

Leif Tronstad.

the homegrown military resistance called Milorg. Through his rich trove of contacts (and by maintaining some of his consulting jobs), he helped supply industrial intelligence to the British. With most of Europe quickly falling under German rule, and the United States not yet in the war, free Britain was the lone beacon of hope for those who wanted to fight the Germans.

In early September 1941, as the Gestapo was breaking up resistance networks across Norway, Tronstad decided to inform the British of a very disturbing development at a place called Vemork. What was happening there could well give the Nazis the power to win the war.

CHAPTER 02

THE URANIUM CLUB

Water ran plentifully throughout the high wilderness plateau of the Hardangervidda, or the Vidda, in Telemark, a region in Norway west of Oslo. It tumbled down from the plateau into its natural reservoir at Lake Møs, and then the Måna River carried the water for eighteen miles through the steep Vestfjord Valley to Lake Tinnsjø.

The river's flow changed when Norsk Hydro, a rising industrial giant, built a dam at the top of Lake Møs in 1906. They redirected the water through tunnels blasted out of the rock,

The dam at Lake Møs.

which ran for three miles underground before they reached the Vemork power station. From there, the water fell 920 vertical feet through eleven steel pipelines into turbine generators that produced 145,000 kilowatts of electricity. It was the world's largest hydroelectric power station.

A fraction of this water was directed into a hydrogen plant thirty feet away on the edge of the cliff. There it flowed into tens of thousands of steel electrolysis cells, which consumed almost all the power generated at the station. The cells created currents of electricity that split the water's two hydrogen atoms from its lone oxygen one. These separated gases were then pumped through a long series of pipes down to Rjukan, a town of 7,000 people at the bottom of the valley. Chemical plants in the town used the hydrogen to make fertilizers — a huge product for agriculturally oriented Norway.

The water, which had by now coursed from the Vidda to Lake Møs through tunnels, then pipelines, then electrolysis cells, was not done yet. A smaller fraction of it was sent through yet more cells and pipelines, reduced and further reduced, until it turned into a steady drip no quicker than a leaky faucet. This water was now something unique and rare. It was heavy water.

The American chemist Harold Urey won the Nobel Prize for his discovery of heavy water in 1931. While most hydrogen atoms consisted of a single electron orbiting a single proton in the atom's nucleus, Urey showed that there was a variant (or "isotope") of hydrogen that carried a neutron in its nucleus as well. The sum of an atom's protons and neutrons is called its atomic weight, so this isotope, deuterium (D), had a weight of 2. It was extremely rare in nature, where there was just one molecule of

The hydroelectric power station at Vemork.

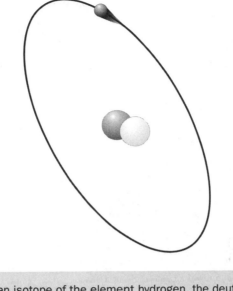

As an isotope of the element hydrogen, the deuterium atom includes a neutron (in white) as well as a proton (gray) and electron (on the outer ring).

heavy water (D_2O) for every 41 million molecules of ordinary water (H_2O).

Building on Urey's work, several scientists found that the best method for producing heavy water was electrolysis. The substance didn't break down as easily as ordinary water when an electric current ran through it, so any water remaining in a cell after the hydrogen gas was removed was more highly concentrated with heavy water.

But producing deuterium in any quantity demanded enormous resources. A scientist noted that in order to create a single kilogram (2.2 pounds) of heavy water, "50 tons of ordinary water had to be treated for one year, consuming 320,000 kilowatt hours [of electricity], and, then, the output had a purity no better than about ten percent." That was a lot of electricity for a very low level of purity in a very small quantity of deuterium.

Jomar Brun in his office at Norsk Hydro.

A man named Jomar Brun ran the Norsk Hydro hydrogen plant at Vemork; he also happened to be a former college classmate of Leif Tronstad. In 1933, Tronstad and Brun proposed the idea of a heavy-water industrial facility to Norsk Hydro. They weren't sure what use it would have, but as Tronstad frequently said to his students, "Technology first, then industry and applications!"

What Tronstad and Brun did know was that Vemork, with its almost limitless supply of cheap power and water, provided the perfect setup for heavy-water manufacturing. They matched the plant's natural advantages with an ingenious new design for the equipment. Think of a group of cans stacked in a pyramid. Now picture that pyramid upside down, with the single can at the bottom. In the Tronstad-Brun design, water flowed into the top row of cans — really 1,824 electrolysis cells, which treated the water with a current. Some of the water was decomposed into bubbles of hydrogen and oxygen gas by electrolysis, and the remainder, now containing a higher percentage of heavy water, cascaded down to the next row of cans in the pyramid (570 cells). Then it repeated the process through the third (228 cells), fourth (twenty cells), and fifth (three cells) rows of electrolysis cells. However, by the end of the fifth stage, with a huge amount of time and power exhausted, the cells still contained only 10 percent heavy water.

Then the water cascaded into the bottom can of the pyramid. This sixth and final phase was called the high-concentration stage. Set in the cavernous, brightly lit basement of the hydrogen plant, it actually consisted of seven unique steel electrolysis cells lined up in a row, surrounded by twisting snakes of pipework, blue tubes, and electrical wires. These specialized cells followed a similar cascade model to concentrate the heavy water in each cell. But they could also recycle the gaseous form of deuterium back into the production process, while it was essentially wasted in the other stages. As a result, the heavy-water concentration

The high-concentration stage at Vemork in its 1942 configuration.

rose on average 11.5 percent from one cell to the next. By the seventh and last cell, the Vidda's natural flow had been purified to 99.5 percent heavy water.

When the plant started production with this method, scientists around the world praised it as a breakthrough. Heavy water froze at 4 degrees Celsius instead of at zero, and some joked it was only good for creating better skating rinks. Tronstad, however, believed in the potential of heavy water. He spoke passionately of its use in the new field of atomic physics, which was a hotbed of scientific activity, and of its promise in a range of fields. Researchers found that the life processes of mice slowed down when they drank small amounts of heavy water. Seeds germinated more slowly in a diluted solution — and not at all in a pure one. Some people believed that heavy water could lead to a cure for cancer.

Vemork shipped its first containers of heavy water in January 1935, in batches of 10 to 100 grams, but business did not boom. Laboratories in France, England, Germany, the United States, Scandinavia, and Japan ordered no more than a few hundred grams at a time. In 1936, Vemork produced only 40 kilograms for sale. Two years later, the amount had increased to 80 kilograms, a sum valued at $40,000; but that meant nothing to Norsk Hydro, which raked in tens of millions of kroner per year. The company advertised its heavy water in industry magazines, to no result: There simply wasn't any demand. Production was shut down on Tronstad and Brun's creation, and dust started to gather on the seven cells in the high-concentration room.

Then, just months later, everything changed.

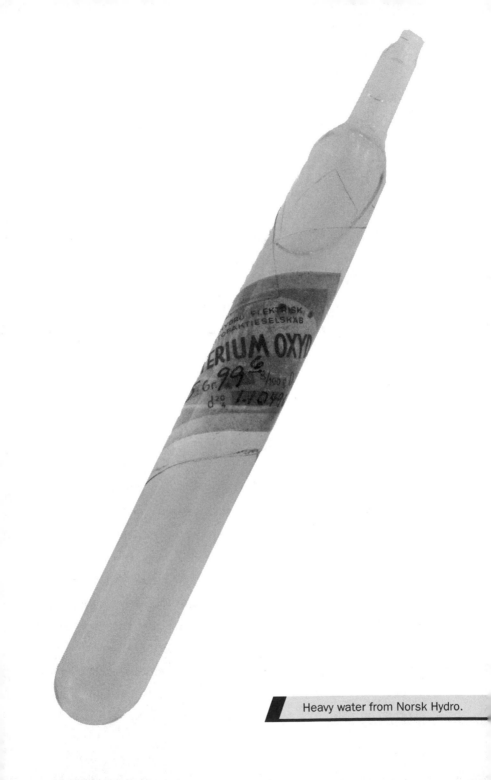

Heavy water from Norsk Hydro.

• • •

For decades, scientists around the globe had been plumbing the mysteries of "atoms and void," which was how the ancient Greeks described the substance that made up everything in the universe. Experimentalists bombarded elements with subatomic particles in dark laboratories. Theoreticians made brilliant deductions on their blackboards. Pierre and Marie Curie, Max Planck, Albert Einstein, Enrico Fermi, Niels Bohr, and other intellectual giants discovered a world full of energy that could be manipulated by humans.

The English physicist Ernest Rutherford observed that heavy, unstable elements, such as uranium, would break down naturally into lighter ones, such as argon. When he calculated the huge amount of energy released during this process, he realized what was at stake. "Could a proper detonator be found," he suggested to a member of his lab, "a wave of atomic disintegration might be started through matter, which would make this old world vanish in smoke . . . Some fool in a laboratory might blow up the universe unawares."

Then, in 1932, another English scientist, James Chadwick, discovered that proper detonator: the neutron. The neutron had mass, but unlike protons and electrons, which held positive and negative charges respectively, it carried no charge to hinder its movement. That made it the perfect particle to shoot into the nucleus of the atom. Sometimes the neutron was absorbed; sometimes it knocked a proton out of the nucleus, which converted that element into a different one. For instance, when a nitrogen atom (with 7 protons in its nucleus, i.e., its "atomic number" on the periodic chart of elements) lost a proton, it became an isotope of carbon (atomic number 6). Physicists had discovered a way to manipulate the basic fabric of the world, and with this ability, they could further investigate its many separate strands — and even create some strands of their own.

Soon they began flinging neutrons at all kinds of elements to transform their natures. They found this process particularly effective when the neutrons had to pass through a "moderator" of some kind, which slowed their progress. Paraffin wax and plain water proved to be the best early moderators. Both contained lots of hydrogen, and when these hydrogen atoms collided with the neutrons, which had the same mass, the moderators stole some of the neutrons' speed, much like when two billiard balls collide. That allowed more opportunity for the atomic reaction to take place.

In December 1938, two German chemists, the elderly Otto Hahn and his young assistant, Fritz Strassman, proved that a neutron colliding with a uranium (U) atom could do more than chip away at its nucleus or become absorbed within it. The neutron could split the atom in two — a process called nuclear fission. When this happened, two lighter atoms were flung apart with a tremendous force equal to the energy that had held the nucleus together. The splitting of one atom could release 200 million

Otto Hahn.

electron volts. Given that a single gram of uranium contained some 2.5 sextillion atoms (that is, 2,500,000,000,000,000,000,000 atoms), numbers alone could not describe the potential energy release. One physicist calculated that a cubic meter of uranium ore could provide enough energy to raise a cubic kilometer of water twenty-seven kilometers into the air.

The atom's potential power became even clearer when scientists discovered that "fissioning" the uranium nucleus released two to three fast-moving neutrons that could act as detonators. The neutrons from one atom could split two others. The neutrons from these two split four more. The four could cause the detonation of eight. The eight — sixteen. With an ever-increasing

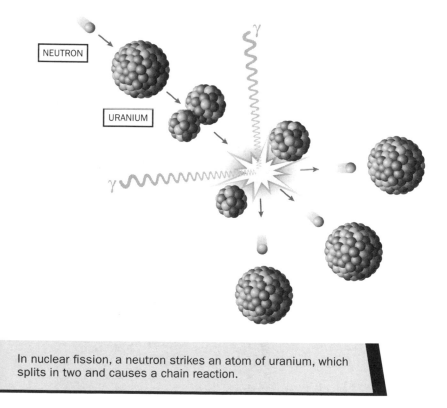

NEUTRON

URANIUM

In nuclear fission, a neutron strikes an atom of uranium, which splits in two and causes a chain reaction.

number of fast-moving neutrons flinging themselves about, splitting atoms at an exponential rate, scientists could create what was called a "chain reaction" — and generate enormous quantities of energy.

Some wanted to use the energy to fuel factories and homes. Others were drawn to — or feared — its use as an explosive. Within a week of Hahn's discovery, the American physicist J. Robert Oppenheimer sketched a crude bomb on his blackboard. Enrico Fermi, who had recently won a Nobel Prize for his work on neutron irradiation, stared out the window of his office at Columbia University. He watched students bustling down the New York sidewalks, the streets crowded with traffic. "A little bomb like that," he said, drawing his hands together as if they held a soccer ball, "and it would all disappear."

● ● ●

On September 16, 1939, Kurt Diebner sat in his office at the headquarters of Berlin's Army Ordnance Research Department, waiting for eight of his fellow German physicists. At thirty-four years of age, Diebner was a loyal Nazi Party member with a presence as modest and retreating as his hairline. His suits fit too tightly over his short, thin frame, and he wore round schoolboy spectacles that constantly threatened to fall off his nose. In meetings, his words came out halting and unsure. But despite his appearance, he was an ambitious and eager man.

Diebner, who came from a working-class family, gained his PhD in atomic physics in 1931. In 1934, the year Hitler became the Führer of Germany, Diebner joined the Army Ordnance, where he was tasked to develop explosives. For years he pushed his boss to allow him to create an atomic research division

Kurt Diebner.

instead. Such work, he was told, was "malarkey," with no practical use. But Hahn's splitting of the atom made it clear that atomic physics was anything but malarkey, and Diebner was finally given the mandate to form a team.

Diebner opened the first meeting of the Uranverein (the Uranium Club) with a statement of its purpose. German spies had discovered that the United States, France, and Great Britain were all pursuing projects in nuclear fission. This team had been called together to decide whether it was possible to harness the atom's energy for the production of weapons or the generation of power — all for the good of the Third Reich.

One of the men present was already dedicated to the atom's weapons potential. In April 1939, Paul Harteck, a physical chemist at the University of Hamburg, had sent a letter to the Reich Ministry of War explaining recent developments in nuclear physics. In his view, he wrote, they held the "possibility for the creation of explosives whose effect would excel by a million times those presently in use . . . The country which first makes use of [this explosive] would, in relation to the others, possess a well-nigh irretrievable advantage." Harteck believed Germany should pursue any such advantage.

Otto Hahn, on the other hand, was distraught that his discovery was being developed into a weapon to kill. He tried to extinguish any enthusiasm by pointing to the many technical challenges involved in engineering an explosive or designing a machine to produce energy. He noted that fission occurred most readily in the rare uranium isotope U-235, while its more common cousin U-238 tended to absorb neutrons into its nucleus, stealing their potential to foster a chain reaction. Natural uranium was made up of only seven parts U-235 for every thousand parts of U-238, and no method to separate the two isotopes existed. They also needed to find an efficient moderator for U-235. Given all this, and likely more unseen challenges, Hahn believed they were on a fool's errand to build a weapon. The debate continued for hours, until the scientists finally concluded, "If there is only a trace of a chance this can be done, then we have to do it."

Ten days later, on September 26, Diebner called another meeting of the Uranium Club. This time, Werner Heisenberg attended. Heisenberg was considered the leading light of German theoretical physics, particularly after Hitler's rise had forced Albert Einstein and other Jewish physicists to flee the country. Initially, Diebner had resisted his inclusion in the group, because he wanted

Werner Heisenberg.

experimenters, not theoreticians, and because Heisenberg had called Diebner's academic research "amateurish." But the others had urged him to reconsider: Heisenberg had won a Nobel Prize at the tender age of thirty-one, and he was too brilliant to leave out.

Heisenberg proved to be a useful addition to the Club. By the end of the meeting, the group had its orders. Some, like Harteck, would investigate how to extract sufficient quantities of U-235 from natural uranium. Others, including Heisenberg, would hash out chain-reaction theory, both for constructing explosives and for generating power. Still others would experiment with the best moderators.

Heisenberg made quick work with the theory. By late October, he started on a pair of breakthrough papers. One showed that if they separated out the U-235 isotope and compressed enough of it into a ball, the neutrons would set off an immediate chain reaction, resulting in an explosion "greater than the strongest available explosives by several powers of ten." Isotope separation, Heisenberg declared, was "the only way to produce explosives," and the challenges of such separation were legion. But constructing a "machine" that used uranium and a moderator to generate a steady level of power was an attainable goal. This machine might look like a giant sphere filled with at least a ton each of uranium and moderator, separated in layers. The amount of U-235 was still key: They would need an enormous quantity of natural uranium to provide enough of the rare isotope.

In his second paper, on the subject of moderators, Heisenberg dismissed plain water and paraffin wax as options. Their hydrogen atoms slowed the neutrons enough to promote the fissioning of U-235, but they also absorbed many of them away from the chain reaction, diminishing its effectiveness. This left two known candidates: graphite, which was a crystalline form of carbon, and heavy water. He recommended further research into these substances.

In recognition of the Uranium Club's work, Diebner was named head of the Kaiser Wilhelm Institute of Physics in Berlin, the country's most advanced laboratory. Heisenberg was appointed to the board as scientific adviser, to placate those who were upset at having Diebner, a physicist of no renown, directing the august institute.

By the end of 1939, Diebner had dozens of scientists under his watch across Germany, refining atomic theory and conducting experiments. They readied advanced laboratories and investigated — and ordered — key materials.

Although the Uranium Club agreed they needed to study the issue further, they calculated that heavy water was the best presently known moderator. Diebner and his scientists required a steady, robust supply of the precious liquid. Unfortunately, the world's sole producer of heavy water, Norsk Hydro's Vemork plant, was far away in a remote valley in Norway, a country whose neutral status in the war made it an unreliable partner. Furthermore, the plant had only recently restarted heavy-water production in November 1939 and could supply little more than 10 kilograms a month. By January 1940, Diebner was sending them orders for 100 kilograms a month, every month. The management of Norsk Hydro — a company whose majority stake was owned by French shareholders — asked for the purpose behind such a large order. Diebner offered no answer, as the German Army had made the use of heavy water, now labeled

SH-200, a high-level military secret. Norsk Hydro refused to fulfill the order.

It was no matter. In April 1940, the Nazis overtook Norway and seized Vemork. Shortly after, a German general ordered production at the plant — and deliveries to Berlin — to increase at a rapid rate. Jomar Brun, who ran the heavy-water plant he helped build, was given no choice but to meet this demand. Although he was sworn to secrecy about his work, Brun consulted Tronstad to see if he knew what the Germans could want with such a large supply of heavy water. Tronstad knew there was interest in the substance in the new field of fission research, but he dismissed the idea that it could be applied to any great military use.

By the spring of 1941, Diebner had increased his orders to 1,500 kilograms of heavy water a year. Then only a few months later, orders rose to 5,000 kilograms. All of Vemork was to be used to produce heavy water. No effort would be spared. If their work achieved its expected results, Diebner and his fellow physicists aimed to deliver an atomic bomb to Hitler.

CHAPTER 03

MINISTRY OF UNGENTLEMANLY WARFARE

Throughout 1940 and much of 1941, Tronstad continued his teaching and research in Trondheim — and his work for the Norwegian resistance. Behind blackout curtains, he met with community leaders active in pushing back against German oppression in the city. Tronstad was also close to several bands of university students. Some published illegal newspapers. Others operated at a higher level in connection with the British Secret Intelligence Service (SIS), sending coded wireless radio transmissions to London to report on German troop movements and naval activity. Tronstad — code-named "The Mailman" — gave them any technical help they needed and provided intelligence of his own from his many industrial connections. He also supplied crucial information about Vemork's supply of heavy water.

On the morning of September 9, 1941, a student visited Tronstad for advice on hiding the wireless radio that he had been using to send messages to the SIS. The Gestapo arrested the student that same afternoon. A week later, they seized the courier Tronstad had tasked to go to London by ship. On the wharf's edge, the courier swallowed the cigarette paper with the information he was carrying, but it was a close call. Tronstad knew the Gestapo would likely come for him next.

On September 22, Tronstad went to Bassa and told her they must flee. That evening, the family boarded a 7:15 train to Oslo with their hastily packed suitcases. In the sleeping compartment, Tronstad wrote the first entry in the small black diary he would keep through the war: "Family, house and worldly goods have to be set aside for Norway's sake."

The next morning, they arrived in Oslo and took another train to a neighborhood a short distance outside the city. From the station, they climbed up the hill to Bassa's childhood home. He made sure Bassa knew to tell anybody who asked that he was headed west toward Telemark, and they hugged. Then he kneeled beside his children. "Take care of your little brother," he told nine-year-old Sidsel. Then he turned to four-year-old Leif. "You must be good for your mother while I'm gone." He promised to bring back a little gift for each of them. "Be kind to each other," Tronstad said before hurrying away, so overcome with emotion that he forgot to hug them.

In Oslo, he collected fake identity papers, and the next morning he borrowed a bicycle and rode twenty miles north, where the Milorg resistance network picked him up and ferried him out of the country. Weeks later in Stockholm, he boarded a transport plane that took him across the North Sea. On October 21, he arrived at King's Cross Station in London. SIS arranged a room for him at St. Ermin's Hotel in the heart of Westminster, a stone's throw from the spy agency's headquarters.

Tronstad knew London well from his student days, but now he found it a war zone. Soldiers crowded the streets, and a floating armada of gray barrage balloons hung in the sky to interfere with German bombers. The streets were strewn with the rubble of bombed-out buildings. Many thousands of people had been killed in the Blitz, and countless more had been wounded and left homeless.

A barrage balloon — designed to keep Nazi planes from dive-bombing their targets — hangs behind a devastated block in London in September 1940.

Within days of his arrival, he sat down with Eric Welsh, the SIS spy responsible for Norway. Tronstad revealed what he knew about Nazi interest in Vemork, particularly the huge spike in heavy-water production. He discovered the British were also pursuing an atomic bomb — and they were deeply concerned about the work of their Nazi rivals.

In September 1939, when Hitler invaded Poland, he boasted to the world that he would soon "employ a weapon against which there would be no defense." This prompted Sir Henry Tizard, head of the Air Ministry's research department, who was already fearful of Nazi advances in atomic science, to look even more urgently into the production of a British bomb.

Two physicists, Otto Frisch and Rudolf Peierls, both Jewish refugees from Germany, put the British firmly on their path. On March 19, 1940, their report, "On the Construction of a Super Bomb," landed on Tizard's desk. They detailed that one pound of pure uranium-235 — divided into two (or more) parts, which were then smashed together at a high velocity — would initiate an explosion that would "destroy life in a wide area . . . probably the center of a big city . . . at a temperature comparable to the interior of the sun." Peierls and Frisch suggested that German scientists might soon "be in possession of this weapon." Britain could only counter this threat, they concluded, by obtaining a bomb as well.

The following month, the British government began exploratory research with some of its best scientists. In July 1941, the group delivered a road map for an atomic bomb program. On receiving it, Prime Minister Winston Churchill wrote to his War Cabinet: "Although personally I am quite content with the existing explosives, I feel we must not stand in the path of improvement." The Cabinet agreed, promising "no time, labor, material or money should be spared in pushing forward the development of this weapon." Thus, the "Directorate of Tube Alloys" — the code name for the British atomic bomb program — was formed.

Winston Churchill.

Throughout this period, fears over the German bomb continued. From far and wide came whispers, rumors, threats, and fact — which, mixed together, made for the typically confusing brew that governments called "intelligence." Two drunken German pilots were overhead on a tram speaking about "new bombs" that were "very dangerous" and had the power of an earthquake. One émigré German physicist warned that there was pressure from high within the Nazi government to build a bomb, and the Allies "must hurry." A military adviser in Stockholm reported, "A tale has again reached me that the Germans are well under way with the manufacture of an uranium bomb of enormous power, which will blast everything, and through the power of one bomb a whole town can be leveled." SIS heard of a mysterious September 1941 meeting where Werner Heisenberg admitted to Niels Bohr, who was living in Nazi-occupied Denmark, that a bomb could be made, "and we're working on it."

The best intelligence the British received came through German activity at Vemork. As early as April 1940, a French spy with close ties to Norsk Hydro had alerted his British allies to Nazi efforts in uranium research using heavy water from the plant. Leif Tronstad provided another gold mine of information. What the Norwegian professor revealed about the increased levels of production left officials at the Directorate of Tube Alloys and high in the British government deeply on edge. Whatever position Tronstad decided to take in his fight against the Nazis, whether as a scientist or as an official in the exiled Norwegian government based in London, the British wanted him to continue to gather intelligence about Vemork and the German atomic program. Tronstad agreed.

• • •

On December 2, 1941, Haukelid was woken up by dogs barking. There was a chill in the air, and frost clouded the windows overlooking the huge wooded estate of Stodham Park, fifty miles southwest of London. He had escaped to Britain in November because of the same intense Gestapo manhunts that had driven Tronstad from Norway. Now he was part of a group of roughly two dozen Norwegians who had volunteered to attend special commando training to fight for their homeland.

Quickly, Haukelid dressed in his new British uniform, its starched collar surpassed in stiffness only by his standard-issue boots. Outside, he stood with his fellow soldiers. They came from every walk of life: rich, poor, and in between; from city, town, and backwoods country. A few had never handled a gun before; others were marksmen. Some were boys, barely eighteen.

Most were in their twenties, and a few were old men — all of thirty, like Haukelid. Before the war, they had been students, fishermen, police officers, bankers, factory workers, and lost types looking for their place in this world — again, just like Haukelid. Together they learned to kill, to sabotage, and to survive, any way and any how. Their grizzled Irish sergeant major, who went by the nickname "Tom Mix," taught them no rules but one: "Never give your enemy half a chance."

The squad of new recruits started their day at 6 A.M. with what Mix liked to call "Hardening of the Feet": a fast march on the estate. A short breakfast was followed by weapons instruction. "This is your friend," Mix said, twirling his pistol around his finger. "The only friend you can rely on." Then he took them out to a grove in the woods and taught them how to stand — knees bent, two hands on the grip of the pistol — and how to fire: two shots quickly in a row to make sure the enemy was down. If circumstances allowed, Mix said grimly, "aim low. A bullet in the stomach, and your German will squirm for twelve hours before dying." Haukelid had grown up hunting, but this was very different.

After two hours of shooting, they spent another hour in a gym. They pummeled punching bags, wrestled, and learned how to take down and disarm an enemy with their bare hands. A break for coffee, then instruction in how to send and receive messages in Morse code. This was followed by lunch, then a two-hour class in demolition. "Never smoke while working with explosives," Mix said, a lit cigarette perched between his lips, again offering the point that rules existed to be broken. They blew up logs and sent rocks skyward. Ears ringing, they moved on to orienteering class, navigating the estate with maps and

A British Special Operations Executive class in demolitions.

compasses, then field craft — stalking targets and scouting routes through the woods. From 5 to 8 P.M., they were free to relax and eat before the night exercises began. Those consisted of more weapons, more explosives, more unarmed combat — now executed in the pitch-dark.

Through day after day of this schedule, his boots and collar softening with each hour, Haukelid turned into a fighter. Though fit at the start, he became fitter still. On occasion, he would be invited into a room with an officer or a psychiatrist and asked if the training was too much, too hard, if he might want to quit. This kind of work wasn't for everybody, they said.

It was for him.

Firing two shots in rapid succession became a reflex, and his aim grew lethally accurate to the range's paper targets. He learned how to time throwing a hand grenade ("One can go from here to London before it explodes," Mix said). He gained expertise in hand-to-hand combat and in the use of a knife. He grew skilled at demolitions, able to light a ten-second fuse without his hands shaking.

After three weeks of this instruction, Haukelid graduated from what his Stodham Park instructors told him was only preliminary training. On December 20, 1941, he boarded a train to Scotland for further lessons.

At Meoble, an old hunting lodge on the windswept coast of the western Highlands, the training began with scrambles through thick brush, crossing ice-cold rivers, and rappelling down steep ravines. Using both British and foreign weapons, he practiced instinctive shooting (shooting without the use of sights) and close-quarter firing. In demolitions, he graduated from blowing up logs to destroying railroad cars. He crafted bombs of all sizes and was amazed at what a small charge placed in the perfect spot at the perfect time could do: It could stop an army, obliterate a weapons plant.

He was taught how to break open safes, how to use poison, how to knock out a guard with chloroform. He practiced how to kill silently with a knife. He learned how to follow a route to a target by memory alone, how to camouflage himself in the field, how to crawl through a marsh and reach his assailant undetected, how to take him down without a sound — without even a weapon. "This is war, not sport," his instructors reminded him. "So forget the Queensbury rules; forget the term 'foul methods' . . . these methods help you to kill quickly." A sharp blow with the side of his hand could paralyze, break bones, or kill.

The members of the Norwegian Independent Company, later known as the Kompani Linge.

Even the occasional night off was instructive. For New Year's Eve, Haukelid and the others in his squad were taken to a pub to celebrate. At first, it seemed like a good time, but they were enlightened later that they were watched all evening to see who drank too much, who made a fool of himself, or, worst of all, who spoke of what he should not, as one had always to be on one's guard. It was a merciless regime, and as before, Haukelid was asked regularly if he wanted to back out. He refused.

On January 14, 1942, Haukelid arrived at Special Training School 26, in the Scottish Highlands near Aviemore, the home of Norwegian Independent Company No. 1. Roughly 150 Norwegians lived in three hunting lodges amidst the cragged granite mountain peaks, steep valleys, and long stretches of moors. The place reminded Haukelid almost too much of his homeland, but that meant it was the ideal terrain to prepare for missions.

The Norwegian company was part of an expansive British organization called the Special Operations Executive (SOE). Founded by Churchill in 1940, its directive was to "set Europe ablaze" with commando missions against the Nazis. Its masterminds, who started the organization from three rooms at St. Ermin's Hotel, called themselves the "Ministry of Ungentlemanly Warfare."

Haukelid was happy to be surrounded by Norwegians like him, who had risked everything to come to England to learn to fight. For two weeks, he trained with his new company and roamed the snowbound countryside. Then, on January 31, several visitors came up from London by night train. The company showed off their shooting and raid techniques, and then hosted a dinner at one of the lodges at STS 26. Oscar Torp, the Norwegian Defense Minister in exile, and Major General Colin Gubbins, second-in-command of the SOE, were the guests of honor. Torp gave a rousing speech, promising a new era of cooperation between the exiled Norwegian government and the British. Their aim in Norway was twofold: the long-term goal of building up Milorg, the underground military resistance in Norway, in anticipation of a future Allied invasion; and the short-term goal of performing sabotage operations and assisting in raids to weaken the Germans. The Independent Company would be at the forefront of any attack. When he finished, the men cheered and pounded on their tables.

Then Torp and Gubbins introduced the two officers who would command them. The first was Lieutenant Colonel John Wilson, the new chief of the SOE Norwegian section. He told them that he had "Viking blood" in his veins but that over the generations it had thinned like his graying crown of hair. At fifty-three years of age, he had a short but upright bearing, a quiet, stern voice, and a determined manner. Wilson had helped design and run the SOE's training schools. Next to Wilson, dressed in uniform and cap, stood Leif Tronstad, whom Haukelid had

Lt. Colonel John Wilson.

briefly met on the fateful morning of the German invasion. Coordinating closely with Wilson, Captain Tronstad would oversee the company's training, planning, and execution of operations, and direct the Norwegian soldiers in their fight for their country. Haukelid pleaded for that chance to come soon, but it was not yet his turn. Others would first have theirs.

CHAPTER 04

THE SIZE OF A PINEAPPLE

On Thursday, March 12, 1942, Einar Skinnarland found himself sitting on an operating table at St. Joseph's Hospital in Kristiansand, a port town in southern Norway. A week before, he had fallen and dislocated his kneecap. He had forced it back into place, but blood now swelled dangerously behind his knee. The doctor was insisting that Skinnarland take anesthesia for the surgery on his left leg.

No anesthesia, Skinnarland said. He was leaving Kristiansand soon, and he feared drugs would hamper his departure. Skinnarland — red-haired, twenty-three years old, all broad shoulders and wiry muscle — leaned back, and the nurses secured his leg. Then the doctor cut into it with a scalpel. His patient did his best not to throw himself from the table.

As the doctor probed into his open flesh, Skinnarland endured the surgery with barely more than a murmur. After draining the blood and

Einar Skinnarland.

fluid from behind the kneecap, the doctor made sure it was set properly in place and then stitched his patient up. He announced Skinnarland would need a few nights to recover in the hospital. Again, Skinnarland refused. A tightly bound bandage would have to do. A couple of hours later, with walking stick in hand, he hobbled down the stairs and into a taxi.

Back in his room, he tried to get some sleep, but the pain radiating from his leg in hot flashes was too intense. Instead, he focused on oiling his revolvers. He planned to persuade the *Galtesund*, a 620-ton steamer that was shortly due into port, to change its course and take him and his friends across the North Sea to Aberdeen, Scotland.

Since the invasion, Skinnarland and his friend Olav Skogen, both natives of the Rjukan area, had set themselves to undermining the Germans in any way they could as part of the town's nascent Milorg cell. At the start of 1942, Skinnarland traveled to Oslo to ask Milorg's signals chief if he could be sent to Britain to train as a radio operator and bring back a radio set with him. He was provided with fake papers under the name "Einar Hansen." In early March, he told his family that he was heading into the mountains on an extended hunting trip. Instead, he left for Flekkefjord, a port town west of Kristiansand, where he was scheduled to be picked up by a boat sent from Britain. Traveling on skis, he injured his leg.

In Flekkefjord, he met with two other members of the resistance: Odd Starheim, twenty-six years old, and his twenty-three-year-old sidekick, Andreas Fasting. Starheim was a legend in resistance circles. Soon after the German invasion, he had commandeered a small boat and gone to Scotland to train. Over the past year and a half, he had developed an extensive intelligence network throughout southern Norway. Now on the run from the Gestapo, Starheim needed to escape the country, and he was charged by the underground to take Skinnarland with him.

On meeting in Flekkefjord, Starheim told Skinnarland that their boat would not be coming because of storms on the North Sea. They needed to find another way, and crossing into Sweden was out of the question. Starheim came up with the idea of hijacking a steamer. Over games of chess, the three hatched their plan to capture the *Galtesund*. But if Skinnarland was to be any use in commandeering the vessel, he first needed to fix his leg at St. Joseph's in Kristiansand.

Two days after his surgery, on March 14, Skinnarland boarded the *Galtesund* in Kristiansand for the trip to Flekkefjord. On the overnight journey, he scouted out the steamer's passengers, crew, cargo, and coal supply, with his walking stick in hand. There was

The steamer *Galtesund*.

only a single passenger, a man traveling to Stavanger, farther up the coast. No Germans. Twenty-two crew. When the steamer arrived in Flekkefjord, Skinnarland disembarked to meet up with his fellow hijackers.

A few hours later, he walked slowly back toward the harbor, the revolvers tucked inside his suitcase. He crossed through a small cobblestone square lined with bright green and yellow wooden houses and then moved onto the quay, where stevedores were loading the last cargo onto the *Galtesund*. He boarded the steamer and made his way to the cabin that he had stayed in the previous night. Half an hour after Skinnarland boarded, Starheim and Fasting showed up. They gave him a short wave, then proceeded to the deck. At 5 P.M., on the third and final ring of the ship's bells, the *Galtesund* shook to life under their feet, its propellers cutting through the black water. Belching black smoke from its funnels, the steamer chugged away from the dock.

Once free of the sheltered harbor, Skinnarland left his cabin with his two revolvers loaded and tucked into his belt and with several lengths of rope around his waist. He was nervous. Starheim was practiced at this kind of action, but Skinnarland felt that he was a novice and might make a mess of things.

At 6:20 P.M., he met Starheim outside the saloon. They were about to open the door, to enter and seize the captain, when the ship's second mate came up from behind. He wanted Starheim to produce his ticket. Skinnarland was not sure what to do, his hand peeling off the saloon door handle, ready to act, uncertain if he should.

"I'm afraid I've arrived too late," Starheim said innocently. "So I thought I would pay on board."

The second mate led him off to pay. Minutes later, Skinnarland and Starheim were back at the saloon. They eased open the door, Starheim first, Skinnarland second, each with two drawn revolvers. "Hands up," Starheim ordered. Only the captain and the passenger heading to Stavanger were inside. Neither knew what to do until Starheim repeated himself. Then he said, "We're officers of the Norwegian Navy, and we're not alone; at this instant my men are seizing the engine room. I'm now assuming command of this ship."

The captain protested, but Starheim cut him off. Soon Skinnarland had the captain and passenger tied up with ropes. The two hijackers then headed to the bridge. The first mate tried to make it out a side door, but Skinnarland, more sure of himself now, prevented the escape. The pilot let go of the helm, but Starheim ordered him to maintain course. Below deck, Fasting secured the engine room with a pair of stokers he had recruited to the effort, and the *Galtesund* was theirs, without a shot having been fired.

Now they had to survive the voyage to Aberdeen. Starheim wanted to set a course directly west, but they were nearing a coastal fortress manned by the Germans, and the pilot warned them that they should proceed on their planned course at least until the sun set. If they were not seen heading to the next scheduled stop, the Germans might suspect something. Once it was dark, they would have until the break of the following day before their absence was noted.

Starheim followed his advice, and once darkness fell, the pilot finally headed away from the coastline. Through the night, Starheim and Skinnarland remained in the bridge, drinking coffee to stay awake. At dawn, as a fog rolled over the sea, they heard the rumble of a plane in the distance. Fearing it might be a German search aircraft, they prepared for the worst. In a momentary break in the fog, they spotted the silver-and-black Nazi cross on the tail. Then the fog blanketed them again — saving their lives.

At 2 P.M., the sky finally cleared, and the hijackers paced the bridge, knowing that the ship was again an open target. Then Fasting saw another plane on the horizon. The red, white, and blue of the Royal Air Force brought cheers and sighs of relief. The seaplane circled over the steamer, and Starheim had the second mate signal: "*Galtesund* making for Aberdeen and wants pilot." A moment passed, and the plane signaled back. "Congratulations." They had an escort. The following morning, an armed trawler from Aberdeen led them through the North Sea minefields to port.

To Skinnarland's surprise, he was sent immediately to London by overnight train. When he arrived at SOE headquarters in London, Tronstad knew he had found the perfect point man for operations near Vemork.

A souvenir spoon Skinnarland bought for his mother during his training in England.

The SOE and the Directorate of Tube Alloys had been talking during the past few months about striking Vemork. The information Tronstad brought from Norway was enough for the British to determine that heavy water was critical to the German atomic program, but since his escape from his homeland, he had limited intelligence on the plant. If there was to be an attack, SOE needed somebody on the ground feeding them information. Furthermore, such a dangerous mission would not be approved without a clear picture of continued activity by the Nazis at Vemork.

Enter Skinnarland. He was born and raised by the Lake Møs dam, which his father supervised. He was employed by Norsk Hydro. He had lots of family and friends who worked throughout the company. Nobody knew he had gone to England for training. Not only could he provide an inside look at the plant, but he could be on the ground to prepare for the arrival of "Operation Grouse." This was a four-man guerrilla organization that Tronstad and Wilson planned to establish in Telemark to prepare sabotage missions and maintain independent wireless contact with London. A hardy outdoorsman, an expert skier, and a trained engineer, Skinnarland was perfect in every way.

Over the course of the next week, he was given the sparest of instruction. Most Norwegian agents sent behind enemy lines underwent at least ten weeks of intensive training, as Haukelid had. Skinnarland spent two days at the specialized training school for radio operators, where he was given a crash course in using a wireless set. From there, he went to STS 51, an airport outside Manchester ringed by a large park, where agents learned how to parachute from planes and land safely. This training usually took place over the course of seven days; Skinnarland got three.

On the clear, moonlit night of Saturday, March 28, 1942, an English Whitley bomber rattled and shook as it crawled through the sky toward its target point north of Lake Møs. Inside, Skinnarland, now a freshly enlisted sergeant in the Norwegian Independent Company, awaited his drop. His white padded jumpsuit, a sleeping bag, and a thermos of tea kept him warm in the frigid air. Beside him was a large steel tube packed with two Sten guns, fourteen Luger pistols, 640 rounds of ammunition, and twenty fighting knives. A smaller container held some spare clothes, fake papers, 20,000 Norwegian kroner, and a camera with enough film for 800 pictures.

As the Whitley approached the drop point, Skinnarland ran through what he had been taught: "Feet together and launch off gently. Relax every muscle when you hit the silk and . . ." It was one thing to parachute in daylight, he thought, the landing zone flat and clear to the eye. It was quite another to fall into a midnight blackness over territory pocked with rocks, steep cliffs, and frozen — but perhaps not sufficiently frozen — lakes. Skinnarland was tough, but he was not fearless.

At 11:44, he was called to his action station. His drop dispatcher sent the large tube container out first. Then Skinnarland edged up to the hole, reluctant to dangle his legs over oblivion. The dispatcher raised his arm and then lowered it, signaling Skinnarland to go. He hesitated, then shouted out that they were not in the right zone, but his words were lost in the growl of the bomber's engines. The dispatcher signaled him again. Skinnarland hesitated still. For twenty minutes, the plane circled around the drop site, Skinnarland unsure whether they were over the right

Norwegian commandos complete a parachute jump.

spot, unsure of himself. At last, a few minutes after midnight, the dispatcher yelled that they lacked the fuel to fly about any longer. Skinnarland took a deep breath and dropped into the dark sky.

●●●

On April 23, 1942, the Tube Alloys Committee met at Old Queen Street in London. As usual, they had a lot to talk about: experimental work on the mechanics of building a bomb, cooperation with the Americans, and the need for more scientists at Oxford and Cambridge. Finally, they discussed the findings of a new SOE source in Norway.

Einar Skinnarland had landed safely in Norway and returned to his job at Norsk Hydro. Over the past month, he had sent a series of coded messages through a system of couriers to Oslo, then on to Sweden. Some were hidden inside toothpaste tubes. Others were taped to the backs of the messengers bringing them across the border, then sent by plane to London.

Whatever method the messages came by, the picture they painted was shocking. Heavy-water production at Vemork was

Underground newspapers of the Norwegian resistance were smuggled out of the country in a hollowed-out log.

up to 120 kilograms a month — and increasing. The plant had fallen far short of its orders for 5,000 kilograms a year, and in January 1942, Jomar Brun had been ordered to Berlin and taken to task for it. Since then, expansion at Vemork had taken off. Over 43,000 electrolysis cells were now devoted to a nine-stage cascade that fed into the high-concentration phase. There, eighteen specialized cells (instead of the original seven) brought concentrations of heavy water quickly up to 99.5 percent purity. In addition, Norsk Hydro was investigating the construction of heavy-water plants at two other nearby hydropower stations. Together they could bring total production up to the 5,000 kilograms target, and possibly more.

Given this intelligence and reports from other sources of Nazi interest in building a bomb, the Tube Alloys Committee decided that something must be done — and soon. In their minutes, sent to Churchill's War Cabinet, they recommended that "an attempt should, if possible, be made to stop the Norsk Hydro production."

Tronstad suddenly found himself working day and night on heavy water. On May 1, 1942, Wilson sent him a note, asking him to determine exactly where in Germany and to whom Norsk Hydro delivered its Vemork supply. The same day, he consulted with Wallace Akers, the head of Tube Alloys, on the construction of a British heavy-water plant. Soon after, Tronstad sat down again with SIS's Eric Welsh, who wanted him to set up a spy network inside Vemork and its surrounds. Germany was largely closed to intelligence work, but Nazi scientists traveled to Vemork, Oslo, and Stockholm — places where Tronstad had close contacts. Skinnarland was already providing great insight into Vemork, but it simply wasn't enough.

On May 11, 1942, Tronstad wrote to Jomar Brun, whom he addressed by his code name, "The Master." The urgency in his tone was clear. He requested detailed sketches, diagrams, and photographs of the Vemork plant, as well as production figures — anything Brun could discover about the German use of "our juice" and the specific address in Germany where it was sent, "so we can give our regards to the people there." Tronstad signed the letter "Mikkel," the Fox.

•••

On June 4, 1942, Kurt Diebner watched a line of guests — some in fine suits, others in uniform — file into the lecture room at Harnack House, the headquarters of the Kaiser Wilhelm Institute. In addition to scientists involved in atomic research,

Albert Speer.

the attendees included high-ranking officials from the Army, Navy, and Air Force. The hawk-eyed Albert Speer, the newly appointed Reichsminister for War Production, had called everyone together to decide the future of the atomic program.

In the first two years of the Uranium Club's existence, they had made steady progress in atomic science. Thanks to the Nazis' military successes, they had access to Norwegian heavy water, Belgian uranium ore, and an advanced French laboratory for experiments. Over seventy scientists across Europe were pursuing research on a number of nuclear projects.

Most excitingly, in September 1941, after several false starts, a professor in Leipzig built a small spherical machine surrounded by two concentric layers of uranium oxide and heavy water. The increase in neutrons was small, but it was there — evidence that the machine was successfully splitting U-235 atoms. With more layers of heavy water and higher-grade uranium, the scientists agreed, this machine would foster a chain reaction. From recent investigations, the Uranium Club had concluded that such a self-sustaining "atomic pile" — what we would today call a nuclear reactor — would do more than produce power. It could also generate plutonium, a new element that was highly fissile, like the rare uranium isotope U-235. Because its atoms split so readily, plutonium could be used as an explosive, and from that point forward, Heisenberg observed, there was "an open road ahead of us, leading to the atomic bomb." Diebner agreed. In his mind, success was now a matter of shifting all their basic research into an industrial program. They just needed to be given the resources.

But two months later, with the Russians attacking Germany on the Eastern Front, Hitler ordered the whole country to bend itself toward meeting the short-term demands of the war. Diebner's supervisor in the Army — no fan of "atomic malarkey" — called for another review of the research. At an Army Ordnance conference held on February 26, 1942, Diebner made his case: "In the present situation, preparations should be made for [harnessing] atomic energy . . . all the more in that this problem is also being worked on intensively in the enemy nations, especially in America." With five tons of uranium, enough heavy water, and a larger, self-sustaining pile, "a bomb of the greatest effectiveness" was in sight. Diebner offered a step-by-step plan to reach this goal. He simply needed the manpower, supplies, and capital to achieve it.

His Army bosses remained unconvinced. Diebner could not promise success with certainty. Unable to justify such expense and effort without the guarantee of a weapon within a year, the Army forfeited control of the Uranium Club's work to the Reich Research Council, a civilian-run, industry-centric body for German scientific research. Abraham Esau, a professor of physics and a man of considerable influence in the Reich, replaced Diebner as the head of the German atomic research group. Diebner experienced a further blow when Heisenberg was chosen to be the new director of the Kaiser Wilhelm Institute of Physics, and he was kicked out of his offices there.

Four months after that disaster, Diebner still believed there was a chance for an industrial-scale nuclear program. Reichsminister Speer, who now controlled the project, had called this June meeting at Harnack House to decide how much backing he should give it.

Heisenberg took the stage to present the scientists' findings. Tall, blue-eyed, with a sweep of straw-colored hair, he commanded the room in a way Diebner never could. With a uranium machine, he said, they could "power ships, possibly even aircraft, with the greatest imaginable range." With plutonium, they could produce explosives that "will be a million times more effective than all previous explosives." One general, who had visions of dropping bombs on New York, wanted to know how big such bombs would be. Heisenberg cupped his hands and said, "About the size of a pineapple."

Once Speer and the generals were excited about the potential, Heisenberg then shifted to downplaying expectations. They were still at the basic research phase, he said. There were many obstacles standing in their way as well, including supplies of heavy water. One day, far in the future, a bomb may "turn the tide of war," he concluded; but first they needed a working reactor, and that was a long way off in its own right.

Speer then asked how much money their project needed. Heisenberg proposed a sum of 350,000 marks (roughly $80,000 in 1942 dollars) — in effect, nothing at all. In other programs, particularly V-2 flying bombs, scientists had demanded billions of marks and tens of thousands of workers in order to complete their projects and see them put to use in the war. Speer was stunned and Diebner furious that Heisenberg would ask for such a trifling sum. The Minister of War Production concluded that, by asking for such a ridiculously small amount, Heisenberg was either uncertain that a pineapple-sized bomb could decide the war, or unwilling to try to build one.

After the meeting, Speer steered his backing toward men more sure of their ambitions. Basic research on atomic power would continue, but all of it would be focused on future potential. There would be no massive project to build a bomb for this war.

Diebner was undeterred. He returned to his laboratory, and with a host of young physicists he had recruited in the first days of the program, he quietly continued building his own uranium machine, with a very different design from the ones that others had engineered. Hard and fast, he pressed on toward a bomb.

●●●

Winston Churchill chewed on a cigar and stared out at the Atlantic's moonlit waters. He was seated in a Boeing Clipper flying boat, and many matters pressed on his thoughts as he flew toward the United States. The whole of Continental Europe remained under Hitler's heel, and though Allied bombers hit Germany night after night, only a cross-channel invasion could liberate the continent. But Churchill knew that his forces were far from ready for such an attack. He needed to convince the US president, Franklin D. Roosevelt, to delay an Allied invasion — one of the two key purposes for his long journey across the Atlantic. The other was to discuss atomic bombs.

When the Clipper finally landed at Hyde Park, New York, the site of Roosevelt's family estate, the American president greeted him on the tarmac. Physically, the two men were a study in contrasts: the short, feisty British bulldog beside the tall, smooth American lion. But Churchill and Roosevelt were both intellectuals as well as cunning politicians, and they shared the terrible weight of leading their people through a great war. In sum, they were friends.

Driving his blue Ford Phaeton, which featured special hand-controlled levers to counter his disabilities from polio, Roosevelt whisked Churchill off on a hair-raising tour along the Hudson River bluffs. For two hours, they spoke of the war, and Churchill was encouraged by how much more they settled zipping across the Roosevelt estate than they would have done on opposite sides of a crowded conference table.

Earlier that week, Roosevelt had read through a report that set out a plan for a massive US Army program, to be run by the Army, to build atomic bombs, with an estimated cost of more than $500 million. Word had just come from Europe that the Germans might have already realized a working nuclear reactor — something the United States had yet to achieve. As one scientist wrote, urging a decisive American effort, "Nobody can tell now whether we shall be ready before German bombs wipe out American cities." Roosevelt responded to the report with a simple "Ok" — and with that authorization, the Manhattan Project was born. In typical bigger-is-better American fashion, its leaders decided that all routes toward a devastating new weapon should be pursued, including heavy-water reactors and plutonium bombs.

On June 20, Roosevelt and Churchill held their formal meeting in a small, dark study that faced the front porch of the Hyde Park mansion. Once, Roosevelt's children had used the space as a classroom, but now it was his quiet hideaway, with bookshelves and nautical prints on the walls.

Churchill and Roosevelt confer during their meeting in June 1942.

Churchill got straight to the point. "What if the enemy should get an atomic bomb before we did!" he later wrote, recounting the meeting. "However skeptical one might feel about the assertions of scientists, we could not run the mortal risk of being outstripped in this awful sphere." Their two countries needed to "pool our information, work together on equal terms, and share the results, if any, equally between us." If Churchill expected a debate, he didn't get one. Roosevelt agreed with the proposal, and given the ongoing Nazi bombing raids on Britain, they decided the United States should be the center of activity. They also discussed the German focus on heavy water — "a sinister term, eerie, unnatural," Churchill later said.

A few days after Churchill flew back to London, the War Cabinet put forward plans, of the highest priority, for a raid on Vemork.

CHAPTER 05

OPERATION GROUSE

Jens-Anton Poulsson wanted a job — and if his commanders would not give him one, he would come up with his own. He had nearly circumnavigated the globe to join the Norwegian Independent Company No. 1, and since his arrival in Great Britain in October 1941, he had heard a lot of plans but seen little execution.

Thus, in late February 1942, Poulsson traveled down from Scotland to pitch his bosses in London a new plan. Meeting with a member of Colonel Wilson's staff, Poulsson proposed the creation of a small team that would organize resistance cells around Telemark. He drafted the details in a report, then returned to Scotland while the plan was considered.

Weeks passed, and no answer came. Poulsson spent time at the British intelligence "Finishing School," where he trained how to be a spy and live an underground life. He learned how to develop a cover ("Your story will be mainly true"), shadow a target, recruit informants, build up an underground cell, and thwart counterespionage efforts. He was taught to burgle a house, to open handcuffs, to read a room for a quick escape. He became skilled in leaving hidden messages, in microphotographs, ciphers, and invisible inks. And he studied the enemy, everything from the Nazis' organizations, uniforms, and regulations to their detective measures, wireless interception abilities, and interrogation techniques. If he was ever to find himself under

Jens-Anton Poulsson.

Arne Kjelstrup.

questioning, his lecturers said, "Create the impression of an averagely stupid, honest citizen." After he finished his spy training, Tronstad informed Poulsson that his proposal to build up resistance cells around Rjukan had been accepted. It was now code-named "Operation Grouse."

Poulsson had been born in Rjukan — the town just below Vemork — where, it was said, one was raised in either the sun or the shadow. Norsk Hydro's top brass lived in grand houses on the sunny northern hillside of the Vestfjord Valley, while the rank and file found themselves living deep in its reaches, down by the river. As his father was a chief engineer at Vemork, Poulsson grew up in the light. His family had a storied history — nobility, ship captains, high-ranking Army officers, English knights — and owned almost 10,000 acres of land in the Vidda region of Telemark, including an island on Lake Møs.

Named after his father and grandfather, Jens-Anton was the sixth of seven children. With his best friend and neighbor, Claus Helberg, he spent his early teens wandering the Vidda, cross-country skiing, fishing, hunting, and hiking. Now a lanky twenty-three-year-old soldier, Poulsson stood six foot two, with a mop of curly dark hair, a lean face, and bright blue eyes. He perpetually had a tobacco pipe stuck in his mouth and usually preferred to stay toward the back of the room, clouded in smoke.

Once the proposal for Operation Grouse was accepted, Poulsson and Tronstad chose the small team. They picked Arne Kjelstrup, twenty-nine, a short, broad-chested plumber, born but not raised in Rjukan, who still carried a bullet in his hip from fighting the Germans in the resistance. Knut Haugland was a slightly built

Knut Haugland.

Claus Helberg.

twenty-four-year-old with a thick shock of fair hair and a thin boyish face that belied his exacting intelligence. A carpenter's son from Rjukan, he had become a first-class radio operator. Finally, Poulsson had come to know Knut Haukelid well while they trained together in Scotland. The two often went hunting together in the Highlands, and it was clear to Poulsson that Haukelid understood what it took to survive and operate in conditions like the Vidda.

Then, during a training exercise, Haukelid stumbled and shot himself in the left foot with his pistol. He nearly blew off his big toe, and the doctors told the crestfallen commando that he would not be "fit for duty" until at least October. Poulsson knew who his replacement would be: Claus Helberg. Now leaner, taller, and fitter than most, Poulsson's childhood best friend had found his own way over to Britain in the spring of 1942 and joined the "Kompani Linge," as the Norwegian Independent Company was now called. He needed parachute training, but he should be ready.

Throughout August, the men prepared for their operation, gathering enough supplies to fill eight tubular containers together weighing almost 700 pounds. The inventory list was two pages long: ski gear, boots, gaiters, windbreakers, undergarments, sleeping bags, cooking utensils, tools, cigarettes, candles, tents, paraffin, backpacks, maps, frostbite ointment, a wireless set and two 6-volt rechargeable batteries to power it, guns, ammo, and food.

Operation Grouse would drop near Lake Langesjå, eleven miles northwest of Rjukan, with Einar Skinnarland on the ground to guide the plane in with lights. Haugland knew Skinnarland well from the local Rjukan resistance, and all of the team were well acquainted with the Skinnarland family. (Einar's

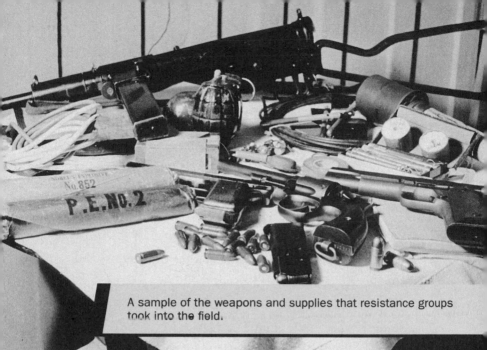

A sample of the weapons and supplies that resistance groups took into the field.

brother Torstein was something of a ski-jumping legend in town.) If, for any reason, it was not possible for Einar Skinnarland to be there, they would blind drop and head to Lake Møs on their own. Their operating instructions were to form "small independent groups" of resistance fighters to prepare for operations. Like the alpine bird for which their mission was named, they were to survive the harshest of winter conditions out in the wild while awaiting sites to attack.

On August 31, 1942, the Grouse team left for Special Training School 61 at Gaynes Hall near Cambridge. The distinguished mansion served as the SOE launch point for foreign agents headed overseas on operations. Grouse would wait and train there until their mission was a go.

• • •

That same day, Leif Tronstad sat in a smoke-filled room on Old Queen Street, the Tube Alloys headquarters, and raised the idea of Grouse leading an attack on Vemork. Seated around the table with him were Colonel Robert Neville, the chief planner of Combined Operations (air/land/sea missions); Wallace Akers; and Michael Perrin, a key member of the British atomic program. The four men considered several potential courses of action to stop the production of heavy water at Vemork.

Tronstad argued against an air attack. The town of Rjukan might be wiped out in the devastating explosions, and it was unlikely any bombs would reach the high-concentration stages in the basement of the plant. As for recruiting saboteurs who already worked at the plant — an inside job — he did not believe they could find enough trustworthy people on the inside to pull it off. Instead, he wanted his Grouse team to stage a direct attack on the plant and destroy the heavy-water equipment. The men knew the area, and according to the most recent intelligence provided by Brun, who was now actively spying for Tronstad, there was only limited security at the plant. With an additional six-man sabotage team to carry out the demolition, the group would have good odds of success.

Neville was unsure: German defenses might be stronger than reported. He favored British sappers (combat engineers) executing the attack with the Grouse team acting as guides. Fifty soldiers could overcome any resistance, and with their strength in numbers, they could perform a larger attack on the plant, beyond destroying the heavy-water equipment, to make certain Vemork was never a threat again. The trouble would be getting the men out and away from Norway. It was a challenge that, Neville recognized, probably made them a "suicide squad." The four men knew the War Cabinet would make the final decision, but it looked like the Grouse team would indeed have a role to play in the Vemork plan.

Tronstad was desperate to be part of any operation on the ground as well. Yes, he was contributing to the war effort. He recruited Norwegian scientists to aid the British defense industry. He helped steer the strategy, training, and operation of Kompani Linge. But at times he felt he was waging battles of paper reports and meetings, that others were suffering the burdens of war while he remained safe in London. Many of his close friends were dead; the Gestapo had evicted his family from their Trondheim home and hounded his wife for information on his whereabouts. Brun was risking his life every day spying for his country. Tronstad wanted to do the same. After celebrating his thirty-ninth birthday that March, he had quit smoking

Norwegian King Haakon VII and Tronstad, in exile in Britain.

and begun exercising diligently. In June, he went through parachute school at STS 51. Each evening, he tried to get in a "little commando work" in the expansive park by his house.

But General Colin Gubbins, the Special Operations chief, told Tronstad that his place was in London. His insight and leadership were too valuable to risk. Coming to an uneasy peace with staying behind, Tronstad threw himself into his Kompani Linge command.

His resolve was strengthened by the news out of his homeland. Across Norway, average citizens were actively resisting the Nazis any way they could. Earlier in the year, teachers had gone on strike, refusing to comply with Nazi demands to teach the New Order to their pupils. Reichskommissar Terboven had ordered the arrest of the most contentious teachers — 500 in number — sending them to a concentration camp in Kirkenes, an Arctic seaport. The journey took sixteen days, the prisoners crowded inside the cargo hold of an old wooden steamer, with little food or water and no toilets. They were forced to work twelve hours a day on the docks, alongside Soviet prisoners of war, and were ill-fed, poorly housed, served rotten fish in a mucky soup, and beaten on a whim. Some died. Others went mad. Still, they resisted.

"War makes the mind very hard," Tronstad wrote in his diary, thinking of the latest news of their hardships. "Becoming a sensitive person again will not be easy."

● ● ●

Throughout September, as Haukelid watched the rains sweeping across Scotland, he wished passionately that he had been able to join the Grouse team instead of injuring his foot. From the team's letters, however, it sounded like they were as stuck as he was. In one, headed "Somewhere in England," Poulsson wrote, "If you think we have left, then you are damned wrong . . . A week's waiting for fine weather which never comes. Otherwise it is alright here — the house full of FANYs [field army nurses]." Then, on September 9, "There is a red light today and we hope for the best. We are now ready to start."

Haukelid awaited word that they had dropped safely. Once they connected with headquarters by wireless and were securely in place in Telemark, the plan was for him to join them with another Linge member. If not for that foot . . .

At the end of September, another letter arrived. "Of course we came back. Motor trouble." The following day brought yet another note from the Grouse team. "Another unsuccessful attempt. Fog in the North Sea. Devil take the lot! But tails up." Then silence. Nothing. Surely they were gone now, landed in the Vidda without him.

● ● ●

General Nikolaus von Falkenhorst, the commander of German military forces in occupied Norway, strode through Vemork's grounds on October 1, 1942. He was impressed by its natural defenses but thought they were insufficient to protect the plant. There needed to be floodlights, more guards, more patrols, barracks for his troops, potentially an antiaircraft battery. The surrounding hillsides and the steep slope running down from the pipelines into the power plant needed to be laid with mines. The fences around the grounds needed to be heightened and topped with rings of barbed wire. The narrow, single-lane suspension bridge leading to the plant needed a reinforced gate. All

General Nikolaus von Falkenhorst and Reichskommissar Josef Terboven visit Rjukan.

of Norway must ready for an Allied attack, Falkenhorst warned the soldiers stationed at the plant, and that included Vemork.

Then, four days after his visit, men in British uniform raided an iron-ore mine outside Trondheim. The Gestapo quickly determined the sabotage had clear help from local people. The next day, the city woke up to find posters declaring a state of emergency. The Nazi governor of occupied Norway, Reichskommissar Terboven, arrived by overnight train, accompanied by SS Lieutenant Colonel Fehlis and scores of his Gestapo. They picked out ten prominent Trondheim citizens — a lawyer, a newspaper editor, a theater director, a bank manager, and a shipbroker among them — "to atone for several sabotage acts." Then Fehlis's execution squad shot them in the back of the head.

Terboven intensified efforts to prevent any future raids and break the will of the Norwegians. New border regulations, ration cards, and travel permits were instituted. The list of violations punishable by death now included "providing shelter to enemies of the state" and "attempting to leave the country." Across Norway, his security services arrested thousands, often without cause, and torture intensified. If a known resistance member couldn't be found, the Gestapo took his or her parents or siblings instead.

In mid-October, Hitler delivered a secret order to his generals across Europe, instructing them to punish the Allies for attacks like the one at Trondheim: "All enemy troops encountered in so-called commando raids in Europe or in Africa, are to be annihilated to the last man. This is to be carried out whether they be soldiers in uniform, or demolition groups, armed or unarmed; and whether in combat or seeking to escape . . . If such men appear to be about to surrender, no quarter should be given to them — on general principle." The order violated the written and unwritten codes of war.

● ● ●

When Colonel Wilson summoned Poulsson and Haugland to London on October 12, 1942, they could not help but fear that the mission was going to be postponed again — or canceled altogether. Their pilot had aborted the first attempt because of dense fog. On the second, their Halifax airplane was already over Norway when one of its engines burned up and they were forced to turn back.

Wilson got straight to the point. The situation had changed. Rather than fomenting resistance in Telemark, Grouse would now be the advance operation for a British Army action against Vemork. They would recon a landing area for either a parachute drop or a Horsa glider. Then they would act as a reception committee, putting out lights to direct the aircraft as well as operating a homing radio beacon. On the night of the attack, they would guide between twenty-five and thirty combat Royal Engineers to the target. Underscoring the top secret nature of the mission, Wilson informed Grouse that Einar Skinnarland would no longer receive them, nor were they to have any contact with him.

They were to leave on the first available date of the next moon phase. Parachute drops into Norway were limited to a very narrow window. For half the year, there was too much light at night for planes to cross over the countryside unseen by the Germans. For the other half, particularly during the long winter, drops needed to occur around the full moon phase, when the darkness was cut by just enough moonlight that pilots could navigate by landmarks — and parachutists could spot a safe place to land. October 18 was the beginning of the next such phase. They could leave then. The sabotage operation would take place the following month.

Then Wilson led them into a room full of maps and reconnaissance photos. He wanted them to pick out a safe spot within the vicinity of Vemork for the sappers to land. The two Rjukan men didn't need a map, as they had crossed every inch of the surrounding area by skis and by foot. Together, Poulsson and Haugland came to the same conclusion: the Skoland marshes, a wedge of unpopulated land at the eastern point of Lake Møs, southwest of the dam and next to a mountain road that was closed during the winter months. The British sappers would have a clear run down the road to Vemork, just eight miles away.

Over the next few days, the two were schooled in what they were to communicate — and when — for the entirety of the operation. All their instructions were given verbally and memorized. "This is Piccadilly," Poulsson was to say on receiving the commandos, naming a famous place in London. "I wanted Leicester Square," they would answer, naming another.

On the day of their departure for Scotland, Wilson brought them in for one final meeting. "This mission is exceedingly important," he said. "The Germans must be prevented from getting their hands on large quantities of heavy water. They use it for experiments, which, if they succeed, could result in an explosive that could wipe London off the map."

The colonel must be a little overexcited, Poulsson and Haugland thought; no explosive could do such a thing. Perhaps he simply wanted to inspire them to the task at hand. Nevertheless, they told him they would do everything they could to see the operation was a success.

The Vidda.

CHAPTER 06

THE VIDDA

"Number one, go!" the dispatcher yelled through the cold wind whipping into the plane. It was 11:36 P.M., October 18, 1942, and a full moon hung in the sky, perfect for a parachute drop. With a surge of excitement and fear, Poulsson edged himself out of the open hatch on the floor of the Halifax's belly. He tipped forward, then suddenly he was falling, falling fast.

Below him spread out the Vidda in the clear moonlight: its snow-peaked mountains, isolated hills, lakes, rivers, and narrow ravines. It was a place both beautiful and terrible, and Poulsson knew it must be respected. At 3,000 feet above sea level, it was exposed to unpredictable weather and high winds that could hurl a man off his feet. In the winter, a skier could be sunning himself on a rock one moment only to find a storm sweeping through the next, bringing blinding slivers of ice and snow and temperatures below minus 30 degrees Celsius. Norwegian legends said it could grow cold enough, quickly enough, to freeze flames in a fire. Simple fact said it could kill the unprepared in two hours.

The Germans had steered around the Vidda when they attacked Norway, and even now they dared venture only far enough into it that they could get out by sunset. There were no roads and no permanent habitations in the 3,500-square-mile expanse of land — larger than the state of Delaware. Only skilled skiers and hikers could reach its scattering of hunting cabins. In the valleys, one could find birch trees, but many areas were simply frozen barren — lifeless hillsides of broken scree, one mile the same as the next.

As his parachute snapped behind him and he prepared to land, Poulsson found himself unable to identify the rockless, flat Løkkjes marshes, twenty miles west of Vemork, where they had expected to be dropped. Instead, there were only snow-patched hillsides of boulder and rocks — ideal for snapping one's neck.

He landed hard, but luckily without injury, and called out to the other members of the Grouse team, who had followed him out of the plane. Kjelstrup and Haugland were in good shape, but Helberg walked gingerly, having come down against the edge of a boulder. On examination, the back of his thigh was swelling, but there was no fracture. He did not complain.

For the next four hours, they searched the hillsides for their eight containers of gear, most importantly their stove, tent, and sleeping bags. If a storm hit, they would be in trouble without those essential supplies. With the aid of moonlight, they found everything, but it was too late to do anything more than take shelter from the wind beside a boulder and settle in for the night. The four huddled together. It was cold but bearable. They each wore long underwear and two pairs of socks, all made of wool, then gabardine trousers, buttoned shirts, and thick sweaters. Over these went parkas and windproof pants, wool caps and two pairs of gloves. If the weather got nasty, they could always pull their balaclavas over their faces and don their goggles.

Poulsson dug into his pouch of tobacco and prepared his pipe, a ritual that somehow eased the nerves of the others. He lit the pipe, puffed a couple of times, and then revealed to Helberg and Kjelstrup, "There's a new order of the day." No longer were they there to build up a network of underground resistance cells, he said; instead, they were the advance team for a sabotage operation. After learning the details of the Royal Engineers plan, Helberg thought it was a suicide mission for the British troops: How would they escape Norway? All four Norwegian commandos, however, were happy they would be in on a bigger job. As Haugland thought, "You don't jump out of a plane over your occupied country to contribute a little something."

Divided into a pair of tents, using their parachutes as groundsheets, the four slept for a few hours in their sleeping bags. They woke to a clear blue sky, the surrounding rugged hills cast in sharp relief. They were home now, far from soggy Scotland, and the air was crisp and dry. Examining the terrain, Poulsson determined that they had landed on the edge of the Songa Valley, more than ten miles west of their intended drop point.

A typical supply and weapons drop during the Norwegian occupation.

The men spent two backbreaking days dragging together the eight containers of supplies scattered about the area. On inspection, they found some serious problems. First, there was no paraffin fuel for the stoves in any of the containers. Fuel would have allowed them to hike a straight course over the barren mountains to the Skoland marshes, where they would meet the Engineers. But crossing the Vidda was too great a risk without some source of heat, so they would have to travel through the valley, where there would be cabins for shelter and birch trees for firewood. That added a lot of distance and at least several days to their journey.

Second, their British packers bungled the radio equipment. They had failed to include bamboo poles, which were used to rig up an antenna, and they had replaced the standard-issue Ford car batteries for the wireless set and their homing beacon with ones that weighed twice as much. Worse, these batteries were stamped MADE IN ENGLAND. The British connection would put anyone involved in recharging the batteries in serious danger if they were caught.

They tried tying together ski poles with parachute cord to form an antenna, but they did not succeed in reaching London by wireless. Now they faced a forty-five-mile trek with heavy packs to the marshes in time to meet the British sappers.

● ● ●

Lieutenant Colonel Mark Henniker was put in charge of the preparation and planning of the Vemork mission, which had been code-named "Operation Freshman." Under his watchful eye, two field companies of the Royal Engineers got a week's training: marching, practicing shooting, sleeping on straw mats, and suffering lectures on how to keep their feet healthy (two pairs of dry socks). Then they were shipped off to northern Wales, where they were sent on long treks through the Snowdon Mountains, using a compass and map, eating hard rations, marching through bogland and up and down steep slopes. They slept huddled closely together, a mound of men sharing not enough blankets.

Combined Operations decided to bring the sappers to their target by plane-towed gliders instead of dropping them by parachute. It was a risky choice: After the planes released the gliders, 10,000 feet in the air, the glider pilots would have to land their crafts at night, in foreign territory prone to shifting weather and uncertain terrain. This would be the first time the British tried gliders in an operation. But using parachutes would require that the sappers be dropped near the plant, which increased the risk of their being noticed. Worse, the sappers might be injured on landing in the rugged terrain, and they might be too spread out to find each another in quick order. Gliders would land silently, and all the men would be together, with all the equipment required for the operation at hand.

The plan took shape. The Grouse team would use lights to signal the two gliders to land in the Skoland marshes. They would also employ the new Eureka/Rebecca system, an untested technology whose radio signals provided a homing beacon to planes. They would then guide the sappers to the plant. At Vemork, the British troops would cross over the suspension bridge, neutralize the small number of guards, and place almost 300 pounds of explosives to blow up the power station's generators and the hydrogen plant. Once away from the plant, they were to separate into groups of two or three men and change into civilian clothes. Then they were to hike the 200 miles to Sweden.

Brickendonbury Hall.

On November 2, Henniker's men were brought to STS 17, the SOE's industrial-sabotage school in Brickendonbury Hall, an old manor house. Leif Tronstad met them there. He gave them blueprints of the buildings as well as photographs and drawings of the equipment to be targeted, which Brun had secreted out of Norway. (Given the impending operation, the Vemork plant manager had been smuggled across the Swedish border and brought to England.) Thanks to information from Skinnarland and Brun, the sappers came to know virtually everything about Vemork, from the type of locks on the doors to the number of steps required to reach the heavy-water high-concentration plant on the basement floor. They even practiced placing explosives on a wooden mock-up of the heavy-water concentration cells.

There was just one problem. It had been more than two weeks since Grouse had left, and Tronstad had heard nothing from them. Without the four young Norwegians on the ground, without regular radio contact, Operation Freshman could not take place.

● ● ●

Like all the members of Operation Grouse, radio operator Knut Haugland was cold, hungry, exhausted, and wet — and worse, he was weighed down with seventy pounds of equipment. The team had buried a depot of supplies that they would not need until after the sabotage in the snow, then left their drop spot on October 21 for the forty-five-mile trek to the Skoland marshes. In ideal conditions, they could have crossed this distance in a couple of days, skiing straight across the frozen surface of the many rivers and small lakes that marked the Vidda. But they had 560 pounds of supplies to carry — 140 pounds for each of them — impossible to haul unless they split it into two journeys. Thus they would ski a few miles with seventy-pound loads, empty their backpacks, and take a short break to eat. Poulsson had rationed them each a quarter slab of pemmican (a pressed mix of powdered dried game, melted fat, and dried fruit — the most treasured part of their ration), four hard crackers, a pat of butter, a slice of cheese, a piece of chocolate, and a handful of oats and flour for the day. Their break over, they returned to their starting point and retrieved another seventy pounds of their equipment and food, to repeat the journey over again. Worse, in late October, the ice on the lakes and rivers was not yet completely frozen. In the few places they tried, the surface water on the ice left their boots and socks drenched.

Given all of this, by the end of the third day, they had advanced only eight miles from their drop site. Before dark, they came across an abandoned farmhouse beside Songa Lake. They broke in and found some frozen meat, which they hacked apart with an ax. They built a fire, melted snow in a pot, then softened the meat in the boiling water. For the first time in almost a week, they feasted until their bellies were full. Better still, they also found an old sledge.

Over the next six days, the team made slow, steady progress east, their supplies now split between their backpacks and their newfound sledge. No longer did they need to make the double journey. Still, the snow was heavy to wade through, the rations strict, the terrain rough, and the stretches of water a risk to cross. Poulsson once fell through the ice of a half-frozen lake, and Kjelstrup, his body stretched flat on thin ice, had to pull him free with a pole. At night, they broke into cabins for shelter, but none held the same booty as the first farmhouse. They ate their pemmican, sometimes cold, sometimes mixed with oats or flour in a hot gruel, but they were always left wanting more. As one day followed the next, the four grew thin and their beards scraggly, their cheeks and lips blistered from the constant wind, cold, and toil. They were almost always wet, as their clothes never dried completely at night. Their skis grew waterlogged. Their Canadian boots were fraying. Had it not been for all their hard training in Scotland, they would already have given up.

As they traveled, Haugland took enough fishing rods from cabins to build a mast for the antenna. One night, he fired up his wireless set, only to have it short-circuit moments later. He cursed his bad luck. Haugland had always wanted to be a radio operator, an ambition fueled by a naval adventure novel he had read as a teenager, which featured a radioman saving his whole crew. Operating a radio set in Morse code had been like learning to play the piano. At first he was all thumbs, slow and stuttery, but after practice, practice, practice, he found that he was a master, tapping out dots and dashes without thinking. He joined Kompani Linge soon after arriving in Britain and attended STS 52, the specialized school for wireless operators, where his teachers said he should be instructing them.

Now, thirteen days into his first operation, Haugland still had not managed to get his radio to function. Determined not to fail again, he set about fixing the wireless set. When ready, he turned it on, hoping that the shortwave signal from his mast would reach the operators at Home Station in England.

Straightaway, he got reception, and then, an instant later, nothing. The battery, all thirty pounds of it, "Made in England," was dead.

The mood in the cabin felt grim. In sixteen days, the moon would be in position for the operation against Vemork. Their team had to be in place to recon the landing site, provide weather reports and intelligence on Vemork, and receive the British sappers. They still had many miles to go, and they had no working radio.

They buried the battery, and Helberg went ahead of the others to Lake Møs dam, seeking help from Torstein Skinnarland, Einar's brother, who served as an assistant keeper of the dam. Even though Grouse had been ordered not to make contact with Skinnarland or any locals in order to maintain the secrecy of their mission, Poulsson felt they had no choice. No radio, no sabotage of Vemork. With new snowfall and a drop in temperature, conditions on the ground improved, and the other three made quick progress east over the next two days. Helberg met them at a river crossing on his return from the dam. Torstein would provide a new battery, he said, but it would take some time. He also suggested an old cabin they could hide in.

In the early hours of November 5, the Grouse team arrived at a cabin beside Sand Lake, three miles east of the Skoland marshes. Once inside, the four collapsed. Dirty, unshaven, their faces chafed from the cold, they looked like mountain men, and half-starved ones at that. They slept that night like the dead.

The next day, Haugland started constructing his aerial antenna again. He lashed together two thin towers made from fishing poles, set them fifteen feet apart, and strung copper wire between them. While he worked, Helberg departed for the dam

to retrieve the battery, and Poulsson and Kjelstrup skied to the marsh to inspect the landing site.

● ● ●

In the woods by the Lake Møs dam, Einar Skinnarland waited for Claus Helberg. Throughout the six months Skinnarland had spent living a double life — working at Norsk Hydro while spying for the British — his fear of discovery had been constant. He had several informants at Vemork, and one had been interrogated recently by Rjukan's police chief. Nothing came of it, but a loose word, a single mistake, by any of a number of people, including Skinnarland himself, and he would be lost. Despite these risks, he was often given less information than he needed from his handlers in London, whether because of communication breakdowns or because of need-to-know secrecy.

News that Grouse had already arrived in Norway, no less at his brother's doorstep, was testament to this problem. Such surprises invited disaster. Still, Skinnarland came instead of Torstein to pass Helberg the freshly charged battery. Einar offered his compatriots any help they might need in the days ahead, whether supplies or intelligence. He quickly became part of the team.

● ● ●

After dark on November 9, Haugland finally thought he had everything set to restart the radio. He had already coded his message, a jumble of letters on the notepad in front of him. It needed to be short and quick because the Germans operated D/F (direction finding) radio stations that tuned in on broadcasts from Norway. If Haugland transmitted for too long and two German stations were close enough, they could zero in on

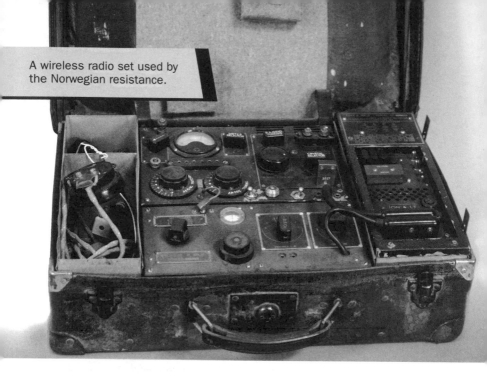

A wireless radio set used by the Norwegian resistance.

Grouse's position. As a radio operator, Haugland knew that brevity and speed were arts that saved lives — his own among them.

The new battery feeding in a steady current, Haugland powered up the wireless set. The three other Grouse team members watching closely, his hand trembling from the cold and excitement, he sent out his identity call sign. He immediately received an answer in return. They had contact. The four cheered. Haugland delivered his first message: "Happy landing in spite of stones everywhere. Sorry to keep you waiting. Snowstorm and fog forced us to go down valleys. Four feet of snow impossible with heavy equipment to cross mountains. Had to hurry on for reaching target area in time. Further information. Next message."

Grouse was in place for its mission, and ready to guide the paratroopers to their target.

CHAPTER 07

TWO LITTLE BIRDS

On November 15, Tronstad sat down with Wilson, Henniker, and several others to go over the plan for Operation Freshman one last time. Despite his misgivings about destroying a plant that he had helped to build, the more Tube Alloys told him about the Germans' atomic research efforts, of "super bombs" that would equal "1,000 tons of TNT," the more Tronstad knew they needed to be stopped.

He delivered the latest messages from Grouse: They suggested the sappers bring snowshoes, but said that even under bad conditions the march to Vemork should not take more than five hours. With the help of Einar Skinnarland, the team would cut the telephone line between the Lake Møs dam and Rjukan on the night of the operation. There were two guards at the door to the hydrogen plant, and the sappers would have no trouble overpowering them. If more forces came from Rjukan, the suspension bridge could easily be held.

Henniker said that he would only need two guides from Grouse on the approach to the plant. Their role would end when the Royal Engineers went across the suspension bridge. The other Grouse men were to operate the wireless and destroy the radio homing beacon, a technology the British did not want to fall into German hands.

Overall, the mood of the meeting was very positive. Toward its close, Tronstad presented diagrams of the plant's layout. He said he understood the mission's importance, but he worried that destroying all the power station's generators would hurt the livelihoods of most of the Norwegians in Rjukan and eliminate fertilizer supplies his country desperately needed. Instead, he sketched out a plan to save two of the twelve generators, which would have the same effect on heavy-water production but keep Vemork alive as a hydrogen plant. Henniker offered to raise the point with his superiors, but time was running short for making changes to the plan.

Tronstad was sure he had been given a polite brush-off, but he prepared a report that finally won him the change. In it, he concluded, "Good policy for destruction of plants in Norway is namely to do just as much damage as strictly necessary — to prevent the Germans from winning the war — and nothing more."

● ● ●

In a dark, windowless corner of the cabin on Sand Lake, Poulsson tended a huge pot of boiling sheep's-head stew. Earlier that day, Haugland and Helberg had come across a sheep that had strayed from its flock and got caught in some rocks. Desperate for food, they killed it. Poulsson fancied himself a bit of a cook, so he had added some canned peas and whatever else he could find in their stores to improve the stew's flavor. Not that the others would complain, he knew, as all of them were starving. The smell wafting from the pot already made their mouths water. The boys had even set a cloth over the table.

Outside, the wind howled, hurling snowflakes into the cabin through the many breaks in the walls. The single, lit candle flickered so much they could barely see one another. On his way to the table with the huge pot in hand, Poulsson slipped on a reindeer rug. An instant later, the stew spilled across the floor, sheep's head and all. Everyone gazed at it, then at their cook. Without a word, the four got down on their knees and scooped whatever they could into their mouths. In the end, there was nothing but picked-over bones and jokes from Kjelstrup about having "hair in my soup."

The British gliders needed the light of the full moon to land. In the three days leading up to November 18, the start of the full moon phase, Grouse stayed busy. They scouted the route down to the target. From a hidden position on the opposite side of Vemork, they watched the guards on the bridge. Helberg continued to venture back and forth from Lake Møs for supplies and batteries. Haugland was the busiest, constantly coding and decoding messages to and from London. Some of his scheduled broadcasts took place after midnight, and he emerged from the shell of his sleeping bag only as far as he needed to tap out his Morse. Mostly he sent word about the weather, which had been very unpredictable. One day it was clear. The next, there were high clouds, and the next the clouds lay low across the valley like a blanket. Some nights it snowed lightly; others were merely freezing cold. The winds came in squalls from shifting directions.

On the morning of November 19, Haugland transmitted that the weather over the landing zone was clear for a second consecutive day. There were no clouds and the northwest winds were light. If the weather held, everything was in place for the British arrival.

● ● ●

That afternoon, twenty-eight Royal Engineers ate sandwiches and smoked cigarettes on the barren seaside moor that made up Skitten Airfield. Some bantered about the upcoming mission, but most handled their nerves in silence. There would be a final briefing, but they already knew what they needed to know: They were heading to Norway to blow up a power station and hydrogen plant. The sappers still had no idea what purpose the "very expensive liquid" produced at Vemork served. However, given the blanket of security everywhere they traveled, and the orders to strip off their uniforms' badges and insignia, they knew it must be important.

After they finished their tea, the sappers kitted up. They wore steel helmets and British Army uniforms with blue roll-neck sweaters underneath. Each of them had a Sten gun, a backpack filled with ten days of rations, an escape kit, explosives, and other equipment. Some of them carried silk maps with the target circled in blue and a false escape route. After the operation, these would be dropped to throw off their pursuers.

Under a slight drizzle, the sappers strode out onto the runway, where two black Horsa gliders waited behind Halifax airplanes. Most of the sappers were in their early twenties, and one observer on the ground noted they looked like schoolboys. While the Halifax crews went through their checks, the sappers boarded the gliders, taking their positions in the fuselage and strapping on their safety harnesses. The floor beneath their boots was corrugated metal, its long channels designed to prevent slipping on the vomit that was a usual result of these glider flights.

After a slight delay, the Halifaxes powered up. At 6:45 P.M., with a wave from the crews, Halifax A roared down the runway. The glider followed behind, connected by a taut rope, 350 feet long. Seconds later, the Halifax and glider drew up into the sky. Soon after, Halifax B and its glider joined them. Including air crews and sappers, there were forty-eight men on the mission.

Having observed the takeoff, Tronstad later jotted down in his diary, "Two little birds following two large ones, off towards an uncertain fate tonight."

● ● ●

When Poulsson and his men arrived at the landing zone, the clear weather was changing. A moderate wind blew across the Skoland marshes, and scattered clouds hung in the sky. Visibility was still good, but knowing the Vidda, this might alter at a moment's notice.

Leaving Haugland and Kjelstrup on a hillside to set up the Eureka beacon, Poulsson and Helberg moved down into the snow-covered marsh to mark out the landing zone. They placed six red-beamed flashlights in the snow, each 150 yards apart, in the shape of an L.

Haugland would be the first to know the Halifaxes were coming. When a plane approached, its Rebecca device would send a radio signal to his Eureka device. A tone would sound in his headset, and his Eureka would send a signal back to the Rebecca, giving the plane's navigator a bead on their landing zone.

Everything ready, the Grouse team gathered together in the dark, certain that they could lead the sappers undetected to the target and that the defenses at Vemork would be overcome. But with each passing minute, the scattered clouds lowered, and a northwest wind rose into a scream.

A Halifax airplane towing a Horsa glider.

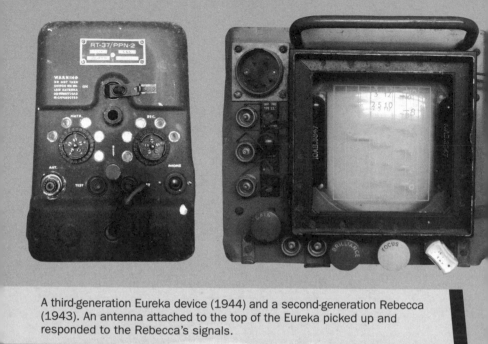

A third-generation Eureka device (1944) and a second-generation Rebecca (1943). An antenna attached to the top of the Eureka picked up and responded to the Rebecca's signals.

At 9:40 P.M., Haugland knelt in the snow beside the Eureka. A tone sounded in his headset, and through the rising winds, he shouted to Poulsson, "I hear the Rebecca. They're coming now." Poulsson skied down toward the landing site. "Up with the lights," he called out. Quickly, they lit the red L in the snow.

Poulsson stood at the corner of the L, covering and uncovering the white beam of his flashlight with his hand. Wind whipped around him. He stared skyward, the low clouds breaking occasionally to reveal the moon. Although he worried that the flashlight beams were too weak for the pilots to see through the cloud cover, he knew the Eureka radio beacon would bring them in close nonetheless.

A few minutes passed before they heard the low grumble of a Halifax approaching. "I can hear it," Haugland cried out, his voice lost to the others. The engines grew louder. The Halifax was surely flying right above them. Spirits high, they waited for the glider to appear out of the darkness. Gradually, though, the roar of the engines faded, and Haugland's headset went silent.

Poulsson continued to flash his signal, and the red lights continued to shine upward into the empty night. No glider. Nothing. They waited several more minutes. At last, another tone sounded in Haugland's headset. "Number two is coming!" he called out. As before, the drone of engines cut through the night. But the sound never grew any louder, nor did any gliders come down.

Over the next hour, the Eureka toned a few more times, and they heard engines from several different directions. Then there was only silence.

● ● ●

Flying with the moon behind them, the crew of Halifax A found it impossible to make out where they were on their map. Every valley, mountain, and lake looked the same. By the navigator's calculations, they should have been within twenty miles of the landing zone. But they never saw any red L on the ground, and their Rebecca was no longer working for some inexplicable reason. In sum, they were wandering in the dark, their fuel running low.

The pilot decided to turn back to Scotland. It was approaching midnight, and after almost five hours of flying, they would just make it home. Having set a new course, they found themselves enveloped in clouds at 9,000 feet. When the pilot tried to rise above them, the glider in tow behind, the Halifax failed to respond to the controls. Ice was beginning to form on the wings of both the plane and the glider.

At full throttle, engines roaring, the plane finally rose. They reached 12,000 feet, but the Halifax could not maintain either its altitude or its speed. It dropped back down into the clouds. The four propellers flung off ice in shards that crashed into the fuselage. They needed to get to a lower altitude to clear the ice or they would not make it. The pilot dipped down to 7,000 feet, but turbulence was worse in the thickening clouds at the lower altitude. The plane shook violently.

The Horsa glider rocked back and forth, surged upward, and plummeted down, its two pilots at the mercy of the towrope. The sappers in the back were hurled about in their seats. The wooden fuselage creaked and groaned as if it would be ripped apart at any moment. Then they lurched ahead one final time, and the icebound towrope snapped.

The glider came down fast, the wind shrieking through the aircraft. The men hooked arms to brace for the landing but had little hope it would do any good. Soon after breaking loose from the Halifax, they crashed into the mountains.

The pilots died instantly, the glider's glass nose providing their bodies no protection. Six sappers perished upon impact. Of the nine who survived, most were too badly injured to move. A few managed to crawl out into the snow. The glider's wings had been sheared off, the fuselage broken apart. Their gear had spilled out all over the mountainside, and the subzero temperatures bit at their skin. They had absolutely no idea where they were.

Halifax B had circled around the landing zone, its Rebecca device sending out its signal, but it had failed to zero in on the target close enough to release its glider. Running low on fuel, the pilot aborted the operation and decided to return to Scotland.

He experienced the same treacherous thick layer of clouds as Halifax A and, at 11:40, lost his glider near Egersund on the southwest coast. He lowered altitude and crisscrossed over the valley, trying to locate it in the darkness.

Suddenly, he found himself staring straight out at a mountainside. He attempted to maneuver the Halifax away but failed. They clipped the top of the mountain with terrible force, throwing the rear gunner from the plane and killing him. Still traveling at great speed, the plane hurtled over the summit, then across a plateau littered with huge stones that tore it apart over the course of 800 yards. The bodies of its six crew members were scattered about the flaming wreckage.

Four miles away, across the valley, their glider rested on its side in a steep mountain forest, its nose sheared off, its two pilots dead. Their efforts to land in the darkness and fog had saved the lives of all but one of the fifteen sappers. As the weather worsened, the fourteen surviving Royal Engineers tended to one another's injuries as best they could and wrapped the fatalities in their sleeping bags.

The ranking officer on the glider, Lieutenant Alexander Allen, sent a pair of his men to find help. At 5:30 A.M., a group of Norwegians and a patrol from the German garrison at Slettebø, outside Egersund, approached the crash site. Allen and the others had decided to surrender, even though they were heavily armed and could easily have surprised the dozen approaching Germans. The German lieutenant promised Allen, whose men were still dressed in their British uniforms, that they would be classified as prisoners of war and that a doctor would treat the wounded.

The fourteen sappers from the glider, some too severely

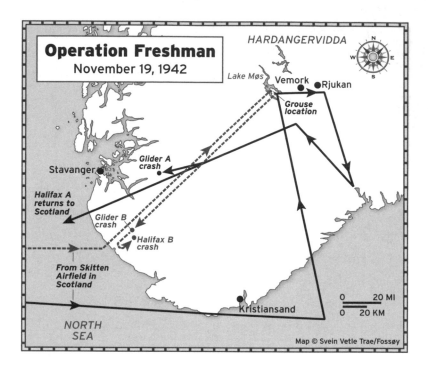

Map labels:

Operation Freshman
November 19, 1942

HARDANGERVIDDA

Lake Møs · Vemork ●Rjukan

Grouse location

Glider A crash

Stavanger●

Halifax A returns to Scotland

Glider B crash

●*Halifax B crash*

From Skitten Airfield in Scotland

●Kristiansand

NORTH SEA

0   20 MI
0   20 KM

Map © Svein Vetle Trae/Fossøy

---

injured to walk, were brought down from the mountain and boarded onto trucks. Walther Schrottberger, the captain in charge of the Slettebø garrison, did not know what to do with them. Clearly, they were British soldiers, and given that explosives, radio transmitters, Norwegian kroners, and light machine guns were collected at the crash site, they were saboteurs, too. He remembered that, according to Hitler's orders, "no quarter should be given" to any saboteurs.

The Gestapo sent SS Second Lieutenant Otto Petersen, known as the "Red Devil," to investigate. He wanted the sappers placed in his custody. Schrottberger instead gave him an hour to interrogate the British. One after the other, the sappers were brought before the Gestapo officer, shouted at, threatened, and beaten. They revealed only their names and ages.

Then, in the late afternoon, Schrottberger and his soldiers led the prisoners out the garrison gates to a sparsely forested valley, where they were shot, one by one. Bodies still warm, the fourteen Royal Engineers were stripped to their underwear and brought to a seaside beach, where they were buried in a shallow trench of sand.

SS Lieutenant Colonel Fehlis was furious over the rushed executions of the British soldiers. He sent a damning note to his chief in Berlin. "Unfortunately, the military authorities executed the survivors, so explanation scarcely is possible." When it became known, on November 21, that there were nine survivors of a second glider crash, Fehlis wanted to make sure that every bit of intelligence was wrung from them. He ordered that the five saboteurs from the second downed glider who were in good enough shape to travel should be brought to Oslo, along with everything collected at the crash site. They would be interrogated, then shot. The other four survivors, all badly injured, could be executed immediately.

Fehlis already knew most of what he wanted to know. Among the gear scattered around the glider, the patrol had found a folded silk map with a planned escape route. Circled in blue: Vemork.

● ● ●

On that bleakest of days, November 20, Tronstad sat with Wilson in his Chiltern Court office. Nothing was certain in war, Tronstad understood. But reading through the Freshman messages, he could not help remembering the meeting with Henniker several days before the team left, when the prospects for success had been so high. Now those plans were shattered. The air crews were lost. Those brave young sappers, many of whom Tronstad had come to know at Brickendonbury Hall, were yet another terrible sacrifice in this awful war.

In silence, Tronstad and Wilson stared up at the giant map of Norway on the wall. It was dotted with symbols of operations under way by Kompani Linge. Some would go right. Others wrong. That was the nature of things. Despite the disaster of Freshman, the two men were determined to learn from it and try another way at Vemork. There was no other choice: They needed to stop its production of heavy water or the threat of greater losses — losses unimaginable if the Nazis obtained the bomb — might become real.

The two men could not know if the Germans had found out the target of the sappers' mission. If they had, the risks for the next operation would multiply. The Nazis would crack down on any person in the area who might aid such an attempt, putting Skinnarland and the entire Grouse team in danger. Wilson made it clear to Tronstad that it was unlikely the British would try to send another big team of Royal Engineers. He and Tronstad agreed that was for the best. A small group of commandos would have the likeliest chance of slipping inside and destroying the plant, they decided. They should be Norwegian, comfortable with and able to navigate the winter terrain. They would be dropped into the mountains by parachute, if possible by the next full moon in December. They would join Grouse, hit Vemork's heavy-water facilities, and get out.

CHAPTER 08

GUNNERSIDE

Poulsson and his men packed up their gear in the Sand Lake cabin. Their latest direction from London instructed them to retreat into the Vidda as soon as possible. "Vitally necessary you should preserve your safety. . . . It is equally important we have earliest possible information in regard to increase of enemy troops in neighborhood of target . . . Advise you to move yourself and your station . . . Keep up your heart. We will do this job yet."

Reports from London of the failure of the glider operation, and the deaths of so many men, struck the Grouse team hard. That there were clear skies for the next two nights made the disaster even more difficult to accept. Their only solace was that the mission to sabotage Vemork had not been canceled. The next attempt was set for mid-December. Poulsson assured Tronstad that his team would do anything they could to help.

On the night of November 23, the four commandos left the cabin at Sand Lake. They had a freshly charged battery for the radio and the key to a cabin owned by the local Milorg leader, Olav Skogen. They skirted around the German troops stationed at Lake Møs and trudged a dozen miles northwest to Grass Valley, deep and high enough into the Vidda that few ventured there in wintertime. Skogen's cabin was surrounded by nothing but snow and a few scraggly juniper bushes that struggled to survive in the windswept hills. Inside, they found some salted reindeer in a barrel, but otherwise it was as barren and cold as an ice locker.

The next day, their backpacks emptied to the essentials, they headed west toward the Songa Valley, where they had parachuted in over a month before. They needed to pick up the food and supplies they had left in their depot. On the way, they spent a night in a dilapidated hay barn. The next evening, they reached their landing site and used shovels to dig a snow cave for sleeping.

The morning of November 26 welcomed them with a misty fog, and they searched for several hours in the deep snow before finding their containers. The stores of food were limited — some sacks of coffee, sugar, and flour — but they were desperate for it. Starvation and the tempestuous Vidda were their enemies now. After dividing up the supplies, Haugland and Helberg skied

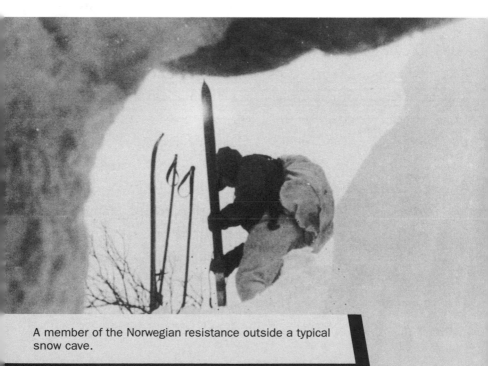

A member of the Norwegian resistance outside a typical snow cave.

east, back to Grass Valley, their packs filled with most of what they had found. Poulsson and Kjelstrup went in the opposite direction to connect with underground resistance cells in the area.

That night, a blizzard hit. Crossing an ice-blue lake that had been blown clear of snow, Helberg and Haugland became separated. Helberg, whose skis had steel edges, managed to make it to the other side without incident. Haugland did not have the same advantage. He was driven across the lake in whatever direction the ferocious gusts of wind blew. At one moment, unable to get a grip on the ice, he found himself being hurled toward a patch of open water at the lake's edge. Stabbing the ice with his poles, he narrowly avoided a deadly plunge.

To the west, Poulsson and Kjelstrup were also caught in the Vidda's monstrous jaws. They skied down into a gully, but each time they tried to climb out on the opposite side, the wind threw them back in. Hounded by squalls, they were forced to crawl on their knees to keep moving.

At last, they came across a shack in the valley. The dirt-floored shelter barely fit the two men, but it was a retreat from the storm. In the morning, they managed to push open the door, only to find that the shack had been completely buried by the blizzard. Handful by handful, they scooped the snow into the shack in order to ease the door open. Finally, Poulsson squirreled up and out into a bright, clear day.

●●●

On November 24, back in Scotland, Joachim Rønneberg was called into Drumintoul Lodge, STS 26's headquarters. The twenty-three-year-old Rønneberg stood to attention, all six feet

Joachim Rønneberg.

and three inches of him. He had a long dome of a forehead, narrow-set gray-blue eyes, and the edged jawline of a silver-screen star.

"You're to be the leader of an operation," his commander said.

"What is it?" Rønneberg asked.

"I haven't the faintest idea, but you're to pick five men for the job."

"Yes, but Lord God, I have to know if we'll be operating on the coast or in the mountains. Are we going in by boat or plane? Will we be there a long time? Do they need to be good skiers?" Rønneberg asked. "Any advice you can give me in my choice of men?"

His commander shook his head. The only thing he did know was that one of the five men had to be Knut Haukelid, who would be Rønneberg's second-in-command. Why? The commander did not know that, either.

Three days later, Rønneberg was in London to meet with Wilson and Tronstad. "Where are we off to?" he asked straight out.

"To Vemork," Tronstad said. "To blow it up."

Rønneberg and Haukelid were to organize and train a six-man team that would parachute into the Vidda. Haukelid had been chosen because he knew the area and was close to the advance team, Grouse. They would be met by Grouse, hit the heavy-water facility at Vemork, then escape on skis to

Sweden. The operation was code-named "Gunnerside," after a hunting cabin owned by a chief SOE officer. Wilson and Tronstad wanted Rønneberg and his team ready to leave by December 17 so they could arrive at Vemork on Christmas Eve. The holiday might prove their best chance at finding diminished defenses. It was a tight schedule: three weeks until launch.

Rønneberg already knew which four other men he would select for the mission. He had instructed them all at STS 26, and he cabled them now from London, telling them to get down to some hard training in the Highlands. Birger Strømsheim was his first choice, and the easiest to make. A thirty-one-year-old builder from Ålesund with a broad, honest face, he was good with his hands, a fine skier, and a hard worker, as steady and

Birger Strømsheim.

Fredrik Kayser.

Kasper Idland.

Hans Storhaug.

reliable as a rock. Next was Fredrik Kayser, twenty-four. During sabotage schemes, Kayser proved to be adaptable and cheerful under pressure. Third was Kasper Idland, also twenty-four, a former small-town postman. Even as a boy, Idland had been taller and bigger than most. As a soldier, he was intelligent, an excellent shot, tough, and loyal. Rønneberg's fourth choice was Hans "Chicken" Storhaug, a short, pencil-necked twenty-seven-year-old. Although not the deepest of thinkers, there were few better in the woods, hunting or skiing. The fifth member of his team, Haukelid, was a concern for Rønneberg. Considered more a loner than a team player by some within Kompani Linge, he might prove a problem for Rønneberg's command, but Tronstad wanted him on board.

Joachim Rønneberg had been raised in Ålesund, a peaceful, quiet harbor town on Norway's northwestern coast. During his first months of training with Kompani Linge, he sometimes had trouble sleeping, disturbed that he was essentially in a "vocational school for butchers." Nonetheless, he excelled at the lessons, particularly with explosives and raid exercises. He also made peace with the brutality he was taught, as he knew it would allow him to survive in any situation.

He was sure he would be sent on a mission straightaway, but instead he was made an SOE instructor, involved first in translation and liaison activities, then increasingly in the training itself. He became an expert in demolitions and devised many of the sabotage schemes against bridges, railway stations, and military barracks that his students went on to execute. New arrivals were shocked that someone so young, with so little experience, who seemed as "gentle as a lark" (as one said), was already an instructor. Then they got to know him. Rønneberg was intelligent, clever, tireless, and determined, strategic, thorough in his preparations, and a professional in every way. What distinguished him most was his innate ability to lead. "He had a quality that made him stand out alone," said one in his company, "without being envied, without making enemies or rivalries." He did not need to dominate, raise his voice, or inspire with flourishing words. He always pursued his own best and allowed others to realize their own. And that was what elevated him.

On his return to STS 26, Rønneberg gathered the five men together and said, "Now, I do not know you all equally well personally, but if there is any disagreement between you, then put it aside until we're done with the job. Or get out." Everyone stayed where they were. He then outlined the operation and its purpose. Whatever this heavy water was, it must be

Knut Haukelid.

important if SOE wanted to make another attempt on a target that had already cost so many lives. They were to understand that if they were caught, the Germans would show them no mercy. Afterward, Rønneberg drew each man aside by himself and gave him the opportunity to back out. No takers.

Haukelid did feel that, given his extensive experience, he should be the one leading the mission, not Rønneberg. However, an order was an order, and he was man enough to swallow his pride if it meant he could go back to Norway at last.

• • •

Before dawn on December 3, air-raid sirens blared throughout Rjukan. Looking outside, the town's residents discovered German soldiers and Gestapo coming through their streets. Soldiers were posted on street corners and on bridges. Bundled in heavy coats, their breath heavy in the air, they looked none too happy to be there on the frigid morning. Orders were given for all residents to remain inside their homes — or they would be shot.

Throughout the town, the same scene played out over and over again. A hammering on the door. Shouts to open up. Soldiers, sometimes led by the Gestapo, storming into the house, asking

for the names of every-
one who lived there,
rummaging through
rooms, looking for ille-
gal material — guns,
radios, underground
newspapers. If anything
was found, the occu-
pants were taken away
by truck. Often, the sol-

Rolf Sørlie.

diers broke furniture, punched holes through walls, and stole
whatever food they could find.

Rolf Sørlie, a twenty-six-year-old Vemork engineer, pleaded
innocence when they came to his house, using the fluent German
he had learned while studying in Leipzig. A short, slight young
man with fair hair, Sørlie had been born with a condition that
left the muscles of his hands and feet in constant spasm. Surgery
had corrected his twisted feet, but not his hands, which were
stuck in a half clench. He had never let it stop him from wandering the Vidda with his childhood friends Poulsson and Helberg.

As soldiers filed into his house, Sørlie was scared. Not only
was he close to the local Milorg leader, Olav Skogen, but there
were two radios hidden in his attic. Fortunately, the soldiers gave
the house only a brief search, either out of laziness or a lack of
concern over this young Norwegian who spoke such nice
German. They left without finding anything. In total, twenty-
two Rjukan townspeople, including several members of the
Milorg cell, were arrested.

That same day, Hans and Ellen Skinnarland threw a little
party to celebrate their son Olav's thirty-second birthday. Their

younger son, Einar, who was working on the Kalhovd dam at the eastern edge of the Vidda, was the only member of the family not present when the Gestapo roared up on their motorcycles. The Germans arrested Torstein, thinking he was the Skinnarland who was rumored to be involved in resistance work. Nothing was said about Einar, but the family knew the Gestapo would soon mark him for arrest as well. The Germans were clearly keen on protecting Vemork for some sinister purpose.

● ● ●

Late in 1942, in two rows of buildings at the Army Ordnance Kummersdorf Testing Facility in Gottow, fifteen miles southwest of Berlin, Diebner and his team of experimental physicists and engineers labored over their first uranium machine, the Gottow-I (G-I) experiment. It had been assembled with whatever cast-off materials they could find. Inside a cylindrical aluminum boiler, eight feet in diameter and height, they stacked honeycombs made of paraffin wax around an empty center. The team then spooned uranium oxide into each cell of the honeycomb, wearing heavy, breath-stealing protective gear to shield themselves from the uranium's toxicity. The work, which took weeks, was "dreadful drudgery," one man said.

When complete, the honeycomb was made up of nineteen horizontal stacks, with 6,902 uranium oxide cells, weighing almost 30 tons (25 tons of uranium, 4.4 of paraffin). Ready to test the design at last, the boiler was lowered into ordinary water, and Diebner told his men to insert the beryllium neutron source into the center of the honeycomb. Eagerly, he waited to see if his design was better than the machines constructed by others in the Uranium Club.

The building at Gottow, near Berlin, where Diebner's team built their G-I and G-III piles, using heavy water.

Earlier that summer, Heisenberg had demonstrated a modest, but still impressive, increase in neutrons, in a machine built with two spherical layers of powdered uranium metal submerged in heavy water. The machine was clearly fostering the splitting of atoms, but not at a rate that would become self-sustaining. However, he predicted that using the same design, but with substantially more heavy water and uranium (five and ten tons, respectively), they would have a self-sustaining reactor. Then, on June 23, bubbles rose to the surface of the heavy-water tank. While Heisenberg and his assistant were figuring out what to do, the machine's aluminum shell swelled like a balloon. They ran from the laboratory moments before an explosion sent streams of flame and red-hot uranium powder through the ceiling.

The disaster did not negate the experiment's achievement. Still, Diebner thought their design was inferior to his own, because the fast-moving neutrons in Heisenberg's machine could escape the uranium mass into a moderator in only two dimensions. The cubes of Diebner's design made the neutrons move through heavy water in three dimensions, which slowed them down to a point where they were more likely to split other U-235 atoms than be absorbed by U-238 — or lost outside the machine.

Near the year's end, after months of labor, his theories proved true. His G-I machine beat the neutron production rates of machines like those Heisenberg had built. Up until this point, Diebner had used cheap, spare materials like uranium oxide and paraffin. Now he asked his new boss at the Reich Research Council for pure uranium metal and heavy water. With these, Diebner promised he would soon have a working reactor.

CHAPTER 09

SURVIVAL

On December 11, a week before their scheduled drop, the six Gunnerside men arrived at Brickendonbury Hall. Major George Rheam, the British master of industrial sabotage who had trained the Royal Engineers, was waiting for them. He invited them to dinner that evening; then his adjunct led the men to their dormitory room. On each bed was a kit bag with the clothes and gear they would need for their training. There was also a factory-new Colt 45.

They each put down the stuff they brought with them. Then, to a man, they grabbed their new guns and tested the action. Rønneberg cocked his, but when he pulled the trigger, the gun fired. As his ears rang and plaster dust fell about him, he realized that he had, by mistake, fired the loaded gun he had brought with him, which he had set beside the new one.

One of the school's guards rushed into the dormitory, quickly followed by Rheam's adjunct. "What the hell's going on?" he asked.

Straight-faced, Rønneberg looked up, pointed at the hole in the wall, and said, "I've tried my new weapon and it works perfectly."

The adjunct shook his head and walked out. Crazy Norwegians.

It was a rare moment of carelessness for Rønneberg. In the ten days since being charged with Gunnerside, he had been punctilious in his preparations for the mission. He had gathered several sets of maps of southern Norway from the High Command's intelligence office in London. One, a large-scale map at 1:250,000 scale, had been nailed to the wall at the base in Scotland and used to chart out the team's routes. The others, at 1:100,000 scale, were given to the team, so each man could memorize every valley and mountain along the way.

When an item of equipment fell short of his needs, Rønneberg redesigned or altered it. He picked out the best wood skis, then had them sealed with fresh pine tar and painted white. To improve the design of the steel-frame backpacks, he added gaiter pockets, drawstring tops, extra-long shoulder straps, and white coverings. For rations, he chose lightweight blocks of dehydrated food, manufactured through a process developed by a Norwegian professor and dieticians at Cambridge University. Given how far they would have to travel in escaping from Vemork to Sweden, every ounce mattered. Using Rønneberg's design, a London bedding maker created a sleeping bag that would allow them to survive the Vidda. It was essentially two bags woven into one (the outer bag a waterproof shell, the inner one filled with down), and large enough to sleep in while fully dressed in their gear. A hood over the top had a drawstring tie that would close almost completely, leaving just a small opening for breathing. By the time Rønneberg and his men arrived at Brickendonbury Hall, they knew their routes to and from Vemork, and most of their gear was ready to be packed for the drop.

Now they could focus on the operation itself. They trained on the same wooden model that the Freshman sappers had used. Rheam showed them where on the base of each heavy-water high-concentration cell they should place the explosive charges.

The machines featured two rows of nine cells. The team needed to place a series of nine half-pound charges connected by a detonator cord on each row. This cord would then be rigged with two-minute fuses to allow them to clear the room before the explosion. The aim was not only to destroy the machinery but also to puncture the cells and drain them of their precious contents. Using children's putty, the team operated in pairs to rig the explosives.

They repeated the maneuvers so many times that they could nearly do them in the dark. For the operation itself, they would use Nobel 808, a rust-colored plastic explosive that reeked of almonds. Soft and malleable, 808 could be cut, shaped, stretched, thrown against the wall, and even shot at, and it would not explode. But set off a small explosive charge (essentially, a detonator) buried within it — even underwater — and . . . boom.

Tronstad came down to Brickendonbury one last time to go over the mission and to bid the men farewell. It was an emotional moment. Each of the saboteurs had been given a cyanide capsule;

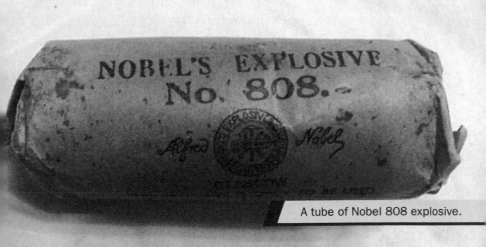

A tube of Nobel 808 explosive.

each knew that his chances of hitting the target and escaping with his life were, at best, even. Tronstad reminded them of the executions of the Freshman sappers and warned them that they would likely be treated the same — or worse — if caught alive.

Then he said, "For the sake of those who have gone before and fallen, I urge you to do your best to make the operation a success. You do not know now exactly why it's so important, but trust that your actions will live in history for a hundred years to come."

There followed an awkward pause. Some on the team felt Tronstad was looking at them like they would never come back.

"You won't get rid of us so easily," Rønneberg said.

● ● ●

At the Grass Valley cabin, the Grouse team was starving. Every morning, one of them went out hunting for reindeer, only to return without spotting a herd. Haugland had managed to kill several grouse, but they picked those bones clean within a day. Even their treasured supplies of pemmican were gone. The four suffered constant pangs of hunger and resorted to digging in the snow for the rust-colored moss the reindeer ate. "It's full of vitamins and minerals," Poulsson promised. They boiled it with a handful of oatmeal and made a bitter soup.

On December 12, this hardship was finally lightened by some good news from London: They were to take an "active part" in the new operation against Vemork, as Gunnerside would need a covering party to give them the time — and security — to carry out the attack. But there was much to be done before the new team arrived on the 18th. Grouse had to secure some food, get the latest intelligence about security at Vemork, retrieve the

Eureka device that had been left at Sand Lake, and recharge their batteries. Then they needed to travel to a new hideout, twenty miles northwest of Vemork, where Gunnerside was to be dropped.

Misfortune hounded them at every turn. German patrols delayed their fetching the Eureka device. Helberg was caught in a storm while returning with a freshly charged battery. They continued to fail to track down any reindeer, and some salted meat they found in a cabin by Lake Møs turned out to be rotten. All of them became too sick to hold down the little food they had left. Helberg and Kjelstrup were in particularly bad shape. Still, they went out every day to ready for the new operation. Skinnarland and a band of local farmers, who assisted him however they could, provided them with some spare food, recharged batteries, and details on new Vemork defenses.

On December 17, Haugland received a signal from Tronstad that Gunnerside was set to leave on the next clear night. It was time to head north. Starving, sick, and against the clock, they trudged deeper into the Vidda.

The four bearded, haggard men struggled with every lift of their skis in the sticky, wet snow on Lake Store Saure. Over the surrounding peaks, a mist hung like cotton wool. Finally, they arrived at Fetter, a hunting cabin Poulsson had built with his cousins before the war. Positioned high on the plateau, near a copse of birch trees and unmarked on maps, there was no better place to hide and await Gunnerside.

On entering, Poulsson found Fetter looking much the same as it had when he had last left it in the summer of 1940. There were four beds; a square, rough-hewn table; some three-legged stools; and a stone-lined stove that heated the ten-foot-by-twenty-foot

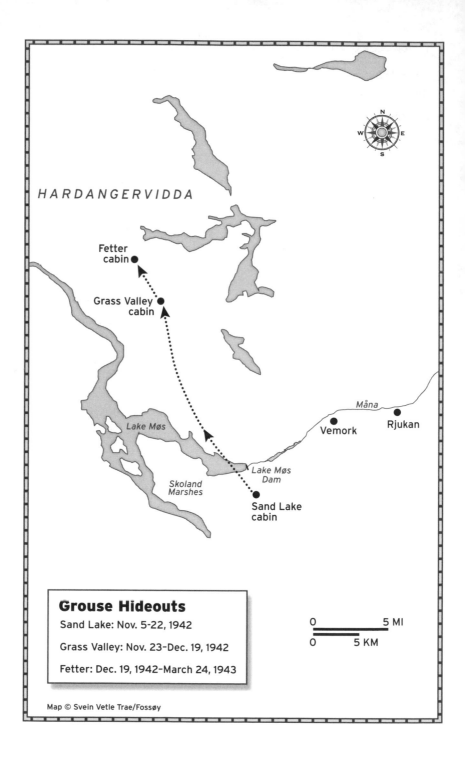

HARDANGERVIDDA

Fetter
cabin

Grass Valley
cabin

Lake Møs

Skoland
Marshes

Lake Møs
Dam

Sand Lake
cabin

Måna

Vemork

Rjukan

N
W · E
S

Grouse Hideouts

Sand Lake: Nov. 5-22, 1942

Grass Valley: Nov. 23-Dec. 19, 1942

Fetter: Dec. 19, 1942-March 24, 1943

0 _____ 5 MI
0 _____ 5 KM

Map © Svein Vetle Trae/Fossøy

room. Poulsson scoured the cupboards for food but found only a bottle of cod-liver oil and a scoop of oatmeal.

The others followed him inside, more exhausted from the journey than they should have been. If they continued to starve themselves, they would have no strength for the operation. The sun set early, and the four lit a single candle and ate reindeer moss for dinner again. Gusts of wind howled around them as they awaited radio contact with London. Finally, they learned Gunnerside would not drop that night. Stomachs rumbling, they settled into their beds. Poulsson promised, "Just wait until there's game in the area. Then we'll have plenty to eat." The others were losing hope he might be right.

Day after day passed in the same pattern, and Gunnerside did not come. Each morning, soon after sunrise, Poulsson left Fetter to hunt. He knew that herds traveled into the wind so they could smell any predators, and unless the wind changed direction, the reindeer would continue to drift far out of range of the cabin. Even so, he trudged from mountain to mountain, often through a heavy fog. Each afternoon, he returned to Fetter empty-handed. His team was becoming dangerously weak. Either Gunnerside came soon or Poulsson tracked down a herd, or they would not hold out much longer.

Rønneberg and his team now waited at Gaynes Hall, the holding camp for SOE foreign agents set for operations. In the five days since they first arrived, terrible weather between England and Norway — dense fog, rainstorms, low clouds, blizzards, tempestuous winds — had shuttered any chance of a flight. All of Europe was suffering the same weather, and Gaynes Hall was rapidly filling up with anxious men. Rønneberg and his team ruminated over when the weather would improve, how the approach to Vemork would go, would they be engaged in a firefight, was it better to be shot or captured, should they have another go at the letters they had written to their wives and families in case they did not come back. One evening, they took a car into Cambridge, drank champagne, and dined at a good restaurant. They knew they might not have another chance.

● ● ●

On December 23, after a week of snowstorms and cloudy, fog-swept days, Poulsson stepped outside to a beautiful morning. It was still freezing, but the sun felt good on his face. Skis fastened, he was just lifting his Krag rifle over his shoulder when Kjelstrup came out of the cabin to get some firewood. Of the four, Kjelstrup was in the worst state, suffering from cramps that left him too worn out to leave his bed for more than a few hours a day. "Crisp and clear," he said, his eyes ringed with red. "Maybe today will be your day."

Poulsson headed away. The frost that had blanketed the Vidda in the night made for fine skiing, and he settled into a nice, steady tempo. Over the many years since his grandfather bought him his first gun, Poulsson had tracked and killed numerous reindeer on the Vidda. But now, when he needed a kill the most, he could not even find a herd. Then, five miles out from the cabin, his legs beginning to weaken, he came across a band of fresh reindeer tracks in the snow. He nearly leapt from excitement. On inspection of the tracks, the herd looked to be a good size. They would be moving slowly, maybe a couple of miles every hour, grazing on moss and resting as they wished.

His men would eat this night, Poulsson thought. He set off

for the nearest hilltop but saw nothing in his binoculars apart from the endless stretch of white. The reindeer were likely down in a valley or on top of a plateau. He followed the tracks for several miles, almost reaching the northern end of Grass Valley. Still nothing. If they had caught wind of a wolf or some other predator, they might already be far away. Bolting reindeer could travel twenty-five miles in less than an hour.

After zigzagging to the top of another valley, Poulsson stopped. He wiped his binoculars clear with a square of flannel he kept under his watch and examined the horizon again. Far to the north, in a small valley, he spied some dark spots. At first he thought they were only stones, but they were moving together. The herd.

Slowly, Poulsson skied closer. He made his way to the eastern side of the valley to keep downwind of the herd and prevent them from picking up his scent. He ascended a ridge and, after unfastening his skis, eased himself up onto a boulder. The herd stood in the valley over a half mile away. They were roughly seventy in number. Several grazed on moss beside a small patch of lake. Others rested on the ice or stood like statues. Their winter pelts had faded to a long, shaggy, whitish-gray, camouflaging them within the landscape. Farther to the north, up on a raised plateau, was a second herd, smaller in size.

To get a good shot with the Krag, Poulsson needed to be within 200 yards of the deer. He did not see how he could get within that range without the herd spotting him across the flat approach or catching his scent. He would have to hope they came toward him, or moved off to steeper, uneven ground where he would have more cover to stalk them. Perched on the boulder, he waited ten minutes, then thirty, then an hour. The cold settled deep into his bones, and he grimaced and contorted his face to keep away frostbite.

More time passed. The herd looked to be staying there for eternity, munching on moss, milling about.

Poulsson had to act. After almost two months of living off the sparest of meals since their arrival in Norway, his men needed food. With the dwindling light of the day, he must make a kill soon or risk losing the herd in the dark — and being caught out on the Vidda. Resolved, he climbed down from the boulder. As he made his approach, two bucks strayed from the herd. Poulsson stood motionless, still too far away for their eyes to distinguish him from the terrain. When they turned back to the herd, he eased his way toward a small mound that would bring him within range. Nearly there, he slipped and almost tumbled down the hill before catching his fall.

The two bucks stamped the ground, then took off toward their herd. Their flight spurred the others. With the pounding of hooves, the lot of them vanished over a hillock toward Grass Valley.

Poulsson lay back in the snow, suddenly unable to stand. He swore at the empty sky. When the anger settled, his desperation almost brought him to tears. Chasing after the beasts was fruitless. They might have stampeded one mile or five. He turned his eye to the high plateau, a short distance away to the north. The smaller herd was still there, grazing.

He climbed back up the slope to gather his gear and then skied fast. When the rise to the plateau grew steep, he went by foot. Heart twisting in his chest, he crept up the last few yards on his belly. He rose up slightly on his elbows to see thirty reindeer, a cloud of mist hovering over them from their breath.

A herd of reindeer on the Vidda.

The wind on the plateau shifted every few seconds, leaving the reindeer ill at ease. Rifle in his right hand, Poulsson crawled forward inch by inch in the snow until he was within range. Carefully, he drew up to his knees, took aim, slid his finger on the trigger, and fired. His target did not drop. The panicked herd fled toward the peak of the plateau. He took aim at another reindeer and fired, then at another. None fell. The herd kept moving, leaving a trail of swirling snow behind them. Then they disappeared.

Rising to his feet, Poulsson felt confused. It was impossible to think he had missed all three. He trailed the deer in the direction where they had fled. Specks of blood were dribbled in the snow along three separate tracks. He followed one track a hundred yards over the top of the plateau and found a wounded doe, trying to rise. Poulsson fired another shot. The doe stilled. He chased after the next track of blood for a short distance but then turned back. He hated leaving wounded animals to a slow death; however, this was a matter of his and his men's survival.

He returned to the doe. It was a fair size. Relief, then joy, rose within him. For the first time in two months, his team would eat their fill. Poulsson drank some of its blood for a quick jolt of sustenance. Then he began skinning and quartering the carcass with a knife and ax. Its head and tongue, rich in nutrients and flavor, went into his backpack, followed by its stomach, with four chambers filled with half-digested moss. Then the heart, liver, kidneys, ribs, and legs. While he worked, he sucked some of the milky white marrow from the small bones near the hooves. He left the leanest cuts of meat in a heap in the snow to be retrieved the next day. First and foremost, his men needed fat and nutrients.

With almost fifty pounds of reindeer in his backpack, Poulsson made his way back toward Fetter in darkness. After wiping his hands clean in the snow, he left the backpack by the door and entered. He said nothing to the others, and seemed to have returned as empty-handed as on previous days. They gave him a pitiful look, sorry for him, sorry for themselves. Haugland reported that Gunnerside would not be coming that night. The chances they would come anytime soon were slim.

Something in Poulsson's look gave the men pause. Then Kjelstrup spotted a smear of blood on his white anorak and roared. They rushed out of the cabin to the heavy, blood-soaked backpack. Cheers rang out. The next night, Christmas Eve, the four gathered at the table. As a centerpiece, they had a twig of juniper decorated with little paper stars. They listened to Christmas carols on the radio, the headphones set on a tin plate so they could all hear. Then the radio was switched off — the precious power in the battery had to be conserved.

They dined: fried reindeer tongue and liver, blood-and-moss soup, boiled meat, and marrow. Helberg had found some salted trout in a nearby cabin, a further treat. Stuffed, they sat in silence. Poulsson puffed on his pipe, and they all listened to the wind surrounding their cabin. It shook the roof and sent a dusting of snow underneath the door.

●●●

Many miles away, alone at a table, Einar Skinnarland celebrated Christmas Eve with some pancakes. He was hiding in a small, dark cabin called Nilsbu, a thirty-minute trek from the shore of Lake Møs. The place was almost indistinguishable from the surrounding terrain. In winter, it was often entirely buried in snow. In summer, it was well hidden amidst the heavy pine forest. If Skinnarland lay flat on the floor, he could almost touch every wall with his outstretched arms and legs. There was no place he felt safer.

Only a few days before, the Gestapo had arrested his best friend, Olav Skogen. Skinnarland was now at the top of their arrest list. As his underground activities were finally known to the Germans, Tronstad had given Skinnarland the choice to escape to England or to remain behind, living on the run and helping Grouse any way he could. He chose to stay and help his friends.

On December 27, Skinnarland headed toward Lake Store Saure. After several hours of skiing through a biting southwest wind, he finally arrived at Fetter. Inside, he found Poulsson stirring some kind of stew on the stove: reindeer flank with cuts of intestine, windpipe, and fat, all flavored by the clots of reindeer fur floating on top. Skinnarland welcomed the meal nonetheless, and they invited him to stay as long as he wanted. With the moon phase at its end and the next chance of a drop a month away, they all had need of company.

CHAPTER 10

THE WHITE TEMPEST

On January 16, when the new standby period came into effect, Tronstad sent a message to the men at Fetter: "Weather still bad but boys eager to join you." As the five waited for the weather to change, one day blended into the next. They cut wood, hunted, cooked, and sat by the wireless, eager for news. By 4 P.M. each day, the sky darkening, they gathered at the table for dinner. Afterward, they retreated into their sleeping bags to endure another night of the raging storms that threatened to tear the cabin apart.

There were petty flare-ups. One man was accused of not keeping the cabin in good enough order. Another didn't get up early enough to cook breakfast. With the men crowded in a small space, isolated from civilization, and always either cold, wet, tired, or hungry, these moments could easily have escalated into war. Skinnarland's presence helped. During the standby period, he alone could leave Fetter, and after miles of skiing, he always seemed to come back in good cheer, often with a pat of butter or some dried apricots that he stirred into their reindeer stew for a change of flavor.

Without Poulsson, the team would have fallen apart. During the short days, he kept the men busy with chores, but it was the long sixteen-hour nights that were the real danger. They could not sleep the whole time, and they did not have either the kerosene or the candles to keep the cabin lit all night to whittle, play cards, or the like. One evening, to occupy them, Poulsson gave a thorough lecture on the art of hunting. This inspired Kjelstrup to take a turn and instruct everyone in the science of plumbing. Haugland followed with a study on radios, Skinnarland about building dams. When they ran out of lecture subjects and poems, they talked about their lives at home, their families. Instead of tearing them apart, as they might have done, the winter nights drew them closer together.

● ● ●

At long last, on January 23, 1943, Haukelid spied surf breaking against the coastline of Norway. Jostled about in the fuselage of the Halifax, he kept his eyes trained on the view through the window. He saw a fishing boat and imagined its captain swinging his lantern to welcome them home.

To avoid German radar, the pilot flew low over the valleys toward Lake Store Saure. The forests and mountains were as

A Halifax in flight.

clear under the bright moon as they were during the day. Their navigator should have no trouble finding the drop site. Sitting in silence inside the Halifax, the five Gunnerside men looked to their dispatcher to give the sign that they were nearing the drop. They drank tea to stay warm.

The plane zigzagged across the Vidda. Its pilot relayed to Rønneberg that he could not yet see any signal from their reception party. Fog hugged some of the valleys. The Halifax veered back toward the coast so its navigator could get a new bearing; then they returned to the drop zone. Out his starboard window, Haukelid saw Lake Langesjå.

Finally, the dispatcher gave the call for them to prepare to jump, and the hatch in the fuselage floor opened. A six-minute warning was called, but no signal to jump followed. The navigator was not able to spot the drop site. Regardless, Haukelid wanted to go — Rønneberg, too.

The Vidda passed underneath them. Wind gusted through the hole, and the Halifax continued to circle. After midnight, they were told the plane was running low on fuel and needed to go back to Britain. It felt like a crater was opening in each of their hearts. To return, on the brink of action in their homeland . . . they simply could not reconcile themselves to it.

Suddenly, there was a burst of antiaircraft fire. The sky around the plane lit up with what looked like sparks. The Halifax banked sharply from left to right, trying to avoid the bullets, throwing the Gunnerside team about in the fuselage. The plane was hit in the wing and rocked violently. One of the engines burst into flames and then cut out. The Halifax corkscrewed. Another engine went dead.

Then all was silent but for the sound of the remaining two engines. They had escaped. The Halifax continued over the North Sea, limping home.

• • •

Haugland deciphered the January 28th message from Tronstad they knew was coming: After the failed flight and bad weather afterward, Gunnerside would not arrive this moon period. "Do hope you can manage to keep going. Take care."

With weeks ahead until the next potential drop, Poulsson and his men knew they must hold on. Once more, they ate reindeer, gathered wood, hunted, met with their web of helpers and informants, hauled batteries back and forth, ate reindeer again, radioed London, and huddled in the dark at Fetter. Their brief diary entries spoke to the constant, monotonous toil and the isolation of a winter that many considered the worst in generations.

A Norwegian resistance fighter, in camouflage, outside a cabin in the Vidda.

As the next standby period approached, the men found themselves at breaking point — perhaps beyond it, after almost four months of living in the wild. They had plenty of reindeer now, but their bodies were suffering from a lack of diverse nutrients. The cold, the constant effort, the tension — these all took their toll as well. One or another of them was always sick, whether from stomach trouble, fever, or sheer exhaustion.

In mid-February, another blizzard left them stuck in the cabin for days. At times their thoughts darkened. Unlike soldiers on the front, whose courage was tested in the immediacy of battle, the five men in Fetter were fighting the relentlessness of time and the faceless, remorseless Vidda. There were moments when they wanted to surrender. "What was the point of our suffering here in the mountains?" Poulsson wondered. "What was the point of carrying out the job we had been ordered to carry out? Was there any chance that it might succeed and that we might escape alive?"

● ● ●

After the failed January drop, Rønneberg insisted the Gunnerside men take a break from Gaynes Hall. While waiting for the full moon phase, they spent two weeks in a lonely stone cottage in western Scotland. The place had no electricity and was accessible only by boat or by foot across the moors. Surrounded by mountains, it was the perfect training location — far rougher than the easy meadows around Cambridgeshire. When not trekking, they fished for salmon and hunted seals and stags. Their time in Scotland both readied them physically and brought them closer together as a team.

Finally, they returned to Gaynes Hall. On their first day back, Tronstad met them to review the latest information from

Grouse. They had feared that the long delay in launching the operation would give their enemy time to reinforce security at Vemork, and that had now happened. Since the Freshman disaster, the Germans had increased their garrisons stationed at Lake Møs from 10 to 40 men; at Vemork, from 10 to 30; and at Rjukan, from 24 to 200. Several Gestapo bloodhounds were stationed in town, sniffing out any trouble. The Germans had also laid additional minefields around Vemork, positioned searchlights throughout the grounds, and posted more guards at the top of the pipeline and on the suspension bridge. Patrols ran around the clock. The winter fortress was now prepared for an all-out assault. All these defenses signaled the importance of the atomic program to the Nazi war effort.

●●●

On February 16, the Gunnerside men boarded a Halifax at Tempsford Airport, squeezing in beside all their gear. They were clad in white camouflage suits and ski caps, their weapons at their sides. At 7:10 p.m., the plane rumbled down the runway and lifted off.

Over the North Sea, the clouds disappeared, revealing the moonlit water below. Both Rønneberg and Haukelid had made it clear that if the navigator was unable to spot their new drop site (Bjørnesfjorden, one of the largest bodies of water on the Vidda and a short day's journey from Fetter), they should be called into the cockpit to help. Reception lights or none, sure of the position or not, they would be jumping that night.

"Ten minutes," the pilot called out just before midnight as the Halifax crossed over the Vidda. The team prepared themselves for the jump.

Rønneberg led the way, vanishing into the darkness and rushing wind. In quick and sure order, four of the remaining five men and several steel tubes with their supplies followed. Haukelid edged toward the hole, his heart thumping in his chest. No matter how much he had practiced, his nervousness about jumping never abated. A thousand feet of empty air was a lot to fall through.

Suddenly, he saw that the cord that released his parachute was wrapped around the dispatcher's leg. If he jumped then, the dispatcher would come with him. Swiftly, he rose, shoved the man out of the way to free the line, and then, without hesitation, leapt through the hole. A moment later, his parachute opened, and with a sharp tug, he was momentarily lifted upward by his shoulder straps. Sixteen other parachutes, attached to containers and packages of gear, floated down with him.

He landed in a snowbank. For a moment, Haukelid sat on the ground, cupping a ball of white in his hand, savoring his return to Norway at last.

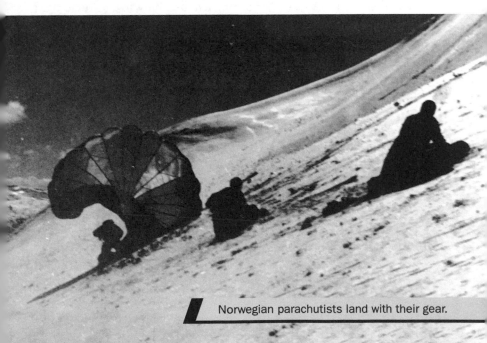

Norwegian parachutists land with their gear.

The team got straight to work. Storhaug, who was the strongest skier, scouted the area while the others looked for their supply containers. A short while later, he returned with the news that he had found a cabin a mile away. Over the next several hours, they collected the steel tubes, placed them in a long trench they dug in the snow, set rods around them that would stick out from any new snowfall, and used a map and compass to take a navigational bearing on their supply depot.

At dawn, they arrived at the empty cabin. To enter, they removed the doorframe with an ax. After lighting a fire in the stove and enjoying a short sleep, they returned to the depot and sorted out the weapons, equipment, explosives, and food they would need for the sabotage. After the operation, they would retrieve the remaining supplies for their retreat to Sweden.

At 6 P.M., they set off toward Lake Store Saure. They were carrying almost sixty-five pounds each on their backs and towing two toboggans of equipment, each weighing 110 pounds. Four miles into their journey, the winds picked up, blowing against their backs. Soon after, they were caught in a storm that surged across the high plateau. With each slide forward of their skis, the winds cut harder, and it became very difficult to see through the snow.

Forging ahead, Rønneberg came across a twig sticking up from the snow. He thought it curious but continued, only to come across some underbrush a couple of hundred yards later. If they were cutting across Bjørnesfjorden — a water channel — there should be no vegetation on it. Then the thought struck: They had not landed at the intended drop site.

He stopped, and the others came alongside him. Through the sweeping winds, he yelled, "I don't think we are where we think we are —"

The rest was lost in the storm.

They started back in the direction from which they had come. As they headed straight into the gale, ice and snow bit at their faces. Visibility cut to zero, and their tracks now gone, Rønneberg led them only by his compass.

They pushed on, hauling their gear through the snow. The darkness was impenetrable, and the cold overwhelming. If they missed the cabin by even a few feet to either side, they would continue endlessly into the Vidda, into the arms of the storm.

● ● ●

A tempest enveloped Fetter. Inside the cabin, the Grouse team and Skinnarland were very worried. On the morning of the 16th, clear weather over the surrounding mountains had given them hope that Gunnerside would launch. Soon after, Haugland received word that the drop was moving forward. Poulsson led his team to Bjørnesfjorden. They set out the Eureka and prepared the lights, but besides hearing the distant drone of engines, there was no other sign that the plane had come.

Through the night of the 17th, the blizzard continued, almost burying the cabin in snow. They talked of sending out a search party, but Poulsson thought better of it. They would have to wait until the winds subsided. But with each passing hour, the storm seemed only to grow more angry and murderous. Huddled in their sleeping bags, the walls of Fetter thick with hoarfrost, they shivered and feared the worst.

● ● ●

Rønneberg took a map down from the wall. A few hours earlier, he and his team had run blindly — and luckily — into the very cabin they were hunting. Stamping their frozen feet and trying to thaw their frostbitten faces, they were well aware that they had barely escaped the Vidda with their lives. Looking at the map, he tried to figure out exactly where they had landed. Starting at Bjørnesfjorden, he ran his finger in a broadening circle, watching out for terrain that matched their surroundings. Someplace flat, a sizable lake, bordered by hills. . . . On the third encirclement, his finger settled on Lake Skrykken, twenty miles northeast of their targeted drop and forty miles from Vemork. In the morning, they found a fishing logbook. In it, they learned the cabin was named Jansbu, and it was located exactly where Rønneberg deduced.

With no wireless set and the storm still raging outside, the Gunnerside team could only sit and listen to the wind. The gale blew with such force and duration that they began calculating how much they and their equipment weighed and whether the sum total was enough to keep the cabin fixed to the ground. Foot after foot of snow fell.

All six became ill from the swift change in climate. Only two days before, they had been near sea level in the moist, relatively warm English weather. Now they were suffering cold beyond measure almost a mile above sea level. Swollen glands made it hard to swallow. Their eyes became rheumy and their temples pressed hot with fever.

On the third night of the storm, Rønneberg wrote, "Same weather. Storm and driving snow. We attempted to reach the depot to fetch more food to save the rations. This had to be given up because of the danger of losing our way."

CHAPTER II

THE PLAN

As quickly as the storm swept into the Vidda, it blew itself out. On February 22, the six Gunnerside men woke up to silence. They stepped from the cabin into a clear, windless day. The blizzard had transformed the landscape into high drifts and flat, indistinct planes of snow. Stalagmites of ice and snow stood like quiet sentries.

Rønneberg gave the order that they must depart for Fetter by early afternoon. For six days, they had been out of contact, and, as far as Tronstad or Grouse knew, they might be dead and the operation off. They must hurry.

They returned to the general area of their depot and marched about the drifts of snow until they found one of the rods marking its position. They retrieved some extra rations, but given the distance and steep terrain they had to travel to reach Lake Store Saure, Rønneberg decided to minimize their loads. They would only carry explosives, uniforms for Grouse, rations for ten men for five days, and their operational equipment: weapons, hand grenades, shears, axes, field glasses, detonators, time fuses, and first-aid equipment.

At 1 P.M., the team was back at the cabin, ready to head out, when Haukelid spotted a man towing a sled. He was heading straight toward them. There was no doubt that he had seen their ski tracks and was coming to investigate. When the man was a few steps from the door, they sprang out. With six gun barrels pointed at him, his weathered face paled.

"What are you doing in the mountains?" Rønneberg asked.

"I'm a hunter," he said, innocently enough.

They searched him and his equipment. His identity card stated he was Kristian Kristiansen, forty-eight, from a valley due east on the edge of the Vidda. On his sled was over fifty pounds of reindeer meat. He was carrying rifles and several thousand kroner, and his pocketbook contained a list of names and addresses in Oslo. He was clearly who he said he was, the list clients for the meat. That did not mean that he was not a threat, particularly when he gave contradictory statements on his feelings about the Nazi occupation.

From the looks of the others, Haukelid knew they were thinking they might need to kill him. If they let him go, he might reveal their presence to the Germans or the police. He was in all likelihood harmless, but they could not be sure. Rønneberg needed to decide what to do.

Idland asked to speak with their leader outside the cabin. They came out into the bright day. "I'll shoot him for you," Idland said. Rønneberg knew Idland was trying to relieve him of the responsibility. It was a kindness. He tried to put himself into Kristiansen's shoes. He might not pose a threat. Rønneberg's instructions were that if the unforeseen occurred, he must act with the mission foremost in mind. Finally, Rønneberg said to Idland, "We'd better take him with us for now."

Kristiansen immediately proved useful. They cooked some of his reindeer meat, saving their own rations. Then Rønneberg asked if he could guide them to Lake Store Saure. He agreed. They decided to leave that night to avoid any further chance encounters. When they departed at 11 P.M., Kristiansen was in the lead, a sled tied to his waist loaded with rations and the uniforms. Rønneberg stayed close behind, compass in hand, to ensure they were following a proper course.

The hunter proved a fine guide. Not only was his path sure, but he skied a course that used the natural contours of the land, economizing effort. It was, Rønneberg thought, beautiful to watch.

At dawn, February 23, the sun rose, first bronze, then gold, over the mountains. Kristiansen chatted easily with them now and even attempted to buy one of their Tommy guns. When they came across a herd of reindeer, Kristiansen asked to be allowed to shoot some of them, to be collected later. Rønneberg refused, but he was coming to the conclusion that their captive was a simple mountain man and not a threat.

Seven miles from Fetter, they spotted a man crossing the lake below. They dropped quickly behind some boulders. Rønneberg waved Haukelid over and handed him a pair of field glasses. Given that the skier was headed toward Bjørnesfjorden, he might well be a member of Grouse out searching for them. Haukelid would know better than anyone if it was indeed one of them.

Although the skier was only a few hundred yards away, Haukelid could not make out who it was. He had a heavy beard and was bundled up in thick layers of clothes. Then he sighted another skier coming around a bend, a hundred yards behind the first. Haukelid made his way quickly along a ridge to get a closer look.

The two skiers came up from the valley toward Haukelid. Near the crest, they stopped. One, then the other, scanned the surrounding area. They were looking for somebody, for

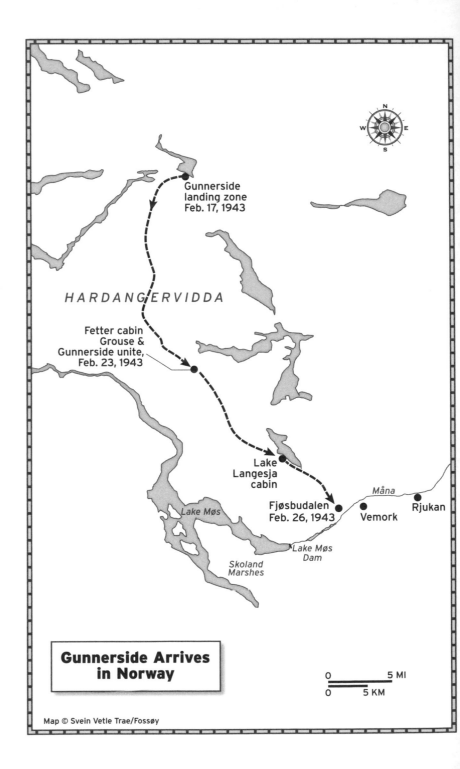

Gunnerside
landing zone
Feb. 17, 1943

HARDANGERVIDDA

Fetter cabin
Grouse &
Gunnerside unite,
Feb. 23, 1943

Lake
Langesja
cabin

Måna

Fjøsbudalen
Feb. 26, 1943

Vemork

Rjukan

Lake Møs

Lake Møs
Dam

Skoland
Marshes

N
W   E
S

**Gunnerside Arrives
in Norway**

0   5 MI

0   5 KM

Map © Svein Vetle Trae/Fossøy

something. As one of them turned, Haukelid recognized a weather-beaten Helberg. Beside him, in an unkempt red beard, was Kjelstrup. For a second, Haukelid remained hidden, over-joyed at the sight of his friends. He wanted to say something funny, but seeing how thin and wan they looked, he thought better of it. Instead, he simply coughed, and the two swung their heads around, startled, hands on guns. When they recognized Haukelid, a shout, a whoop, then a holler rose over the valley.

Poulsson had sent Helberg and Kjelstrup out to search for Gunnerside. By pure luck, their paths had crossed.

The men decided to release Kristiansen with a warning that if he spoke to anybody about them, they would make it known that he had helped guide their party. "Stay on the Vidda and say nothing," he was told. Nobody felt completely at ease with the situation, but it was a risk they measured in favor of taking an innocent life.

Helberg went ahead to Fetter before the others to warn Skinnarland so that he could get away before being seen. His identity had to be kept secret even from Gunnerside in case any-one was captured during the operation.

Crowded into Fetter that night, February 23, the men had a feast. Gunnerside provided biscuits, chocolates, powdered milk, raisins, and, most welcome to Poulsson, tobacco. Grouse offered reindeer meat of every sort, including marrow, eyeballs, stom-ach, and brain. Their guests were happy to stick with plain meat.

After a night's rest — every bed and inch of floor taken over by curled-up, sleeping figures — the ten men had some cof-fee and a breakfast of reindeer, boiled or roasted. Then they gathered to hash out their operational plan. First, Rønneberg assigned each man his task. He would lead the demolition party,

Vemork in winter, with a view of the railway and gorge.

accompanied by Kayser, Strømsheim, and Idland. They would split into pairs to double their chances of reaching the target. Haukelid would command the covering party, which would be composed of himself, Poulsson, Helberg, Kjelstrup, and Storhaug. They would see that nobody interfered with the setting of the explosives. Haugland would go to Jansbu, the cabin beside Lake Skrykken. With his radio equipment, he would establish and maintain contact with London. Skinnarland (who was only ever referred to as their "local contact" in front of Gunnerside) would join him there.

Now they needed to figure out the best way in and out of Vemork. Pencil and paper in hand, Rønneberg sketched out the plant and surrounding area. He had never actually been there, but he knew every detail from their prep work and drew it true to scale. Rjukan to the right. Vemork in the middle. Lake Møs to the left.

The Vestfjord Valley split the rudimentary map from left to right, following the course of the Måna River. Vemork was perched on a ledge of rock above the river gorge, on the south side of the valley. The pipelines that fed its turbine generators rose above the power station along the valley wall. A single-track railway line curled east to Rjukan along this same wall. A seventy-five-foot-long, single-lane suspension bridge connected Vemork to the valley's north side. Located in the hills by the bridge was Våer, a hamlet with a scattering of houses for the plant's staff, through which the road between Lake Møs and Rjukan ran. A long, high trek up the valley's northern wall led to the endless Vidda.

They debated three main routes. They could approach across the top of the southern side of the valley and descend to the plant alongside the pipelines. This idea was quickly dismissed, because a guard had recently been placed at the top of the pipes, and numerous minefields lined this approach. They could make a straightforward attack: ski down to Våer, neutralize the guards on the bridge, and head across to the plant. This had the advantages of being fast and easy, but if the guards were able to raise the alarm, the team would have to make their attempt on the heavy-water cells in the middle of a firefight. Any escape would be doubtful. Last, they could cross down through the gorge, climb up to the railway tracks, and enter the plant through a gate that was patrolled but not permanently guarded. This was their best chance of reaching the compound unseen, but at certain places along the railway line, there was a 600-foot drop straight into the river below. Rønneberg decided not to make a decision until they had secured a new update on the plant's patrols and defenses.

●●●

After a trip into Rjukan to gather the latest intelligence from his old friend, Rolf Sørlie, Helberg waited for the others at a cabin in Fjøsbudalen, high up in an isolated side valley. From its vantage point, one could see Rjukan in the far distance. Vemork was two miles away on the opposite side of Vestfjord and was not visible. On Friday, February 26, the others joined him there. Helberg recounted what he had learned from Sørlie, and the nine men reviewed their potential plans again.

The gorge was unguarded and the entrance to the railway line only lightly patrolled, but, Helberg explained, this did not make this approach a better option. The climb from the gorge to the railway was all but impossible in summertime. With added ice and darkness, it was surely madness. Idland urged them to choose the bridge. It was swift and sure. They would kill the guards, then run up to the plant. Poulsson and Helberg doubted it would be so easy, but they agreed that the bridge was the better of the two approaches. Rønneberg sided with them. Only Haukelid insisted they should attempt the gorge. Otherwise, he said, they would likely face a pitched battle to reach the high-concentration plant.

From his backpack, Rønneberg produced a set of aerial photographs of Vemork, taken the previous summer. He had studied these in detail with Tronstad in Britain. Haukelid pointed to some scrub and trees rising along the sides of the gorge. "If trees are growing," he said, "you can always find a way." The others nodded. Rønneberg instructed Helberg to return the next morning to scout a potential route that would not have them plunging to their deaths.

An aerial view of the Vestfjord Valley.

An hour after sunrise, Helberg journeyed down toward Vemork, wearing civilian clothes. Because it was the weekend, he would blend in with others skiing in the populated valley. Passing Våer, which lay straight across the gorge from Vemork, he continued east through the woods above the road and along the northern wall of the valley. There he came upon a power-line track that ran parallel to the road. At last, he sighted what might serve as a path. Stashing his skis and poles, he made his way down into the gorge. Eventually, with the aid of some juniper bushes and pine branches, he reached the Måna River. Its surface was frozen, but the ice was very thin in places. In a warm spell, the river would prove impassable.

He hiked back and forth along the river's edge, trying to spy a manageable route up the gorge to the railway line, which ran along a ledge cut into Vestfjord's southern wall. Finally, he spotted a groove in the cliff that was somewhat less steep than the surrounding wall. Some bushes and small trees rose out of the splintered crevices of rock, and they could provide hand- and footholds for climbing. Weather and luck permitting, he figured it was possible.

Smiling broadly, he returned to the Fjøsbudalen cabin after lunchtime to give his report. Overwhelmingly, the team agreed with the proposal to climb up the gorge on the night of the operation. It would not be easy, but this route would give them a far better chance of sneaking into the plant, blowing up the heavy-water cells, and getting out before the guards were alerted. Rønneberg assented. The plan was set.

This image from a film about the Vemork raid shows the men in camouflage.

At 8 P.M. on February 27, white camouflage suits covering their British Army uniforms, the nine men skied away from the cabin in silence: Rønneberg, Strømsheim, Idland, Storhaug, Kayser, Poulsson, Helberg, Kjelstrup, and Haukelid. Though they did not talk about it, most of the team, including their leader, believed that the odds of their escaping the mission alive were thin at best. Either they would be trapped at Vemork or hunted down by the hundreds of soldiers in Rjukan. They kept cyanide pills hidden in their uniforms, knowing all too well what became of those who were brought in for interrogation by the Gestapo.

Helberg led the way down the Fjøsbudalen valley. Obscured by low clouds, the moon shone dimly, so he navigated mostly by memory and an instinct for the terrain. He kept a steady pace, sweeping around boulders and twisting through the scattering of pine and mountain birch. Roughly a mile from the cabin, the valley became steep and thick with boulders and shrubs. The men unfastened their skis. When they were not sinking up to their waists in the snow, they slipped and scrambled to remain on their feet. Their heavy backpacks and weapons only threw them further off balance.

An hour into their descent, they reached the road between Lake Møs and Rjukan. Free of the woods, the wind gusting through the valley, they saw Vemork. After months of thinking about this leviathan, months of examining every facet and corner of it in blueprints and photos and in their minds' eyes, there it was. To a man, they stood mesmerized by the dark winter fortress.

It was no wonder, Haukelid thought, that the Germans felt they only needed thirty guards on hand to defend it. Set on the edge of a cliff, bordered by the precipitous southern wall of the Vestfjord Valley, Vemork looked all but impregnable. As they stood in awed silence, they could hear the distant hum of the power station's generators.

Then they were off, back on their skis and heading east along the road to Våer. Given the mild temperature and the warm wind coming down the valley, the surface of the road was covered in a treacherous slush. They kept their eyes peeled for headlights coming up from ahead or behind. In spite of the risk of discovery, using the road to reach Vemork was better than attempting the whole distance through the uneven hillside terrain.

They made it to the first sharp turn in the Z-shaped segment of the road without incident. To bypass Våer and avoid spying eyes, Helberg steered them back into the forest, and they followed a narrow path made for the line of telephone poles that advanced like sentries through the thick woods. Then the slope became almost a sheer drop through the trees. Backs flat against the snow, feet acting as brakes, they edged themselves downward.

Helberg finally dropped onto the road east of Våer, followed by a few of the others. While they were waiting for the rest of the men, headlights suddenly cut through the darkness. They hurried to hide behind a roadside snowbank as two buses rumbled toward them. Those still sliding down the steep slope frantically tried to anchor themselves to keep from falling into the road. Two of them narrowly missed landing on the roof of the first bus. The driver and Vemork night-shift workers inside saw nothing.

Once everyone was down on the road, they put their skis on again and traveled east, away from Vemork and toward Rjukan, for about half a mile. Beside an open field, Helberg led them up seventy-five yards to the power-line track that ran parallel to the road. A short distance down the track, they unloaded anything they did not need within Vemork, including their skis and poles. Then they stripped off their white camouflage suits to reveal British Army uniforms. It was essential that the sabotage be seen as a British-only military operation to prevent retaliation against the local Norwegian population.

At 10 P.M., they made their final checks. Rønneberg and Strømsheim each had a backpack with a set of explosives, detonators, and fuses, either one capable of destroying the high-concentration plant. The covering party carried Tommy guns, pistols, spare magazines, and hand grenades. Kjelstrup had the added burden of heavy shears to cut through any locks that stood in their way.

"All right, let's go," Rønneberg said.

Helberg guided them across the road and down into the gorge. They hung on to shrubs and branches as they descended to the Måna River at the bottom of the valley. Time and again, they lost their footing and slid, creating small rockfalls that tumbled down the slope. Then they were at the river.

The wind continued to blow, and melting snow dripped down the rocks on either side of the gorge. Helberg and Poulsson both feared the thaw might have caused the Måna to rise, sweeping away the ice bridges they were planning to use to cross the river. The nine men trekked along the riverbank, seeking a still-frozen

The gorge below Vemork.

section. The cliffs of the gorge soared upward on either side of them. Rønneberg felt like he was walking down a blacked-out street with skyscrapers to his left and right.

After a few minutes, they found an ice bridge that might hold their weight. Helberg went first, quickly stepping across the wide span. In single file, the others followed. The bridge did not break, but they knew it might well be gone by the time they made it back — if they made it back.

Now Helberg searched for the groove in the gorge wall he had seen on his scouting mission earlier that day. He felt no relief when he found it: This mountainside, rising almost 600 feet to the railway, was much steeper than the one they had just come down. Nevertheless, this was the approach they had chosen, and there was no turning back. Rønneberg gave the signal with his hand. Up.

Each man took his own silent path up the rock wall, guiding his hands and feet into holds, feeling his way by touch. Water trickled down the cliff, and they often slipped on patches of ice and encrusted snow. On some stretches, the ascent was more like a scramble, grabbing tree trunks and rock outcrops just to gain a fast few feet. On other stretches, they dug their fingers and toes into crevices and inched their bodies sideways, always tight to the gorge wall to avoid the wind that gusted around them. Sweat soaked their clothes as they forced themselves up from ledge to ledge, burdened by their heavy guns and backpacks filled with explosives and other gear. Now and again they rested, flexing numb fingers, rubbing cramped muscles, waiting for pulses to calm, before venturing up again.

A half hour into their climb, more than 300 feet up and the railway line still out of sight, they were all starting to weary. Their fingers hurt. Their toes were numb. Their limbs ached.

Nobody had started the mission in optimum shape, and they had skied and trekked for miles through rough, snowbound terrain before reaching the base of the gorge. But not one of the nine men felt alone. If one found an easy path, the others followed. When one sank into a pocket of snow and found himself in need of a good shove from behind to get him moving, he didn't need to ask.

At last, several minutes past 11 P.M., the first man scrambled up a final bit of scree to the railway line. The others followed — dazed, exhausted, relieved to be at the top. For a spell, nobody spoke. They rested on the tracks and looked toward the fortress at the end of the line.

● ● ●

In their cabin retreat, thirty miles from Rjukan, Skinnarland and Haugland sat on their beds as a snow squall blew outside. Neither had wanted to remain behind to deliver the news of the operation. They wanted to be in on the job. But that was the curse of the radioman: He was the eyes and ears of the mission but rarely the hand in its execution.

Well-trained radio operators were limited in number within the SOE and were considered too valuable to risk in sabotage operations. Their transmissions — and their need to move around with heavy equipment — made them traceable targets for the Germans, and in fact, radio operators suffered the most casualties among SOE agents. At that moment, though, Skinnarland and Haugland were safer than anybody else, high up in the Vidda, in the middle of winter.

Both men knew that their families might suffer reprisals if the Vemork sabotage succeeded. The Germans would suspect any commandos would have had local help. There was nothing to do but wait and wonder, and hope that all the intelligence they had gathered and all the preparations they had made before Gunnerside arrived were contributing to the operation's success.

• • •

Leading the advance, Haukelid was sure he would not be seen coming along the railway: There was very little moonlight, and patrols were not known to travel down these tracks. Across the gorge, a lone vehicle snaked along the road to Rjukan that the team had crossed just an hour before. As Haukelid came around a bend, the team following silently behind him, he saw the suspension bridge down to their right and the silhouettes of two German guards. Straight ahead, 500 yards away, was the railway gate into Vemork, and beyond that the hulking shapes

The railway leading to the Vemork plant.

of the power station and the hydrogen plant. Squeezed between them was the German guard barracks.

At 11:40 P.M., Haukelid stopped beside a snow-covered shed. He waited for the others to catch up with him. This was the perfect vantage from which to watch the bridge and wait for the changing of the guard at midnight. Using the shed as a windbreak, the nine men settled down on the tracks and ate chocolate and some hard crackers.

A few minutes before midnight, a new set of guards descended toward the bridge. Soon after, the men they had relieved from duty plodded up to their barracks. Bundled in coats, caps drawn tight over their heads, they carried their weapons in the casual manner of men who felt they had nothing to fear.

Eventually, Rønneberg's watch told him it was almost half past midnight — enough time for the new sentries to ease into their duty and get lazy. With barely a nod from him, the men rose to their feet. They checked their guns and explosives one last time. "In a few minutes we'll be at our target," Rønneberg said. He echoed the words Tronstad had told them all before they left for the mission: "Remember, what we do in the next hour will be a chapter of history in the hundred years to come. . . . Together we will make it a worthy one." Then Rønneberg gestured to Haukelid, who left first with the others in the covering party.

Conscious of land mines, Haukelid was careful about where he put his feet. Then, a few yards down the track, he found some footprints in the snow, probably from one of the plant's workers. The trail of footprints provided him with a safe route. Kjelstrup followed close behind him, then the seven others. They quickly came within 100 yards of the gate and stopped behind a short row of sheds. At this range, the hum of the generators was now a roar.

At 12:30 A.M. sharp, Rønneberg motioned Haukelid and Kjelstrup ahead to cut the gate lock. "Good luck," he whispered as they headed, in a crouch, over the final yards to the gate. Kjelstrup snapped off the padlock, and Haukelid drew aside the chain and pushed open the twelve-foot-wide gate. The five-man covering party entered first; the demolition party followed.

Within moments, Haukelid and his team had taken up their positions. Tommy gun at the ready, Kjelstrup covered the steps down from the penstocks. Helberg stood at the railway gate, protecting their retreat. Storhaug was posted by the hydrogen plant with a clear view of the suspension bridge. Haukelid and Poulsson got behind two steel tanks, fifteen yards from the guard barracks. While Haukelid lined up a row of hand grenades, Poulsson trained the barrel of his Tommy gun on the barracks door. "Good spot," he said.

In the meantime, the demolition party cut a hole in the fence fifty yards down from the railway gate. Farther down again, they snapped the lock off another gate that led to some warehouses outside the factory grounds. These would serve as alternative paths of escape.

With Kayser and his Tommy gun close by, Rønneberg crossed the open yard to the eight-story hydrogen plant. It looked even more formidable in the half-light. Strømsheim followed, Idland covering him. The two men with the explosives were to be protected above any others.

The demolition team edged around the eastern wall until they reached a steel door near the corner. Gun ready for any guards who might be inside the door, Rønneberg pulled at the handle. The door didn't budge. "Locked," he said.

He sent Kayser up an adjacent concrete stairwell to see if the first-floor door was open. "No." Rønneberg tensed. They needed a way into the plant — a way that did not involve blasting one of the thick steel doors or breaking the windows, both of which would alert the guards. He rechecked the basement and first-floor doors himself. Kayser stayed with him, searching the shadows for any sign of a patrol coming their way. Strømsheim and Idland looked for another way in. They knew they had only so much time before a guard crossed their path or came across someone in the covering party.

Rønneberg was struck by the thought of the cable tunnel on the northern wall. Racing down the steps, he waved for Kayser to follow him. At Brickendonbury Hall, they had discussed alternative entry points into the plant, and Tronstad had told them about this narrow tunnel filled with pipes and cables, which ran below the first floor of the plant and out a small access hole in the exterior wall facing the gorge. Maintenance workers sometimes used it to fix leaks. If it had not been blocked up as part of the heightened security, it might provide a way in.

Rønneberg and Kayser hurried around the building. "There it is," Rønneberg said, spotting the ladder that led up to the hole. The two climbed the slippery steel rungs, Rønneberg first. Fifteen feet up, he found the tunnel entrance half-filled with snow. He swept the snow out of the opening, then crawled in, headfirst. There was barely enough room for his own body, and he had to drag the backpack of explosives behind him.

Kayser squirreled into the tunnel after him. They crawled on their bellies over the cables and pipes for several yards. Rønneberg tried to turn his head to check if the others had come in after them. There was too little space to see, but Kayser confirmed that Strømsheim and Idland had not followed them. They would have to execute the sabotage alone.

Rønneberg kept crawling. After a few minutes, he spied some water pipes that bent through a hole to his left into the ceiling of the basement floor. Through the hole, he could just make out some of the high-concentration cells. They were close. They continued to worm their way forward. Twenty yards into the maze of pipes, Rønneberg arrived at a larger opening. He looked through it into a large hall. After taking off his backpack of explosives and making sure there were no guards in the room, he slipped through the opening and dropped the fifteen feet to the floor. Remembering his parachute training, he collapsed into a roll to blunt the fall. Kayser tossed him his backpack, then came down after him.

On the double doors into the high-concentration room, a sign read NO ADMITTANCE EXCEPT ON BUSINESS. Pistols drawn, the two saboteurs flung open the doors. A portly, gray-haired Norwegian swung around from his seat at the desk. Kayser was beside him in an instant, his pistol barrel aimed straight at the man. "Put your hands up," he barked in Norwegian.

The man did exactly as ordered. His eyes flicked back and forth between Rønneberg and Kayser, clearly scared. Rønneberg locked the doors behind them. "Nothing will happen to you if you do as you're told," Kayser said. "We're British soldiers." The worker looked at the insignia on their uniforms. "What's your name?"

"Gustav Johansen."

Kayser kept guard over Johansen, telling him about life in London, trying to cement the idea in his mind that they were British. Meanwhile, Rønneberg unpacked the explosives from his backpack. The high-concentration cells looked exactly like the replicas at Brickendonbury Hall. Each cell tank was fifty inches tall, ten inches in diameter, and made of stainless steel. A twisting cord of rubber tubes and iron pipes ran out of the top.

After putting on rubber gloves to avoid electrical shock, Rønneberg moved to the first cell and pressed the plastic-explosive charge to its base. The first charge secure, he moved to the second, then the third, his movements almost automatic after so many hours practicing at Brickendonbury.

Hands held high, Johansen was becoming increasingly nervous as he watched Rønneberg work. Finally, he blurted, "Watch out. Otherwise it might explode!"

"That's pretty much our intention," Kayser replied.

Just after Rønneberg stuck on the ninth band of explosive, glass shattered behind him. Both he and Kayser swiftly turned their guns to the threat. It was Strømsheim and Idland, now knocking a few more pieces of glass out of the window. The other demolition team had decided that they had to force their way into the room — and only narrowly missed being shot by their own compatriots.

Rønneberg hurried to help clear the glass so Strømsheim could enter. In his rush, he cut his hand on a broken shard. He told Idland to stay outside and cover the broken window with his body to prevent any light from shining out. The guards would come running if they saw it in the darkness.

Then Rønneberg and Strømsheim began attaching the rest of the explosives to the cells. Working together, they finished quickly, then double-checked everything was in place before securing the 120-centimeter-long fuses to the charges. After they were lit, the team would have exactly two minutes to get clear of the room.

Rønneberg told Strømsheim to open the locked basement door so they could make a quick escape. Johansen pointed out the key on his lanyard, and Strømsheim took it and disappeared from the room. Crossing the large hall to unlock the door, he heard footsteps. The night foreman, a man named Olav Ingebretsen, flung his hands up and yelped in surprise when he saw Strømsheim point a gun at him. Kayser then watched their two hostages in the hall while Strømsheim unlocked the basement door and pushed it open.

In the high-concentration room, Rønneberg made one final check of the chain of explosives. Almost forty-five minutes had passed since they first entered by the railway gate. They were pressing their luck. With the explosives ready, he tore off his bloodied gloves, dropped a British parachute badge on the floor, then struck a match and brought the flame to the fuses.

Idland was still standing outside the window. As the fuse began to burn, Rønneberg barked at him to get clear, then dashed into the hall, counting down the seconds in his head. To the two prisoners, he said quickly, "Run up the stairs. When you reach the first-floor landing, lie down and keep your mouth open until you hear the bang. Otherwise you'll blow out your eardrums."

As the Vemork workers raced upstairs, the three saboteurs pushed through the basement-level steel door. Kayser threw it closed behind him; then they sprinted away from the plant. Idland joined them on their run. The four were twenty yards away when they heard a muffled boom, and flames burst through the shattered windows of the high-concentration facility.

Making their escape toward the railway line, they were alive with the thrill that they had done the job.

CHAPTER 13

ESCAPE

On hearing the faint thud in the distance, Haukelid and Poulsson shared a long glance. "Is that what we came here for?" Poulsson asked. It must have been the explosion, they knew, but it sounded too small. Something must have gone wrong.

In that instant of doubt, the barracks door opened, casting a fan of light into the darkness. A guard stood in the doorway for a few seconds, looking left and right, before stepping out into the snow. He wore a thick, heavy coat but was unarmed and had no helmet. Even so, Poulsson cocked his Tommy gun for the first time that night, and Haukelid placed his index finger through the ring of a grenade's safety pin. Both waited to see what the guard would do.

At a slow walk, clearly not alarmed, the guard started to cross the fifty-yard gap between the barracks and the hydrogen plant. He gazed up at the plant building. If he saw the light coming from the broken basement windows, he did not react. Seconds later, he returned to the barracks and closed the door behind him. Perhaps, Haukelid and Poulsson thought, he had taken the noise to be a land mine set off by an animal or some thawing snow.

There was no sign of the demolition team, but Haukelid knew they could have retreated to the railway line through the hole they had cut in the fence. One way or the other, enough time had passed for them to get away. He was about to tell

Poulsson that they should fall back when the barracks door swung open again.

This time, the guard came out fitted with a steel helmet and a rifle and flashlight in hand. Advancing from the barracks, he shone the flashlight beam close to where Haukelid and Poulsson were positioned.

Poulsson brought his finger to the trigger and took aim. The guard was only fifteen yards away. A single shot would take him down.

The guard swept his light in an arc and slowly approached their hideout behind the storage tanks. Poulsson looked back at Haukelid, his expression clear: *Shall I fire?* Haukelid sharply shook his head and whispered, "No." They were not to kill unless absolutely necessary. Until that beam of light came right onto them, they would wait.

The guard swung around again, the beam creeping across the snow, almost touching their feet. Poulsson drew a tight bead on the man with his sub-automatic. Then the German turned on his heel. He gave a couple more glances about the grounds and returned to the barracks.

Haukelid and Poulsson waited another minute, then raced toward the railway gate. On reaching it, they heard a voice call out from the darkness: "Piccadilly!" They would have answered with the matching code phrase, "Leicester Square," but before they could, they were already upon Kjelstrup and Helberg. "Piccadilly," Kjelstrup urged, his training ingrained.

"For God's sake, shut up," Haukelid and Poulsson said together with a laugh.

Helberg told them that the demolition team was already moving down the railway track. Haukelid closed the gate and looped the chain back in place. Hiding the direction of their retreat from the Germans — even for a few seconds — might make all the difference in their escape.

They were a couple of hundred yards down the track when the first sirens rang out. Hearing the alarm quickened their steps. Soon they caught up with Rønneberg and the others. They shook hands and pounded one another on the back. The mission was a success, without a single bullet fired or grenade thrown. They could hardly believe it themselves.

But there was no time to celebrate. Sirens now sounding throughout the valley, they flung themselves into the gorge, hurtling down the southern wall with little thought to breaking bones or falling to their deaths. They simply wanted to get away. Helberg found a slope that was slightly less steep than the one they had ascended, and they hopped and scooted from ledge to

The steep wall of the north side of the gorge, with the Måna River at the bottom.

ledge through banks of heavy, wet snow, exercising a controlled fall into the gorge.

Throughout, Rønneberg ran through their chances of escape. Since they had not crossed the bridge, nor retreated up the penstocks, the guards might think they were still inside the plant. Once they tracked their footprints in the snow or found the clipped gate locks, they would know different. How much of a head start would they have? Would the Germans use dogs? When would troops arrive from Rjukan? Where would they be stationed? Why had the plant's searchlights not been lit? For now, they could only move as fast as possible, and as far as possible, away from Vemork before the manhunt started.

When they reached the valley floor, the thaw had weakened the ice bridges across the Måna River. Deeper pools of water rested above the surface of the ice. Helberg crossed first, jumping from one hunk of ice to the next until he was on the opposite bank. The others raced after him, soaking boots and pants on the way.

They came to the other side of the gorge and began their ascent toward the road. They clutched at whatever they could find on the hillside — a root, a boulder, a tree — to help gain purchase and move upward. They were sweating, their clothes clinging to their bodies. Their throats ached with thirst. Still, they climbed.

Approaching the road, they turned to see guards with flashlights walking along the railway line, roughly 150 yards down from Vemork. The direction of their escape was known. They would have to move faster.

● ● ●

Alf Larsen, who had replaced Jomar Brun as the chief engineer at Vemork after Brun mysteriously disappeared, had just finished a long game of bridge when he heard the explosion. Straightaway, he rang the hydrogen plant. Soon, he was on the line with Olav Ingebretsen. The night foreman explained that three men had broken into the plant and had taken him and Johansen prisoner. They spoke Norwegian ("normal like we do") but were wearing British uniforms and insignias. "They blasted the plant into the air," Ingebretsen told Larsen.

Now Larsen stepped over the blasted door and shone his flashlight around the high-concentration room. Everything lay in ruins. The heavy-water cells — what was left of them — stood at an awkward angle on the floor, their wooden stands in splinters. The electrical system was blown out, the pumps were broken, the walls scorched, the windows shattered, and the web of tubes overhead a twisted wreck. Shrapnel had sliced through

The ruins of the high-concentration stage.

the copper pipes of the cooling system, leaving the whole room drenched in a continuous spray of water.

Soaked through, Larsen walked across the debris-strewn floor to one of the rows of high-concentration cells and bent down to inspect the damage. All nine of the steel-jacketed cells were in shreds. The other row was the same. The precious heavy water inside the eighteen cells had poured out and swirled down the room's drains. Whoever these saboteurs were, they knew exactly what to destroy, and they had done their work well.

●●●

The saboteurs ducked behind a bank of plowed snow as a car from Rjukan rushed past. The car disappeared around a bend, and the nine men set across the road, which had become little more than an icy stream in the thaw. Just as the last of them made it to the other side, another car came barreling down the road. They jumped into the ditch to escape its headlights. Trucks containing soldiers would be next.

After locating their supply depot, they put on their camouflage suits and collected their gear. Then they skied along the power-line track toward Rjukan. Roughly a mile and a half down the track, they took off their skis and headed into the woods. After a short hike, they came to the Ryes Road, a series of switchbacks cut through the forest, which ascended steadily to the Vidda. Weary from the long operation, and now carrying heavy packs, their weapons, and their skis, they still had to climb through deep, wet snow for a half mile, vertically, to reach the plateau.

It was already past 2 A.M., and they wanted to be at the top of Vestfjord Valley and away before dawn. They trudged in single file, each trying to follow in the footprints of the man in front.

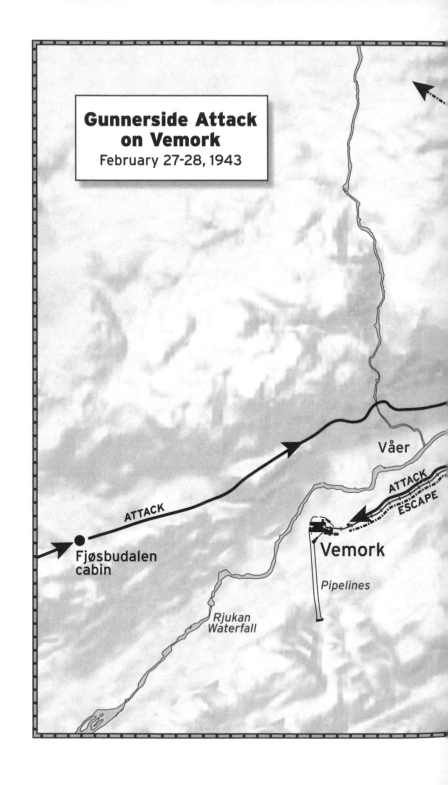

Gunnerside Attack on Vemork
February 27-28, 1943

Våer

ATTACK

ATTACK

ESCAPE

Fjøsbudalen cabin

Vemork

Pipelines

Rjukan Waterfall

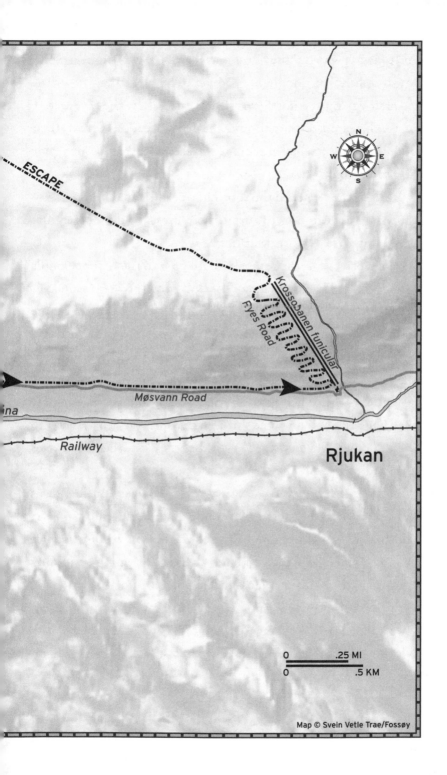

ESCAPE

Krossobanen funicular

Ryes Road

Møsvann Road

na

Railway

Rjukan

0   .25 MI

0   .5 KM

Map © Svein Vetle Trae/Fossøy

At times, a gap in the trees gave them a view of Vemork. Mysteriously, the floodlights had yet to be turned on.

Halfway up the northern wall of the valley, they were long past exhaustion. Pure will and the fear of capture drove their bodies now. When one of them fell back, another came alongside him to urge him on.

At last, they reached the top. They celebrated only briefly — the wind was beginning to gust in their faces, and the temperature was falling fast. A storm was on the way.

For a brief time, they struck a path up into the first open hills of the Vidda. Then, with dawn breaking and their legs sapped of strength, Rønneberg called for a rest. The men sat down on the hillside, ate some chocolate, and quietly gazed toward Vestfjord Valley. Silvery blue clouds hung overhead, and to the southeast, the towering peak of Mount Gausta was framed in red by the rising sun. Unseen, a bird chirped. They thought about how they had somehow all come through the operation alive and with the job done. Having expected to die, they now had their lives ahead to consider.

After everyone was rested, they readied to leave. Helberg was heading back to the cabin in Fjøsbudalen to retrieve his passport and the civilian clothes he had used during his reconnaissance around Rjukan. "I'll see you later," he said, planning on joining back up with the team at Jansbu. Then he skied off.

The other eight set a course north for Poulsson's brother-in-law's cabin near Lake Langesjå. Around 7 A.M., the winds struck with such force that the men barely could stand. Hour after hour, they struggled on, until at last they sighted the cabin. Inside, they stripped off their backpacks and collapsed. Most remained awake just long enough to raise a toast to their success from a bottle of whiskey they had found in the cabinet. There was no need to post a watch. The Nazis would never venture into the Vidda during such a storm. The men slept almost eighteen hours straight.

The next night, March 1, Poulsson led the saboteurs through a blur of driving snow and biting winds to Fetter. When they arrived at the cabin, the storm strengthened further still. There they stayed for thirty-six hours.

When the weather cleared, the eight men departed for Lake Skrykken in the north. As previously arranged, Rønneberg left a message for Haugland hidden in a hut along the way, to pick up and send to London: "High-concentration plant totally destroyed. All present. No fighting."

At Jansbu, the cabin where Gunnerside had spent its first night in Norway, the team got ready to split up, portioning out food, weapons, ammunition, clothes, and other supplies. All of Gunnerside, except Haukelid, were heading on a ten-day trek to the Swedish border and then to England. Haukelid and Kjelstrup were off to the southwest to organize resistance cells. Poulsson alone was going east, to Oslo, where his sister lived. There was no sign of Helberg, but Poulsson figured he had probably been delayed by one of the storms. The two men had a backup plan to meet in the capital in a week's time, where they would hide out with family and friends until any searches around Vemork abated.

The next day, March 4, the Gunnerside five departed. The men shook hands and wished one another luck. Before Rønneberg turned to go, Haukelid said, "Give our best regards to Colonel Wilson and Tronstad. Tell them we shall manage whatever happens."

Wearing civilian clothes and carrying only a few supplies in his rucksack, Poulsson was the next to leave. He grabbed

Haukelid's hand and wished him well. Then he moved to Kjelstrup. "Remember the day you carried those heavy batteries through miles of fog and snow?" Poulsson asked. "You looked just like a snowman when you got back."

"I felt like one," Kjelstrup said.

They recalled the sheep's-head stew spilling over the floor, Haugland tapping at his wireless in the dark, cold night, Helberg grinning on his return from yet another successful reindeer hunt, Skinnarland stirring up a masterpiece of porridge and marrow on the stove. "Well, Arne," Poulsson said finally to Kjelstrup. "Goodbye and good luck. If we don't meet sooner, we'll meet after the war." Skis fastened, he started away.

Haukelid and Kjelstrup watched him disappear into the distant white of the countryside. They felt very much alone now and worried that Poulsson was even more so.

CHAPTER 14

100 PERCENT SUCCESS

On March 5, after thirty miles of skiing, a night in a cold hut, and spare rations, all Poulsson wanted was a good sleep in a soft bed. Although he was prepared to remain out in the woods, the sight of the warm lights of a small roadside inn was too much to resist. He had a fake Norwegian passport in the name of Jens Dale, and nobody had seen him during the Vemork operation. A hot meal alone was worth the risk, he finally decided.

He went in. "On holiday?" the innkeeper asked.

"That's right. Good skiing," Poulsson replied. There appeared to be few guests. After a meal of fish, potatoes, and mushrooms, he retired to his room on the second floor. He took a bath, washed out some of his clothes, and relaxed on the bed, half-dressed. Months on the Vidda made the simple room a luxurious experience.

Then he heard voices downstairs. Easing open the door, he could make out two men asking who was staying there. Then footsteps, fast and heavy, ascended the steps. Poulsson shut the door, threw on pants and a shirt, and considered leaping from the window.

There was a sharp rapping on his door. Sticking his pistol in his right pocket, he opened it. A police sergeant came into the room, followed by a burly younger man — clearly his deputy. The sergeant asked Poulsson for his identification, while the deputy searched the room with his eyes. Poulsson saw him glance at the clothes hanging out to dry, then at his rucksack, half-open on the floor. Unwisely, it contained military rations, printed maps, chocolate, and English cigarettes.

While the sergeant inspected his passport, Poulsson sat on the edge of the bed, his hand tight around the pistol in his pocket. If either policeman reached for the bag or appeared ready to arrest him, he would shoot them both.

The deputy stepped toward the worn sleeping bag on the floor. He commented on its high quality. Stitched on the inside was an English label, but the deputy did not examine it that closely.

"What are you looking for?" Poulsson asked, his hands beginning to sweat.

"Something happened in Vemork. Saboteurs attacked the hydro plant," the sergeant said, passing the passport back to Poulsson. He then explained that the Germans wanted any strangers in the area inspected.

"Hope you have luck finding these men," Poulsson said.

"No," the sergeant said. "I think they're armed. . . . I'd rather not meet them." The two policemen apologized for the disturbance and closed the door behind them.

Poulsson eased his hand from his pocket. Leaving the inn now would only raise suspicions. Instead, he dressed, packed, and slept under the feather-filled comforter, his pistol close at hand.

● ● ●

A wireless radio set and Eureka device on his back, Skinnarland neared Skårbu, a cabin some fifteen miles northwest of Fetter, which would serve as a new base for him and Haugland. He needed to rest. On each of the past three days, he had skied roughly twenty-six miles back and forth across the Vidda, bringing food, equipment, and weapons to this new location.

By March 6, he still had not received word from Gunnerside about the operation. Haugland had gone to check the prearranged dead drop, but if this day was like the others, there would be no note. Approaching Skårbu across a frozen lake, Skinnarland spotted a pair of tracks in the snow, then saw skis leaning against the cabin wall. He was not expecting anybody. Then, out through the door came Kjelstrup and another man, a stranger. Skinnarland was introduced to Haukelid and given the good news. Finally, the sabotage was done.

Inside the cabin, Skinnarland brewed some coffee. They spoke of the operation, then of what lay ahead. All three were staying in Norway to build the underground resistance. Skinnarland would be the radio operator for their team once his training with Haugland was complete.

Near midnight, Haugland returned to the cabin in a terrible temper, his face red from the cold. For several hours, he had dug through the snow at the dead drop, looking for the tin box with the note, which he had not found. He was glad to see Haukelid and Kjelstrup, but he wanted to know what happened, why the delay, where was everybody else?

"Don't worry, Knut, keep calm," Haukelid said, easing his feet onto the table. He paused. "It all went according to plan."

His news started a stomping, cheering celebration in the cabin. Once they settled down, the four began drafting a message for London. Tronstad and Wilson would be desperate to learn everything.

Haugland tried to get a connection on the wireless transmitter, but something must have broken during transport. They would need to find a fix for it, all while evading the Nazi manhunt.

●●●

It took them several days to get the radio fixed. Finally, on March 10, Tronstad had his long-awaited confirmation from Grouse. "Operation carried out with 100 percent success. High-concentration plant completely destroyed. Shots not exchanged since Germans did not realize anything. Germans do not appear to know whence the party came or whither they disappeared."

More messages followed over the course of the day: General Falkenhorst had inspected the damage at Vemork; 300 were arrested in Rjukan; reprisals from the Nazis; the information that only three of the party had been sighted at Vemork — and only three were being hunted; a note from those Grouse men who wanted a firm mandate to continue their work in Norway, Haukelid among them. Tronstad could not help but be moved by this last request. Here were men who had already risked so much, and they wanted to stay and do more. He and Wilson sent a message back of their own: "Heartiest congratulations on excellent work done. Decision to continue your work approved. Greetings from and to all."

On March 12, Tronstad delivered his report to the SOE. His best estimate was that between 600 and 700 kilograms of heavy water had been destroyed — about four months' worth of production. The Germans would need at least six months to reconstruct the high-concentration cells, and an additional four to six months to return production to previous levels. In total, this would delay German heavy-water supplies by ten to fourteen months.

"It's justified to say the Germans have suffered a very serious setback of their project in utilizing the atomic energy for war or other purposes," Tronstad wrote. Winston Churchill was informed of the mission's success, and he urged that the commandos and their officers be awarded the highest medals. The operation gave both the SOE and Kompani Linge a major victory, elevating their reputations.

● ● ●

Rønneberg knew the escape to Sweden would be a trial over many days. They must cover 280 miles over punishing terrain through enemy-occupied country, with the Nazis now on alert for five men in British uniforms. In England, he had prepared exhaustively for what he saw as a ten-day journey: They would travel northwest from the Vidda, across the Hallingdal Valley, then northeast until they circled around the town of Lillehammer (a Nazi stronghold). From there, they had to cut southeast through three other long valleys, after which they would finally reach the Swedish border. They had brought Silva compasses and twenty-five separate topographical maps, which they burned ceremoniously each time they completed a stage.

But for all their plans and preparations, their maps could not foresee thawed ice bridges, random patrols, Norwegian hunters, blinding storms, checkpoints. The hand that Rønneberg had cut on the broken window at Vemork became infected and swelled up. They steered far from any German garrisons and slept outdoors when they could not find uninhabited cabins or farmhouses. By March 13, the tenth day of their trek, Rønneberg and his men were still roughly 100 miles from the Swedish border.

Idland asked to speak with Rønneberg alone. Idland had

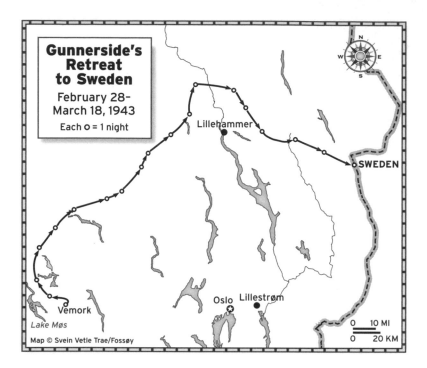

Gunnerside's
Retreat
to Sweden
February 28–
March 18, 1943

Each O = 1 night

Lillehammer

SWEDEN

Oslo Lillestrøm

Vemork

Lake Møs

Map © Svein Vetle Trae/Fossøy

0   10 MI

0   20 KM

been struggling to stay with the team, and there had indeed been some stretches of tough terrain that they would have traversed on skis if he had had the skill. "You must all speed up and get yourself to Sweden," Idland said. "I'll follow."

Rønneberg felt that even though Idland was not as efficient a skier as the others, his workhorse attitude bridged the difference. "Stop it now," he said. "You're imagining things." Idland tried to protest, but Rønneberg cut him off. They would arrive in Sweden together.

Finally, they reached a frozen marsh fewer than twenty miles from the Swedish border, and they took a long rest. Shirts and boots off, sleeping bags spread out to dry, they ate what was left of their food and relaxed. "Guys," Idland said. "When we get to London, I don't want to bloody see your faces for fourteen days, because I'm completely sick of you." The others laughed, at ease for the first time in weeks.

At 8:15 P.M., March 18, they passed Border Marker #106 into Sweden, where they shook hands with one another. They settled down around an open fire and burned the final map; then they fell into their sleeping bags. In the morning, they buried everything that marked them as soldiers, including their guns. Wearing civilian clothes, they hiked twelve miles over the border and surrendered to a patrol. Their cover story was that they had escaped a German prison where they had been held for underground activity.

The Swedes believed their story, and the five were quickly brought to a refugee camp. From there, they reached out to Norwegian officials tied into SOE. They were safe at last.

CHAPTER 15

THE CHASE

On March 24, SS Lieutenant Colonel Fehlis launched a massive manhunt for the Vemork saboteurs. No effort was to be spared in rounding up them and those in the resistance who supported them. Fehlis sent an army to accomplish the task: thousands of Wehrmacht infantry; hundreds of German and Norwegian police, Gestapo investigators, and SS shock troops; and, finally, dozens of Jagdkommando platoons. These were composed of elite soldiers who specialized in destroying guerrilla groups where they lived and operated. Numbering close to 8,000 men in total, Fehlis's army was guided by locals who knew the

German soldiers in Norway.

countryside and supported by roving patrols of Fi-156 Storch spotter planes. Its chief focus was on the Vidda.

● ● ●

In the late afternoon of the 25th, Helberg skied across Lake Skrykken to Jansbu. A month before, after the Gunnerside mission, he had been caught in a storm and failed to rejoin his compatriots before they had scattered in different directions on the Vidda. In Oslo, as planned, he met up with Poulsson. His friend had decided to return to England to await a new mission, while Helberg chose to go to Notodden, a town southeast of Rjukan, to connect with the underground cell there.

On his way to Notodden, he needed to fetch some weapons and explosives left by Gunnerside that were buried in a depot near Jansbu. When he reached the cabin, he saw that the door was ajar but there were no skis outside or trails up to the cabin. He unfastened his skis, stuck his pistol in his pocket, and entered with his backpack in hand. The place was a wreck, the furniture upended, mattresses ripped open, cupboards broken. The thought of Germans intruding so far into the Vidda — territory Helberg considered safe and his own — left him deeply unsettled.

Then he was struck with fear that they might still be close at hand, perhaps even hiding in wait. He moved to the window. Peering through, he didn't see anybody. Still uneasy, he ventured outside.

From the direction of the lake, he saw three Wehrmacht soldiers in white camouflage suits skiing toward the cabin. They were roughly 400 yards away and coming fast. Helberg had only a Colt 32 pistol. Outnumbered and almost certainly outgunned, he knew that he had no choice but to run. He raced inside, grabbed his backpack, returned to his skis, then dashed away.

A soldier shouted in German to halt. When Helberg continued to ski, he heard the crack of gunfire. All around him, the snow mushroomed up from the missed shots. He looked over his shoulder and realized that his pursuers were all skilled skiers. He would have to be better.

He veered to the west, straight into the setting sun. Its piercing light was sure to make him a harder target to hit. For the next hour, he cut around hills, down into ravines, up short valleys, and past rocky outcroppings. He hoped to find some way to mask a change in direction, but they were hanging on too close. He knew the terrain better than they did, but he had already skied many miles that day and was only just recovering from the months on the Vidda and the night of the sabotage itself.

Ten miles from Lake Skrykken, Helberg finally began to distance himself from all but one of his pursuers, a giant of a man. No matter how hard Helberg pushed, the soldier maintained a distance of about 100 yards behind him, his task made easier by Helberg's plowing a track through the snow for him to follow. For another hour, Helberg kept at it, glancing over his shoulder now and again to see if he had finally broken free. But as the terrain flattened, the soldier drew closer than ever. "Halt! Arms up!" the German shouted.

In that instant, Helberg made his decision. Pulling the Colt from his pocket, he stopped and spun around. The soldier came to a sharp halt as Helberg fired a single shot from forty yards. He missed.

The soldier drew a Luger. If it had been a submachine gun, Helberg would have been dead. Now he knew how this would play out: Whoever emptied his magazine first would lose, unless he had already managed to kill the other. He calculated that the soldier was not in the best shape to aim true. The setting sun was in his face, he would have sweat in his eyes, and his muscles would be burning with strain.

Helberg stood his ground. The soldier quickly fired his shots, eight in total. They all missed. Then, knowing that he would not have time to reload his weapon, the soldier spun around and skied off. His poles struck the snow fast and forcefully as he sped up the hill.

Helberg followed him, Colt in one hand, both poles in the other. He could not allow the soldier to get clear, reload, and come after him again. As the man approached the top of the hill, Helberg leveled his Colt and fired.

The soldier stumbled forward slightly, then hung over his poles in the snow like he was taking a much-needed rest. Helberg turned straightaway and raced downhill. It would be dark soon, but he knew that his pursuers would try to follow his tracks the next day. He needed to get as far away as possible and cut across some bare ice to throw them off his trail.

For two more hours, he journeyed south. He could see little, but the terrain was mostly flat and his instincts guided him well. Then, suddenly, he felt himself falling.

He had skied straight off a cliff.

Helberg crash-landed in a hard-packed bank of snow. Once he caught his breath and realized he was still alive, pain enveloped him. He rolled over, his left shoulder and arm useless. Looking up at the precipice outlined by the starry sky, he figured he had fallen 100 feet or more. He inspected his upper left arm and felt sure that it was broken. His shoulder was mangled, too. He knew that he could not remain in the mountains in such a state. He brought himself to his feet. At least his skis were still intact. With one pole, he pushed off.

Since that morning, he had journeyed some sixty or seventy miles. Thirty-six hours had passed since he last slept. Now he had farther to go, crippled, exhausted, and hungry. His shoulder was throbbing, his arm pulsing with agony at any awkward movement. If cornered by the Germans, he would have little fight left.

At a slow, steady pace, his left arm hugging his side, he continued down to the tail end of Lake Møs, where a friend of Skinnarland's gave him some food. Barely warmed up, Helberg skied along the lake, then down toward Rauland, a village twenty miles to the south, where he had a contact he knew would help.

A mile outside Rauland, he ran straight into a patrol. The German soldiers asked for his papers, and he presented his, with the name Sverre Haugen. They told him that nobody was meant to be traveling about the area. Concealing his wounded arm, Helberg pleaded ignorance, saying that he was only out to visit a friend. The soldiers allowed him to pass.

At 9 P.M., he reached the house of his contact. When the door opened, several Germans flanked the owner. Helberg knew there was only one course open to him: to talk his way out of the situation. He explained that he had been injured while guiding the Germans in the mountains; now he needed medical treatment. When one of them offered to put his arm into a sling, he took off his coat, revealing his pistol. Coolly, he recounted how the company he was with allowed him to carry a gun in case of trouble.

The soldiers accepted his story. They played cards with him and even offered to take him in a medical truck to the neighboring town, from where he could go on to an Oslo hospital. Helberg smiled and thanked them. True to their word, the next day they drove him twenty-two miles south, past one checkpoint after the next, to Dalen. *"Auf Wiedersehen,"* he said, waving to the soldiers before they drove off.

There were scores of Germans in the town, but it was beyond the restricted zone. Helberg felt that he would be safe there. The boat for Oslo left the next morning, so he checked himself into a hotel. After an early dinner of fried trout, seasoned carrots, potatoes, and thick bread spread with strawberry jelly, he returned to his room and crawled gingerly into bed, his arm and shoulder still throbbing.

Soon after he fell asleep, there came a pounding of fists on doors and barked commands in German. SS soldiers emptied every room of its guests and led them all to the lobby. They informed the sleepy guests that Reichskommissar Terboven and his security chief, Fehlis, were taking over the place for their headquarters.

With soldiers guarding every entrance, Helberg knew there was no escape. He presented his false papers, lied about his injury, and, indeed, was one of the few who were allowed to return to their rooms instead of staying in the sitting room all night. He did not dare leave.

At 10:30 A.M., his arm in his sling, Helberg slowly descended the stairs from his room. A soldier trailed behind him. The Gestapo was sending all but a few of the hotel's guests to the concentration camp at Grini in retaliation for some disrespect shown to Terboven the night before. Once at the camp, Helberg knew he would no longer be able to talk himself clear. His identification would be double-checked and determined false. Then the interrogations would begin — if he did not swallow his cyanide capsule first.

Helberg was pushed into the line of prisoners filing out of the hotel. They were all led to a rickety old bus with blacked-out windows. He was one of the last to enter and found a spot on the floor at the back. From the front, a single SS soldier in a steel helmet, armed with a rifle and grenades, watched over them. The bus rolled out of Dalen for the 140-mile ride to Oslo, escorted in front and behind by SS riding in motorcycles with sidecars. Somewhere along the way, somehow, Helberg was resolved to escape.

The afternoon passed in silence, the bus straining to get through the mountains. Two young women were in the seat beside Helberg, and he could not resist flirting with one of them. In the middle of their conversation, their guard came down the aisle. "You sit there," he said to Helberg, pointing to the front of the bus.

Helberg shuffled down toward the driver and eyed the pull handle that operated the door. From the passing landmarks, they must be thirty miles from Oslo. The bus started up a hill and slowed down to a crawl. Helberg rose, grabbed the handle, pulled, and jumped.

He tumbled onto the road, slamming into his broken arm, then scrambled through the snow-covered field toward the woods. He fell several times, each time certain that the Germans were about to reach him. The field ended in a thick, tall hedge that stopped Helberg in his tracks. He couldn't get past it. "Stop!" a German guard yelled.

Helberg knew what he had to do. He was sure to be shot, but he saw no other choice. He turned around and barreled back across the field toward the soldiers and SS. A grenade exploded in the snow behind him. Unhurt, he continued. Several gunshots sounded. Nothing hit him. He dashed across the road between the bus and a motorcycle, zigzagging to avoid being tackled by the Germans, who were shocked still by his coming straight at them.

He ran across the field on the other side of the road. Another grenade exploded behind him, too far away to cause harm. Something hit him in the back, hard: a third grenade. He couldn't possibly get clear of it.

The explosion never came — the grenade was a dud.

He sprinted into the woods and darkness. There were several more gunshots, but Helberg was out of their aim. He slowed to recover his breath, then threaded through the trees, his arm now ablaze in sheer agony.

Finally, after a long hike through the forest, he found a long rectangular building lit up from inside. He climbed over the barbed-wire fence surrounding it and staggered to the front door.

An old man answered it. There was no more room for lies. If this man was a good Norwegian, he would help. If not, Helberg was lost. His arm was shattered. He was bloodied and his head hurt. His clothes were in tatters. He could go no farther.

The man welcomed Helberg in and told him he had arrived at a state psychiatric hospital. They had food, doctors, clothing, and beds. Helberg was safe.

● ● ●

On April 17, when the Nazis' search moved away from Lake Møs, Skinnarland returned to Nilsbu after several weeks hiding in the mountains with Haugland. He discovered two sets of skis leaning against the cabin wall. Fearing they belonged to Germans, he retreated back into the mountains. The following morning, with no sign of any patrols down below, he and Haugland skied back to Nilsbu. As they edged their way over to the cabin, they sighted the trespassers: Haukelid and Kjelstrup.

The four men warmly reunited and recounted their narrow escapes from the Germans over the past month. They were ready to launch their own resistance work. Skinnarland could now run a wireless station. Haugland was headed to Notodden, then on to Oslo, to help build a network of radio operators. After gathering all the supplies brought by the Gunnerside team, Haukelid and Kjelstrup would begin recruiting and training resistance cells in the district. Their mission had been accomplished. As far as they knew, they would have nothing more to do with Vemork.

CHAPTER 16

ANOTHER GO

In mid-April 1943, a military truck drove across the suspension bridge into Vemork. Secured in the truck bed was what looked like a steel drum of ordinary potash lye, an ingredient used in the electrolysis process. The drum actually contained 116 kilograms of almost pure heavy water from Berlin. It had originally been produced at Vemork.

Soon after the sabotage on February 28, a stream of Norsk Hydro company men and German officials had come to the plant to decide its fate. Some argued that it should be rebuilt. Others wanted all the salvageable equipment shipped to Berlin. Since destroying Vemork had become a "national Norwegian sport," they contended, a new plant should be built in Germany. The Army Ordnance Office was asked for a "swift decision," which it delivered: The cells should be repaired and the plant expanded as soon as possible at Vemork. Heavy-water facilities at two other locations should also be completed. The German command provided any materials and manpower required (including slave labor from abroad) and warned workers that if they did not revive the plant quickly enough, there would be reprisals.

By the time the secret shipment of heavy water arrived at Vemork, the round-the-clock work on the high-concentration plant was almost complete. The shipment was used to fill the new high-concentration cells, overriding the slow process of accumulating the precious substance drop by drop, and accelerating the return to production by several months. With three new stages and a number of cells added to the preliminary electrolysis process, the Germans projected that daily output would soon reach 9.75 kilograms. Given the plans to double the size of the high-concentration plant yet again, the daily yield might reach almost 20 kilograms.

On April 17, at 2 P.M., heavy water began to flow through the cascade of cells.

● ● ●

Three weeks later, on May 7, the Uranium Club met at the Reich Physical and Technical Institute in Berlin. The scientists were under pressure for results like never before. With German fortunes in the war deteriorating, the Allies set to retake all of North Africa, and the Soviets continuing to defeat the Wehrmacht on the Eastern Front, the Nazi brass felt a desperate desire for something that would quickly turn the tide in their favor. One report stated that "rumors abound in the general German population about a new-fangled bomb. Twelve such bombs, designed on the principle of demolishing atoms, are supposedly enough to destroy a city of millions." Worse yet, Abwehr intelligence had revealed that the Americans were on the path to creating "uranium bombs." The German atomic program was riven by factions, and its scientists and research centers now exposed to attack by Allied bombing. They needed a breakthrough to focus their efforts.

The first item on the agenda for the May 7 meeting was heavy water. Only the previous day, at a German Academy of Aeronautical Research conference, Abraham Esau had placed part of the blame for their slow atomic progress on the recent lack of heavy water. But with Vemork back online and investigations beginning on some new methods of production, Esau felt confident they would soon have all the heavy water they needed.

Diebner was less sure there was enough to go around. He made it clear that he needed every drop for his next two experiments. His team's most recent uranium machine (G-II), which used uranium metal cubes suspended in frozen heavy water, showed neutron production at a level one and a half times greater than any German experiment so far. The machine proved that a cube design was far superior to any other in fostering a chain reaction, he said, and at the right size, it would likely be self-sustaining.

Heisenberg disagreed. In his mind, the best design was still an open question. He claimed the dimensions of his latest machine, a sphere with alternating layers of uranium metal and heavy water, were "too small to yield absolutely certain values." But he added that the company producing uranium metal for them was already casting it in plates like he needed, rather than cubes, as Diebner demanded. Thus his experiments — and the heavy water they required — should be first in line. "This doesn't rule out a subsequent cube experiment, if one is needed," Heisenberg offered.

The tension in the room was sharp. Diebner had his supporters, including Harteck, who believed that Heisenberg was blind to the value of any experiment that did not originate from his own brain. Esau, who had appropriated heavy water from

A spherical pile of the kind Heisenberg built.

Heisenberg for Diebner's latest experiment, said he needed to think further about whose work should be given precedence. Eventually, both men received a share of heavy water and uranium to allow them to proceed with small-scale experiments, but both were left dissatisfied.

• • •

On July 8, Tronstad received a message from Skinnarland: "Vemork reckons on delivering heavy water from about August 15."

Until that point, Gunnerside had been judged an unqualified success. Their target was destroyed. Not a shot was fired. There had been no major reprisals. Every single member of the team had escaped to safety, their identities unknown to the Germans. Tronstad could not have dreamed of a better outcome. Praise came from every quarter, from the Norwegian High Command to Churchill himself. The success had raised the profile of the SOE and its Kompani Linge, giving them more opportunities for future missions in Norway. Skinnarland's news did not blemish the Gunnerside achievement, but it was disturbing information nonetheless.

Later that month, on July 21, seven of the nine men involved in the operation had assembled in uniform in London. On behalf of King George VI, Lord Selborne awarded Rønneberg and Poulsson the Distinguished Service Order, and the others present (Helberg, Idland, Kayser, Storhaug, and Strømsheim) were given the Military Cross or Military Medal. Tronstad received the Order of the British Empire. Later, Selborne hosted a dinner for them all at the Ritz Hotel. Naturally, they ate grouse, gnawing at the bones until they were picked clean. After dinner, Tronstad took the men out on the town, the merry group singing songs as they made their way up Piccadilly. Tronstad said nothing of what he had learned from Skinnarland. He did not want to sour the evening.

Tronstad was also carrying another secret. After two German physicists visited his lab in Copenhagen, the Danish physicist Niels Bohr stated that he believed atom bombs were practicable in the immediate future, particularly if there was enough heavy water on hand to manufacture the necessary ingredients. When asked if heavy-water production was "war-important" and whether such plants should be destroyed, Bohr answered yes to both questions. Coming from Bohr, one of the fathers of atomic physics, this declaration put the bull's-eye back on Vemork.

Tronstad sent orders to Skinnarland to investigate progress at

The Gunnerside men in London. Back row, left to right: Storhaug, Kayser, Idland, Helberg, Strømsheim. Front row: Poulsson, Tronstad, Rønneberg.

the plant and the potential for some inside sabotage. More than anything, he wanted to prevent a massive bombing run on the plant, which the Britons' American allies were pushing for. As he had argued several times before, he doubted such a bombardment would destroy the basement-level high-concentration plant. What was more, an attack would inflict enormous collateral damage, on both the lives of the everyday Norwegians living around the plant and the Norwegian postwar economy, which would need powerful industrial plants.

Through all this concern over heavy water, not to mention the scores of other resistance missions Tronstad was coordinating, he deeply missed his family. Their sacrifices, his own, had to be worth it. One night that summer, he tried to make sense of the struggle for his ten-year-old daughter in a letter he wrote to her:

"When we say 'Our Fatherland,' we mean everything we love at home: mother, little boy and you, and all the other fathers and mothers and children. It's also all the wonderful memories from the time we ourselves were small, and from later when we had children of our own. We mean our home villages. We mean the hills, mountains and forests, the lakes and ponds, rivers and streams, waterfall and fjords. The smell of new hay in summer, of birches in spring, of the sea, and the big forest, and even the biting winter cold. Everything . . . Norwegian songs and music and so much, much more. That's our Fatherland and that's what we have to fight to get back."

● ● ●

Through summer and into the fall, Haukelid and Kjelstrup championed this struggle by developing underground cells throughout western Telemark. They stressed security above all else to their seventy-five recruits: "Remember: Keep your mouth shut." They built their own mountain hideout and established a wireless station on a nearby farm. They also scouted German positions throughout the area in preparation for the time when the Allies invaded Norway — or when their cells were called on for sabotage operations.

In late September, Haukelid and Kjelstrup received an SOE supply drop of food and weapons. But no matter how much Kjelstrup ate, he could not get over the stiffness and swelling that had plagued him since the previous winter. A doctor in Oslo had diagnosed beriberi — a disease caused by the chronic lack of the vitamin thiamine — as a result of his eating only reindeer meat for such a long stretch of time. While staying in the capital, he recovered somewhat, but his six months living back on the Vidda had caused a relapse. Kjelstrup realized he would not be able to endure another winter. He decided to cross the Swedish border and move on to Britain. The two made their farewells. When Kjelstrup cycled away, Haukelid found himself alone again.

Soon after, Haukelid closed up the cabin. With a heavy backpack on his back, he set off by foot toward Lake Møs. Approaching Nilsbu, half-hidden in fog, he was grateful that there was no shovel on the cabin roof, which would have been a warning signal telling him to keep away. Skinnarland welcomed him into the cabin.

For almost a year now, Skinnarland had largely been alone in the old reindeer hunter's cabin. He was completely cut off from his family. His father had died during the summer, but Skinnarland dared not attend his funeral; the Gestapo was still looking for him, and it would have been an obvious chance to catch him. Moreover, his brother Torstein and friend Olav

Haukelid and Skinnarland outside a cabin.

Skogen had both been captured and tortured by the Nazis for information on his whereabouts. Though he knew both men would never have accepted his surrender in exchange for their freedom, that did not soften his guilt or grief.

Skinnarland and Haukelid planned on spending the winter together. It was good to have someone to rely on, and frankly, they knew they would need each other's company through the long, dark months. They continued to supply London with intelligence on the ramp-up of heavy-water production at Vemork, and they were ready to act to slow or stop it.

A call to action did not come.

• • •

"The powers that be wish us to consider whether we can have another go at the Vemork plant," wrote one SOE deputy to another on October 5, 1943. Those "powers" were General Leslie Groves, head of the Manhattan Project in the United States, and Lord John Anderson of the British War Cabinet. Groves believed his scientists would have a working bomb in twelve to eighteen months, and the Germans might not be far behind. As a result, every opportunity to strike a blow against German progress must be seized. Whatever "another go" entailed, the two SOE deputies were agreed: The Norwegians, including Leif Tronstad, were against such an attack and must be excluded from further involvement in the decision.

Using the intelligence provided by Skinnarland, Colonel Wilson and his staff drew up a report with three options: (1) internal interference with production, (2) direct attacks along the lines of Gunnerside, and (3) aerial bombing. The first was deemed only a temporary solution. The second was a long shot given the new defenses at the plant. The third, if carried out during a daylight precision attack, likely offered "the best and most effective course."

The order for the attack was sent to the head of the American 8th Air Force, General Ira Eaker. From his base at Wycombe Abbey, an hour's drive west of London, Eaker governed a force of 185,000 men and 4,000 planes. His job was to pummel Germany into submission, chiefly by destroying its ability to fight. At first, the cigar-chomping, soft-spoken general doubted the importance of the target and resisted the mission, but by October 22, Groves made clear he wasn't asking. Eaker informed his men, "When the weather favors attacks on Norway, the target should be destroyed."

CHAPTER 17

BIGASSBIRD II

At 3 A.M. on November 16, 1943, when the duty sergeant roused pilot Owen Roane from his bed, Station 139 — the massive US airbase by the North Sea coast — was already alive with the movement of an impending mission. While Roane shaved his boyish, bright-eyed face — the better to improve the fit of his oxygen mask during flight — fuel tankers rumbled across the foggy tarmac to fill a row of B-17 bombers. The four-engine, long-range B-17 could take punch after punch and still deliver its 9,600-pound bomb load to its target. Crewed by ten men, the bomber was known as the "Flying Fortress" thanks to its size

Flight Officer Owen D. "Cowboy" Roane.

and its arsenal of machine guns.

Dressed for the minus-30-degree Fahrenheit temperatures at high altitude, First Lieutenant Roane gathered with the other pilots and air crews in the huge hut used for briefings. Orders from the 8th Air Force Command had come into the base by teletype earlier that morning. They were headed to Norway, to a place called Rjukan. The target was a power station and hydrogen plant named Vemork, where the Germans made some special explosive. To limit civilian casualties, they would hit the site during the lunch hour. The operations officer did not expect much enemy resistance. He called the attack all but a "milk run."

Although Roane had just celebrated his twenty-second birthday, he was something of an old-timer, only two missions away from joining the "Lucky Bastards Club." Membership was earned by beating the odds and making it through a twenty-five-mission tour alive. At 5 A.M., he made his way onto the hardstand to inspect his plane, the *Bigassbird II*, then circled around with his crew for some tea. A little over an hour later, his B-17 headed down the runway. Throttles at maximum power, Roane lifted the *Bigassbird II* into the dark sky at 120 miles per hour.

At 3,000 feet, they finally emerged from the clouds. A half-moon hung overhead. Three hundred and eighty-eight B-17

The *Bigassbird II* and its crew in October 1943.

The American planes ready an attack on Vemork.

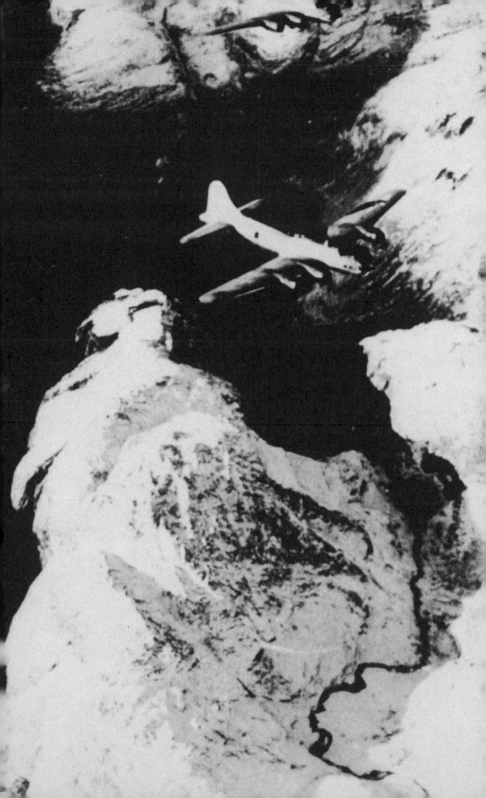

Flying Fortresses and B-24 Liberators were headed to Norway that morning. Roughly half of them were set on Vemork, and the other half were assigned to destroy an airfield outside Oslo and mining operations in Knaben.

They crossed the North Sea at a steady cruising speed of 150 miles per hour. The sun rose over the horizon to their right, illuminating a stunning view: drifts of feathered clouds hanging below them and pure blue skies above. When they neared the coast, Roane and crew donned their flak jackets and steel helmets in case of German antiaircraft fire.

On checking his watch, Roane found that they were twenty-two minutes ahead of schedule. The first bombs were not supposed to be dropped until 11:45, when the plant's workers were eating lunch in the basement-level canteens. The armada had a choice: Drop the bombs early and risk more civilian casualties, or make a 360-degree turn at the coast to delay the run, which would give the Germans time to muster a defense.

"Make a circle over the North Sea," their commanding officer said.

When the bombers came around again, the Germans were ready. Two coastal patrol boats fitted with antiaircraft guns fired away. One B-17 went down, but the rest of the armada continued through the flak. Then German fighting planes scrambled into the sky, a scattering of Messerschmitts and Focke-Wulfs. They were too few in number to press the attack home, but a B-17 in another group was hit. Its crew parachuted out before their plane corkscrewed into the sea. Still, 176 Flying Fortresses and Liberators soared on toward Vemork.

At 11:33 A.M., air-raid sirens blared throughout Vemork. Three minutes later, down in the power plant's shelter, the chief engineer received a call from the phone operator at Våer. She reported twenty aircraft above the valley, then another fifty, then cried out, "There are even more planes!" The families of the workers and engineers who lived on the Vemork side of the Vestfjord Valley ran into the air-raid shelter near their homes. Down in Rjukan, citizen volunteers directed the townspeople into a range of shelters. At the local school, teachers hurried some sixty pupils into a tubular concrete bunker. Four Germans who lived on the first floor of the school joined them. All heard the thunder of airplanes overhead. Fearing what was to come, one of the teachers ventured outside to see the formation of bombers directly overhead. "We're in the center of the circle!" he shouted. "Run to your homes!" The schoolchildren dashed from the bunker and scattered in all directions.

At 11:43, through a slight break in the cloud cover, Roane spotted the plant. The Germans had started to generate smoke screens over the valley to hide the target, but it was not enough. His plane released its six 1,000-pound "eggs," and with the sudden loss of weight, the *Bigassbird II* bucked upward in the sky.

In total, 711 bombs struck Vemork and the surrounding area. Some fell in the valley and woods, causing no harm. Others ripped apart the pipelines, spewing tons of water down the hillside. The suspension bridge was torn in half and hung down over the southern cliffs. Three direct hits on the power station tore away part of its roof, destroying two of the generators and damaging the rest. The western corner of the hydrogen plant was sheared off. Several houses at Vemork and Våer were leveled, and the homes not eviscerated by explosions were destroyed by flying stones and splinters and the fires that followed. Flames — red, green, and orange — rose throughout Vemork.

Just as the main body of the armada banked away from Vemork, a pack of twenty-nine B-24 Liberators flew down the Vestfjord Valley. The pack had been assigned to the bomb run outside Oslo, but they found their target covered in clouds and so had come the 100 miles to Vemork. The B-24s mistook the nitrate plant in Rjukan for the target and released their 500-pound bombs to destroy it. Most of the cluster hit the plant, but some of them struck the town's populated center, only a few hundred yards away.

Once finished with their runs, Roane and the other pilots directed their bombers back toward the Norwegian coast. While they made their way home at 12,000 feet, the residents and workers of Vemork and Rjukan emerged from hiding to reckon with what they had left behind.

The air-raid sirens were still wailing as shouts sounded from every direction. "My God, what's happened to my family?" one engineer shouted as he ran toward the Vemork air-raid shelter. Where it had stood, there were only two craters, the result of

Vemork after the American bombing.

two direct hits from the bombers. The sixteen people who had huddled inside were dead, their bodies irrecoverable: eleven women, two children, and three men. A crowd of workers knelt down in the open smoldering holes, their cries joined together.

Rjukan, four miles away, suffered similar devastation. Several houses were in ruins, as was the nitrate plant. Plumes of heavy, dark smoke filled the sky. The teachers and students who ran from the bunker during the attack had saved themselves. Their shelter had been leveled, just like the one at Vemork. In total, twenty-one Norwegians lost their lives in the attack.

At Vemork, there was much that needed urgent repair, from the pipelines, the suspension bridge, and the power-station generators to the equipment and structure of the hydrogen plant. But after a careful survey, Berlin was told that the high-concentration plant was undamaged. Only a brief period of time and a limited amount of material would be needed to get the heavy water running again.

● ● ●

The Allies had broken their word. Without telling the Norwegian government, they had sent hundreds of bombers to strike Vemork. The whole situation — the betrayal, the needless civilian deaths, and his powerlessness to stop it — left Tronstad deeply angry. He wanted answers, and promises that nothing like it would happen again. Investigations were started and apologies given, but neither the British nor the Americans offered to seek Norwegian approval before future strikes. They made it clear that they needed a free hand to hit the Germans as they saw fit.

The Rjukan nitrate plant after the American bomb run.

Tronstad discovered that the decision to bomb Vemork came from outside the usual channels, and in fact, the highest Allied authorities had ordered the attack. They felt that even if the Germans were unable to manage an atomic bomb, like the ones the Manhattan Project was developing, they might still produce radioactive weapons that could ruin entire cities. Unless and until they had clear intelligence that the Germans were no longer pursuing this kind of weapon, then the Allies had to act with resolve. The threat was too great.

Tronstad knew from his intelligence sources that the Germans had not abandoned the atomic field. Their experiments continued, and they were still eager to produce heavy water for a self-sustaining reactor. There were further reports from Germany that Hitler was heralding "secret weapons," soon to be loosed onto the world. Another report, from a Reuters correspondent who had interviewed several fugitives from Germany, warned of a Nazi bomb "filled with explosive gases of fantastically high destructive power . . . that will be used against Britain soon." Tronstad snipped out the article and tucked it into his diary so that he did not forget what he was fighting against.

Through November and December 1943, as Allied bombers struck Germany day and night, Kurt Diebner and his crew of young physicists continued to work on the assembly of uranium machines. For the Gottow-III (G-III), his team fitted 106 uranium cubes onto thin metal wires, with either eight or nine cubes to each wire. Then they secured the wires to a thick steel lid, with each cube in the lattice an equal distance apart. The whole arrangement was lowered into a hollow sphere filled with 592 kilograms of heavy water. The machine showed impressive results.

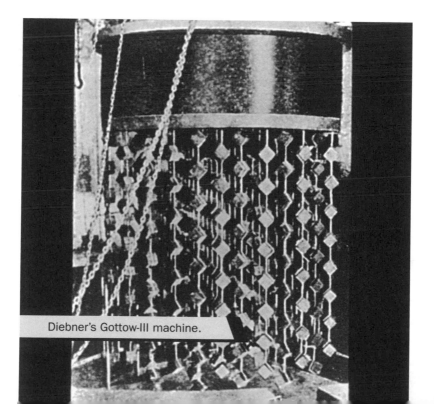

Diebner's Gottow-III machine.

The Gottow team then repeated the experiment, using the same sphere and the same heavy water, but this time with 240 uranium cubes. The design was efficient enough to be assembled in a day, and the results showed a neutron increase of 106 percent. As Diebner reported to his fellow physicists, "Given the relatively small size of this apparatus, these neutron increase values are extremely large." In his estimation, a working reactor was now only a matter of enough heavy water and uranium.

His success came at an opportune moment: The officials involved in overseeing the atomic group were about to oust Abraham Esau as head of the program. Although Esau had overseen a number of advances, from Diebner's cube design, to Harteck's work to enrich Uranium-235, to numerous theoretical papers that laid the groundwork for practical progress, there was still no self-sustaining reactor to produce plutonium, nor any prospect of a bomb. Furthermore, the program continued to lack a steady supply of that essential moderator, heavy water. The recent Allied raids on Vemork had brought into stark relief what a mistake it was to rely on the Norwegian supply.

Esau's replacement was Walther Gerlach, a fifty-four-year-old scientist who had made his name studying magnetic fields. Although he was not a member of the Nazi Party, he was a militarist who wanted to see Hitler remain in power. By late 1943, he felt doubtful that Germany would be victorious in the war, but he was sure that if it possessed a working reactor or a bomb, it could secure whatever terms it wanted in a peace treaty.

Before his official appointment, Gerlach met with Diebner, telling him that he would be given whatever resources he needed. Heisenberg, who continued to resist the superiority of Diebner's cube design over his layered plates, would simply have to adjust.

On December 11, 1943, Diebner visited the Oslo headquarters of Norsk Hydro. Several officials told him that the company could no longer produce heavy water, as they could not "expose the company's workers to further attack, nor invest another fortune in rebuilding a plant that would be lost in the event of a new air raid." Diebner agreed. He wanted to move the plant's high-concentration equipment — including all existing stocks of heavy water, at every level of concentration — to Germany, where a new plant would be constructed. Then he would have all the moderator he required.

At the same time, Diebner was also pursuing a completely different type of atomic explosive, one that used heavy water's deuterium directly. Almost a decade before, physicists had shown that when two deuterium atoms collided at high speeds, pulses of energy were released. Some German scientists had recently perfected the shaped charges that could bring about these collisions. With this in mind, Diebner and his team began putting together a series of experiments that would use explosive shock waves to squeeze deuterium atoms together. One way or another, Diebner aimed to give Germany the weapon it needed to reverse its failing fortunes.

• • •

On January 29, 1944, Skinnarland received an urgent message from Tronstad: "It is reported that the heavy-water appliances at Vemork are to be dismantled and transported to Germany. Can you obtain confirmation of this? If it is true, are there any possibilities of preventing the transport? It is a matter of great importance."

That same day, Thor Viten, a Milorg leader in Rjukan, visited the Vemork engineer Rolf Sørlie. Sørlie was helping the war effort by rebuilding the plant as slowly as possible. While such passive resistance was important, Sørlie wanted to be a part of the bigger struggle, like his childhood friends Helberg and Poulsson. He wanted to fight. Viten told Sørlie to come to Lake Møs with him and bring skis.

They took a bus up to the lake, then started across its frozen surface. The wind blew with such force that Sørlie had to turn his head to the side to breathe. He wanted to prove that his handicapped hands and feet were not a hindrance to his abilities, so although he was struggling mightily, he kept up with Viten. After a few miles, they finally reached a farm owned by the Hamaren family. As he came in from the cold, Sørlie felt like his face was on fire. They were given dinner, then shown to a cabin a couple of hundred meters away. Neither the Hamarens nor Viten explained why Sørlie was there, but he suspected it was to meet Einar Skinnarland, whom he knew to be in hiding in the area.

In the morning, Sørlie was awakened early by a knock on the door. It was Skinnarland himself. He wanted to know if a recent message he had received from London was true: Were the Germans planning on disassembling the high-concentration plant and moving it out of the country? Sørlie replied that they were, but they first planned to ship out their existing stocks of heavy water. Skinnarland suggested contaminating the stocks with cod-liver oil, and Sørlie agreed to look into this possibility. Afterward, he returned to Rjukan, his journey made easier by his excitement at finally participating in a meaningful mission.

Back at Nilsbu, Skinnarland was eager for Haukelid to return from his hunt so they could talk over this new development at Vemork. Over the past few months, the two had become as close as brothers. Both were committed patriots who loved life in the mountains and were tough and skilled enough to endure it in the worst of conditions. While Haukelid was emotional, Skinnarland was able to absorb his friend's moods by not taking them personally. More than anything, they each trusted the other with their survival. When as much as a single track in the snow could lead the Germans to their door, this was essential.

● ● ●

On Sunday, February 6, 1944, Haukelid was coming back to Nilsbu from the west, furious that a herd of reindeer had escaped him after his rifle refused to fire. He reached the cabin long after the sun had set, hungry, his pride stinging from the failed hunt, and his dark beard half-frozen from the cold. He pulled open the door and entered cursing.

Skinnarland was there with a stranger, a slight-looking man. Haukelid was introduced to Rolf Sørlie, who had arrived soon before. Sørlie reported that the Germans intended to move all the stocks of heavy water within the next week. He had attempted to contaminate the cells with cod-liver oil, but workmen had discovered the floating fat and cleaned it off. Any further sabotage would have been too great a risk.

With this troubling news, Skinnarland and Haukelid knew they had to find a way to attack the shipment of heavy water. Skinnarland sent a message to London: "We will probably be able to blow up the transport, but as time is short, I must be told soonest what to do." With a tight schedule and no commando team at the ready, the two knew it would not be an easy operation.

An attack still required approval from the highest level. In London, Tronstad alerted Colonel Wilson and Eric Welsh. Over the next couple of days, everyone from the Norwegian High Command to the British War Cabinet agreed that a strike should be made. Haukelid and Skinnarland were to intercept the shipment, no matter what it took or what reprisals it created in Rjukan. In his diary, Tronstad wondered what the outcome would be: "We will do the best we can, but with a heavy heart for the consequences at home. I fear it will result in a lot of suffering, but we have to hope that it will save us from worse things. The guys are outstanding."

● ● ●

"Einar, you awake?" Haukelid asked late in the night of February 7. They were still waiting for the official go-ahead on the attack, and the thought of it kept him from sleeping.

"I wasn't until you began talking," Skinnarland said.

"You're as fast as anybody in Norway on the British sets now," Haukelid said. "You'll have to stay in the hills as the radio link-up with London."

"Not bloody likely," Skinnarland said. It was true he did not have as much commando training as Haukelid, but it was a lot more than anybody else they would find to help with the job.

"If we 'buy it' — as they say so charmingly in England," Haukelid said, "you'll have to take over to see the heavy water never makes it to Germany."

"I'll sleep on it," Skinnarland said.

The next morning, he received the critical message from Tronstad. "We are interested in destroying as much of the heavy water as possible, especially drums containing high concentrations is of the greatest importance . . . Leave British effects and if possible use uniforms as before . . . Try to make the action to cause the least harm to the civil populations."

Sørlie appeared at the cabin again soon after, with information on the transport route of the heavy water. A train would leave Vemork with roughly forty iron drums labeled POTASH LYE, containing heavy water at various levels of concentration. It would travel down to Rjukan, then to Mæl, at the northern tip of Lake Tinnsjø. Then a ferry would bring the railcars down the long, narrow lake. On the opposite shore, eighteen miles away, another train would haul them the short distance to Notodden, then to the port of Menstad, where a ship would take them to Hamburg, Germany. The Gestapo was aware that the shipment might be attacked, and security would be everywhere.

Sørlie assured them that the engineers at Vemork were going to tap the heavy water into drums as slowly as possible, in order to allow more time for an attack to be planned. Therefore, the train was unlikely to depart before February 16.

Sitting at the table in Nilsbu, the three men hashed over their options. They could try to blow up the drums while they were still at Vemork, but with all the additional defenses put up after Gunnerside — minefields, steel doors, bricked-up windows, and soldiers at every entrance — and more guards expected soon, it was unlikely the commandos could get into the plant. Next, they considered the possibility of hitting the train while it wound its way down the cliffside toward Rjukan. There was a shack along the route where Norsk Hydro kept explosives — the company did plenty of blasting to run its water pipelines in the area. As the train passed, they could use pressure switches on the track to set off a huge detonation that would send the railcars pitching down into the gorge. The heavy-water drums were thick, however, and some of them might survive the fall intact. Such an attack would also kill any Germans guarding the transport — deaths that would be avenged on the people of Rjukan.

The three decided that the best option was to wait until the railcars were loaded onto the ferry and then sink it. Given the depth of Lake Tinnsjø, it was unlikely that any drums would be recovered. But the ferry carried civilian passengers, and some of them were sure to drown, along with the Germans guarding the railcars.

On February 10, they received the green light from London. "Agree to sinking of ferry . . . Must not fail . . . Good luck."

● ● ●

During Gunnerside, now almost a year before, Haukelid had been on a team with nine other hardened commandos. They had trained exhaustively and knew almost every detail of their target and its defenses. In this action against the ferry, he was going in with the brave but inexperienced Sørlie and whatever ragtag collection of men he could assemble. The Germans were on the highest alert. He would have to improvise a plan as events developed. There was only a short window of time to destroy the target while limiting casualties, and if innocent people died, he would carry that burden for the rest of his life. He already carried the responsibility for the recent arrest of his father, who had been tortured by the Gestapo because of his son's activities. Further, he had not been able to see his wife, Bodil, for more than two years now, and she sent him a letter asking for a divorce. Haukelid wired a message to London, requesting three weeks of leave after the sabotage against the transport, in hopes that he could go to Stockholm and reconcile with her. All of it was a lot to bear.

Haukelid decided to give Sørlie a crash course in commando training. Over two bright, clear days, he taught him how to fire a pistol and a machine gun. Using snowmen as targets, Sørlie practiced until it was dark, the ground around him littered with casings. Haukelid also showed him how to throw grenades and the basics of hand-to-hand combat. "You have to know it all," he told his charge whenever he wavered. "You have to be tough." And then he would toss Sørlie into a bank of snow again.

On February 13, Haukelid and Sørlie skied away from Nilsbu into a bitter southwest wind. Skinnarland waved them goodbye from the door. He wished he was going with them, but they all knew that he was more valuable as their lifeline to London during the operation — and after, if things were to go sour.

Haukelid on skis.

Two days later, Haukelid and Sørlie met secretly with Kjell Nielsen, the Vemork transport manager, and Gunnar Syverstad, a laboratory assistant who had been feeding intelligence to Skinnarland for almost two years. Over the past couple of weeks, they had provided Sørlie with details on the exact concentrations of heavy water in the drums (from 3.5 percent to 99.5 percent), the number of drums being shipped, the routes from Vemork to Hamburg, the dates, the security, and even the presence of German scientists at the plant.

The best day to attack the ferry would be Sunday, February 20, because there was only one crossing that day, with the least number of passengers on board. Nielsen and Syverstad could not guarantee that they would be able to delay the transport until that date, but they would try. They also warned Haukelid and Sørlie that a number of Gestapo agents had come to town. A battalion of elite assault troops was expected to guard the train, and a host of other soldiers had just arrived in Rjukan for some "mountain training." Two German planes would sweep the area every day in advance of the shipment.

Both Nielsen and Syverstad pushed for the operation to be called off. Norwegians were likely to die, and reprisals would be inflicted on the local population. Haukelid agreed to communicate their reservations to London but said that his superiors there would have the final word.

On February 16, a heavy snow falling outside, Skinnarland made contact with London and sent Haukelid's message. At the next scheduled hookup, he got the answer from Tronstad: "The matter has been considered and it is decided that it is very important to destroy the heavy water. Hope it can be done without too great misfortune. We send our best wishes for success in the work." Skinnarland did not like the order; he knew it meant the deaths of innocent people.

The following day after dusk, Haukelid and Sørlie came

down from their mountain hideout into Rjukan. They met again with Nielsen and Syverstad, as well as Alf Larsen, the chief engineer at Vemork, who had passed information to them for months as well. Haukelid told them that London sent the order to proceed with attacking the ferry. "I know, it's tough," he said. "Sure, it's tough — but London says there's no other way." They strategized over the best way to sabotage the ferry, finally deciding to "place a time bomb on board and sink the vessel quickly before it could be run ashore." It would work so long as Haukelid could sneak on board the ferry the night before to set the timed explosives, and the ship stayed on schedule. Sørlie promised to recruit a third man for their team.

They also planned for the aftermath of the sabotage. Haukelid urged Larsen to escape with him to Sweden so the Germans could no longer use his heavy-water expertise to their own advantage. He agreed. Sørlie, already underground since the first of the month, would move out to Nilsbu to live with Skinnarland and do resistance work. Nielsen and Syverstad would stay in Rjukan.

After the meeting, Haukelid and Sørlie went to see Ditlev Diseth, a sixty-seven-year-old Norsk Hydro pensioner and member of Milorg. Diseth had a small workshop littered with tools, hollowed-out telephones and radios, and boxes of wires, hinges, springs, and screws. Haukelid needed some kind of accurately timed detonator, as he had no easy way to set an explosion on a long delay. Diseth proposed an alarm clock. Instead of hitting the bell on top of the clock, the strike hammer would close an electrical circuit attached to a detonator and set off the explosive. He promised to have the device ready within twenty-four hours.

CHAPTER 19

THE TICKING CLOCK

On February 18, Haukelid strolled through Rjukan in a borrowed blue suit and nice shoes. He carried a violin case in one hand for camouflage; an orchestra was visiting the town and scheduled to play that night. As he crossed to the train station, it seemed to Haukelid that there were Germans everywhere. Standing on the street corners. Sitting in the restaurants. Driving past in cars. Time and again, he saw residents stopped to have their IDs checked. Neither the Sten gun hidden in his violin case nor the hand grenades in his backpack would be much help to him.

At the railway station, he bought a ticket for Mæl and waited for the train. He knew the schedule for the Sunday ferry, and Nielsen had provided him with a diagram of the vessel, but he wanted to determine when the ferry reached Lake Tinnjsø's deepest point and the best place to lay the explosive charge. If anybody asked why he was riding the ferry back and forth, he could say he was out for some sightseeing before the concert.

The train arrived, and Haukelid took the eight-mile trip down the Vestfjord Valley to Mæl. The ferry terminal had only a fence surrounding it and a single attendant at the ticket booth, but Haukelid knew that when the heavy water came down from the plant, it would have numerous soldiers watching over it.

As his timetable indicated, the D/F *Hydro* was in port, readying to depart. There was nothing beautiful about the *Hydro*.

The D/F *Hydro*.

Launched in 1914, the 174-foot flat-bottomed ferry had a broad, angled bow that could break up the ice. A set of tracks ran along either side of the main deck. Together they could fit a dozen railcars of whatever was to be transported across the lake — usually fertilizer and chemical products. Under this deck was room for 120 passengers. The captain's bridge, flanked by two tall black funnels, stood over the deck.

When Haukelid boarded, these funnels were belching steam into the dreary overcast sky. He watched some railcars being brought down a ramp from the quay onto the deck. Checking his watch and taking notes in his head, Haukelid timed everything, from the boarding of the passengers, to the ship's actual moment of departure, to when they cleared the terminal. From his study of maps of Lake Tinnsjø and using the landmarks on both shores, he knew that they reached the deepest spot in the lake thirty minutes into the two-hour crossing. The lake ran to a depth of

1,300 feet at that point. Recovering anything sunk to that level would be all but impossible.

For the rest of the four-hour round trip, Haukelid kept busy. He headed up to the bridge and chatted with the helmsman about navigating the lake. He walked the length and breadth of the ferry, searching through any compartments to which he could gain access. He dropped his pipe through a metal grate above the engine room, giving him an excuse to go down and get a look at the two 250-horsepower engines driving the ferry. After retrieving his pipe, he offered the chief engineer a pinch of tobacco. They talked about the building of the *Hydro*, and the engineer even gave him a little tour. All the while, Haukelid spied for the best place to put his explosives. He forced away the thought as best he could that this same engineer might die in the sinking.

By the time they returned to Mæl, Haukelid was sure of his plan. He could blow a hole in the ferry with a couple of charges attached to its bow. Water would pour through the front holds, and its weight would pitch the ferry's front end down into the lake. This might cause the railcars to roll forward, speeding up the sinking of the ship. Even if the cars remained in place, the rudders and screws in the stern would rise out of the water, stopping the vessel's forward progress.

The question was, how big a hole should he make? Lake Tinnsjø was narrow enough that it would take only five minutes to steam from its center to either of its banks. Haukelid needed to balance the risk of the captain bringing the crippled ferry to shore against allowing time for as many passengers to escape as possible.

Thinking on it still, Haukelid returned by train into Rjukan. There he met up with Sørlie and the new recruit he had found

Knut Lier-Hansen.

for their operation. Knut Lier-Hansen was a twenty-seven-year-old former Norwegian Army sergeant as well as a local Rjukan boy. He had worked for Milorg as a weapons instructor, radioman, and spy, traveling back and forth between Stockholm, Oslo, and Rjukan. Haukelid liked him straightaway. He was eager for the job, knew how to handle a gun, had seen action, and could use connections of his own in town if they were needed.

Less than forty-eight hours before the ferry was due to be sunk, Haukelid had his team in place.

● ● ●

That same day, Tronstad was hiking through the Scottish Highlands, but the details of the attack on the *Hydro* were never far from mind. According to a recent Grouse report, the Germans were tapping almost 15,000 kilograms of heavy water from Vemork at every concentration, and 100 kilograms of that was 97 to 99.5 percent pure. Tronstad calculated that if the German scientists managed to concentrate this whole supply, they would have 633 kilograms of pure moderator. Added to what they had already received from the plant and any production they had managed on their own, they might have enough to start a working reactor.

When Skinnarland sent word of the plan to hit the ferry, Tronstad knew it was a drastic but unavoidable solution. He could only console himself with the certainty that there was no way to destroy the Germans' supply of heavy water without loss of life. If he refused to send Haukelid to take care of the ferry, the Allies would bomb Vemork again by air before the shipment left the plant, or bomb the train or ferry while they were in motion. Many more innocent civilians would die in these scenarios.

Nonetheless, Tronstad and the British drew up backup plans in case the shipment did make it off the ferry. Wilson sent instructions to a two-man resistance team working in the Oslo area to prepare for a mine attack on the cargo ship in Menstad. They would sink the ship before the heavy water left the harbor for Germany. If that failed, the RAF Bomber Command would ready an aerial attack while that ship was at sea. A lot could go wrong with these attacks. Sinking the *Hydro* was still the best option.

● ● ●

Two pops ripped Haukelid from his dreams. He was on his feet in an instant, gun in hand, moving toward the door of the cabin. Sørlie was already at the window, his Sten gun pointing out. It took a moment for the fog of sleep to lift before they both realized the source of the noise.

"At least they work," Sørlie said, looking at the two alarm clocks on the floor.

Diseth had removed the alarm bells from both clocks, then screwed strips of Bakelite insulation in their place, taken from a broken telephone he had in his shop. On top of these strips, he fixed copper plates, which were then connected by wires to electric detonator caps pilfered from Norsk Hydro. The caps would go off when triggered by a current, supplied by four 9-volt flashlight batteries.

Haukelid and Sørlie had set the clocks to "ring" in the early afternoon to wake them up. At the right minute, the strike hammers on the alarm clocks closed the electric circuit, and pop went the caps. These same caps would trigger the detonator fuses embedded in the long sausage of Nobel 808 they had rolled the night before — almost nineteen pounds of it. Once the explosive was set correctly in the bow of the *Hydro,* Haukelid figured it would blow a hole eleven feet square that would sink the ferry within four minutes. Four minutes was enough time for the passengers to escape, but not enough for the ferry to reach shore.

● ● ●

At Vemork on Saturday afternoon, February 19, Syverstad oversaw the hitching of a locomotive to railcars loaded with forty-three 400-liter drums and five 50-liter flasks of "potash lye." Dozens of soldiers with machine guns encircled the train, scanning the surrounding hillsides and valley for any threat. They had guarded the cars overnight under the glare of spotlights. In a couple of hours, the train would move down to Rjukan. According to the schedule, the train would leave the town at 8 A.M. on Sunday. Two hours later, at 10 A.M., the ferry would start down the lake.

Shortly before midnight, Haukelid and Sørlie made their way through the backstreets of Rjukan to a detached garage behind a house. The garage door was locked. A practiced thief by now, Haukelid easily jimmied it open. The owner had offered to lend them his car but said that it would be best if it looked like it had been stolen. Lier-Hansen and a man named Olav, whom he recruited as their driver, met them at the garage soon after, as did Alf Larsen, who was going to escape with them.

They set off, the car's tire chains churning up a trail of murky white. The short ride to Mæl was made long by the dread they all felt. If they ran into any checkpoints, they would have a tricky time talking their way free. Five men without travel permits in a stolen car in the middle of the night would be bad enough. The presence of weapons and explosives would see them shot — but only after they were tortured.

Roughly a mile from the ferry station, Haukelid told the driver to pull over by a bank of trees and shut off the headlights. "Wait for us," Haukelid told him and Larsen. If they were not back in a couple hours, the two should drive off.

Haukelid, Sørlie, and Lier-Hansen got out of the car. A half-moon hung in the clear sky, providing barely enough light to see their way to the station. The winter chill stung their skin, and the ice under their feet cracked and snapped with every step. If there was a sharp-eared guard ahead, he would hear them coming long before they saw him.

Moving slightly ahead of the others, Haukelid kept his eyes trained on the station, watching for any movement. His pockets were stuffed with grenades and alarm clocks; he had a Sten gun hidden under his parka and nineteen pounds of explosives wrapped around his neck and waist. He felt like an awkward, overstuffed giant.

A single hanging lamp lit the gangway that led to the shadowed hulk of the *Hydro*. Otherwise, there were no other lights. From what he could see, no soldiers patrolled the ground around the ferry. A few nights before, on reconnaissance, they had seen between fifteen and twenty men in the station house. They rarely ventured out in the cold, but Haukelid had figured that they would be significantly more careful tonight.

One hundred yards from the station, Haukelid waved for the others to stop and provide him with cover as he moved closer. He spotted some soldiers in the station house, but again, none outside. For all their defensive measures, the Germans had not thought to guard the ferry the night before its use.

With Sørlie and Lier-Hansen following at a short distance, Haukelid crept along the dock toward the ferry. Again, no guards or lookouts. Fear snaked up his spine. He did not trust that the Germans could be so foolish.

Unchallenged, the three moved onto the ferry at last. Haukelid heard some faint voices below the main deck. Slowly, he continued down into the companionway. Near the door leading to the crew's quarters, he listened closely. By the sound of it, the crew was in the middle of a game of poker. He stole forward, briefly catching sight of the Norwegian crew sitting around a long table, playing cards.

They entered the third-class passenger compartment. Now they needed to find a hatch belowdecks, where they would place the explosives. While Haukelid and Sørlie searched for the hatch, Lier-Hansen provided cover. Just then, they heard the shuffle of feet down the passageway. Before they could hide, the watchman appeared in the door. If he called the alarm, they were lost. "Is that you, Knut?" the watchman asked.

"Yes," Lier-Hansen said coolly, recognizing a man named John Berg, whom he knew from the Mæl Athletic Club. "I'm with some friends."

Haukelid and Sørlie stepped forward. There was another tense moment as the watchman tried to work out why they were on board in the middle of the night.

"Hell, John," Lier-Hansen said. The man knew Knut was in the resistance. "We're expecting a raid and we have something to hide. Illegal things. It's as simple as that."

"Why didn't you say so?" John said. "No problem." He pointed out a hatch in the passageway, which led belowdecks. "This won't be the first time something's been hidden below."

Lier-Hansen kept up the conversation with the watchman as Haukelid and Sørlie climbed down into the bilge. On their hands and knees, a flashlight to guide them, they sloshed through the ice-cold black water until they reached the bow of the ferry.

Sørlie held the light as Haukelid got to work. The minutes passed quickly as he delicately prepared the charges. He secured the explosives underwater, on the bottom of the corrugated-iron floor. The sausage of Nobel 808 was curled into an almost complete circle. Haukelid fixed two detonator fuses to both ends of the sausage. He drew the other ends of the fuses out of the water and taped them together. Then he connected the electric detonator caps to these fuses and fixed them to the ribs of the ship. After connecting the two alarm clocks with their battery packets, he made sure that the wires leading from the clocks were not already electrified. Then he wound the alarm clocks, setting them to go off at 10:45 A.M., and taped them to the ferry's ribs as well.

Hands wet and numb, eyes stinging from sweat, Haukelid began the most dangerous part of setting the charges: taping the wires from the alarm clocks to the detonator caps. With only a third of an inch separating the strike hammer on each alarm clock from the plate that would trigger the caps, Haukelid took great care. If he jarred the alarm clocks, if his hands slipped, if he lost his balance on the slick floor, he and Sørlie would be dead before the thought even flashed across their minds.

His hands remained steady, and he finished his work.

After ninety minutes belowdecks, Haukelid and Sørlie wriggled their way over to the ladder and climbed through the hatch, dirty and drenched. Lier-Hansen and the watchman were still talking away. Berg did not ask any questions about what had taken so long, and Haukelid was not about to answer any. He simply shook Berg's hand and thanked him for being a good Norwegian. Then the three men sneaked off the ferry and away into the night.

They reached the car just a few minutes before their two-hour deadline, drove a short distance, then stopped again on the side of the road. Sørlie got out. He was heading back to Nilsbu to reconnect with Skinnarland. After putting on his skis, he said his goodbyes to the others. "I'll be back before long," Haukelid promised — after his leave to see his wife in Stockholm. Then Sørlie disappeared into the woods. Olav drove the rest of them south toward Kongsberg, where they planned to board a train to the capital. Lier-Hansen decided at the last minute not to leave for Sweden and got out.

Back on the ferry, the clocks ticked.

CHAPTER 20

SABOTAGE

On Sunday at 8 A.M. sharp, whistles blew across Rjukan railway station. The crowd of soldiers guarding the two flat cars settled into their positions beside the drums of heavy water. The freight train was also hauling seven tanks of ammonia and two wagons of luggage. Never had a shipment from the town been so well protected. Soldiers were stationed all along the railway line as well, to make sure there was no attack on the route.

At Kongsberg, a sixty-mile drive from Rjukan, Haukelid and Larsen bought train tickets to Oslo. Olav had dropped off the two men roughly ten miles from the town, and they had skied the rest of the way through the forest.

The D/F *Hydro* at the dock, waiting to be loaded with railcars.

From a hillside overlooking Mæl, Lier-Hansen watched the freight train come down the line. Over the next hour, the train wagons and flatcars were shifted onto the *Hydro* and locked into place. Then the passengers from Rjukan began to arrive. The clerk checked their tickets before they crossed the gangway and took their seats. Lier-Hansen looked at his watch frequently. A few minutes after ten o'clock, the mooring lines were cast free. The ferry moved away from the dock, its propellers stirring up the placid waters of Lake Tinnsjø behind it.

It was a cold but clear morning, and the sun shone brightly overhead. Up on the bridge, Captain Erling Sørensen directed the *Hydro* toward the center of the lake. It was a trip he had taken hundreds of times. Just before 10:45 A.M., he stepped out of the wheelhouse to make a note in the logbook. Belowdecks, the thirty-eight passengers were passing their time in the saloon and other compartments. Some played cards. Others were engaged in conversation or quietly reading their books. An elderly woman thumbed through a photo album. In the engine room, three crew members were eating a late breakfast, taking a break from the cold. Apart from the eight German soldiers keeping careful watch over two of the railcars, all was normal.

As Sørensen descended from the bridge, a sharp bang sounded belowdecks. The whole ferry shook. If they had not been in the middle of the deep lake, he might have figured that they had suddenly collided with another ship or run aground. No, this was something different altogether. Running back up the steps, he saw smoke blanket the deck. "Steer toward land!" he shouted to the helmsman. But before the ferry could change course, it began to keel violently.

Terror struck the passengers. Water poured across the floor in the compartments below, and steam hissed through cracked pipes. The lights went out, and in the third-class saloon, which had no portholes, it was almost pitch-black. "A bomb!" one of the passengers shrieked. "We've been bombed!" Everyone struggled to find the door.

Sørensen knew the ferry was lost. The bow was sinking underwater, and they were nowhere near the shore. He shouted for the passengers to get into the lifeboats and, with a crew member, managed to release one of the boats. He told his helmsman to abandon ship, then took over the bridge himself, swinging the wheel to direct the *Hydro* to the starboard side. It continued to list to port, the bow now completely submerged. One crew member was almost crushed between two tilting railway cars.

Passengers fled from their compartments onto the main deck. Some managed to find life vests before jumping into the water. Others simply took off their thick coats and leapt overboard. Those who could not swim faced the terrible choice between the sinking ship and the treacherously cold water.

Down in third class, several passengers finally found the door out but were confused in the darkness about which way to go. Water poured down the passageway in a torrent. Screams and cries for help rang out in every direction. The floor underneath their feet steepened into a slide.

Sørensen scrambled out of the wheelhouse. The bow was now completely submerged. At the other end, the propellers spun higher and higher out of the water, and the ship tilted to one side. At that moment, there was another huge bang, and eleven railcars broke free and pitched into the lake. Sørensen had only

Lake Tinnsjø.

seconds now before the whole ferry sank, and he would go down with it if he did not move quickly. He jumped.

Four minutes after the explosion, the *Hydro* was gone.

The one lifeboat that had been launched quickly became inundated with passengers. Others held on to the debris left in the wake of the sinking ship, including suitcases and four half-empty drums of "potash lye." Those who had managed to free themselves from the ferry now struggled to get to shore before the ice-cold water overwhelmed them.

Local fishermen and farmers who had witnessed the disaster hurried out in rowboats to rescue those in the water. They pulled at their oars so hard that their hands bled. Of the fifty-three people who boarded the ferry, twenty-seven survived, including the captain and four German soldiers. All eleven of the railcars sank to the bottom of Lake Tinnsjø, and the drums of heavy water went with them.

Barrels from the D/F *Hydro*, recovered from the bottom of Lake Tinnsjø.

● ● ●

RAILWAY FERRY HYDRO SUNK IN THE TINNSJØ. Haukelid read the headline in a newspaper in a cabin north of Oslo. The day before, at 10:45 A.M., he had stared at his watch, picturing in his mind's eye what was unfolding on the lake. The explosion, the ship keeling, more Norwegian lives lost to the battle against Vemork's heavy water. Now he held the news in his hands.

He had followed his orders, tough as they were to bear.

With the help of the underground escape network, Haukelid crossed the border a few days later and made his way to Stockholm. After many months in the Norwegian wilderness, he found it strange to sit in a restaurant and eat his fill or to pass shop windows piled high with merchandise. In a hotel, he bathed and changed into new clothes. Not long afterward, he met with Bodil and tried to reconcile. But much — too much — had passed while they were apart.

Two weeks into his stay in the city, he was ready to return to his resistance work. It was the only life that made sense to him.

● ● ●

On February 26, 1944, Tronstad arrived at Euston Station from Scotland. On the way to his office, he passed a large apartment building cordoned off by police. It had suffered a direct hit twelve hours before during a renewed blitz by German bombers. Across the city, hundreds were dead, and many more left without homes.

He thought further about the sabotage of the *Hydro*. He was deeply saddened at the deaths of his innocent countrymen, but the hard truth was that many more were dying in London during the nightly bombings. Worse, if the Germans had managed to build an atomic bomb, they would have left the British capital — and perhaps other cities, too — scorched ruins with innumerable dead. Tronstad understood that in war, leaders had to measure their decisions against such comparisons, whether on the field of battle or at the planning table. Still, when he read the names and ages of those who perished on the ferry, he felt terribly small inside.

Within days, Tronstad received final confirmation from Skinnarland's spies that the entire shipment of Vemork heavy water — except for a few drums of nearly worthless concentrate — was now at the bottom of Lake Tinnsjø. In his diary, he noted the closing of this "brave chapter" in the fight against the Germans. He would ask Winston Churchill to reward Haukelid and the others involved.

As for Vemork, he lamented having to destroy what he had helped to construct. When the war was over, he hoped to rebuild the plant better than before, for the future of Norway. Until then, Tronstad and his men had succeeded in eliminating the Nazis' source of heavy water for their atomic research — and contributed to stopping them altogether from realizing a weapon unlike any before.

● ● ●

In mid-1944, Hitler, increasingly deluded and desperate, promised anyone who would listen: "Very soon I shall use my triumphal weapons, and then the war will end gloriously. This is the weapon of the future, and with it Germany's future is likewise assured."

Few people believed him. Germany was under assault from land, air, and sea. Allied forces drove their way to Berlin from the west, and the Russians pushed from the east. In July, a bomb run of 567 Flying Fortresses destroyed any possibility of renewing the heavy-water supply in Germany. Other attacks halted uranium production and U-235 separation. By the end of 1944, the best Diebner or anyone else in the Uranium Club could hope to create was a self-sustaining uranium machine.

The Allies knew it. That November, Colonel Boris Pash, a US Army intelligence officer, and his boss, Dr. Samuel Goudsmit, discovered a bounty of secret papers in a Strasbourg hospital commandeered by the German atomic program. For four freezing days and nights, while American forces battled the Wehrmacht on the outskirts of the city, Goudsmit and Pash read through the papers by candlelight, eating little, sleeping less. By the end, there was only one conclusion to draw: "Germany had no atom bomb and was not likely to have one in any reasonable time. There was no need to fear any attack either from an atomic explosive or from radioactive poisons."

But at the start of 1945, with the war's end inevitable, Gerlach and Diebner continued to hope. They crisscrossed Germany, distributing supplies and directing experiments in one last-ditch effort to obtain at least a working uranium machine. In a rock-hewn wine cellar in Haigerloch, a hillside village in southwest Germany, Heisenberg had established a laboratory and constructed a lattice of uranium cubes submerged in heavy water, similar to that set up by Diebner before the evacuation from Berlin. Using 1.5 tons of uranium and heavy water, the machine produced the highest level of neutron multiplication yet achieved. By Heisenberg's calculations, he was sure to have a self-sustaining reactor if he could just have 50 percent more uranium and heavy water.

He would get neither one.

After Germany surrendered in May 1945, ten of the leading Uranium Club scientists were interned at Farm Hall, a quiet country house outside Cambridge, England. Among them were Otto Hahn, Werner Heisenberg, Walther Gerlach, Paul Harteck, and Kurt Diebner. They had been rounded up when the Nazi regime fell, along with their papers, laboratory equipment, and supplies of uranium and heavy water. They bided their time, reading in the library, playing bridge, and wondering if they would see their families again.

At 6 P.M. on August 6, 1945, a short BBC radio bulletin reported that an atomic bomb had been dropped on Japan. Major Terence Rittner, who was in charge of security at Farm Hall, went to Otto Hahn's room to inform him. The man who discovered fission was "shattered" by the news and "felt personally responsible for the deaths of hundreds of thousands of people." Rittner steadied him with a glass of gin.

Then Hahn went down for dinner. In the dining room, he told the others what he had learned. The news staggered them, too. They could not believe it. Surely the Americans and British were not able to build an atomic bomb.

Their doubts were soon answered by another BBC broadcast, with Churchill making a statement: "The greatest destructive power devised by man went into action this morning. . . . The bomb, dropped today on the Japanese war base of Hiroshima, was designed for a detonation equal to twenty-thousand tons of high explosive . . ." He continued, "The possession of these powers by the Germans at any time might have altered the result of the war. Every effort was made to locate in Germany anything resembling the plants, which were being created in the United

States. In the winter of 1942–43, most gallant attacks were made in Norway on two occasions by small parties of volunteers upon stores of what is called 'heavy water,' an element in one of the possible processes. The second of these two attacks was completely successful." Churchill concluded, "This revelation of the secrets of Nature, long mercifully withheld from man, should arouse the most solemn reflection in the minds and conscience of every human being."

Diebner always believed that without the sabotage of Vemork, he would have had enough heavy water by the end of 1943 for a working reactor. He likely would not have stopped his research until he produced a bomb. "The obliteration of deuterium production in Norway," he wrote later, "is one of the major reasons why Germany never obtained one."

An American atomic bomb explodes over Hiroshima, Japan, on August 6, 1945.

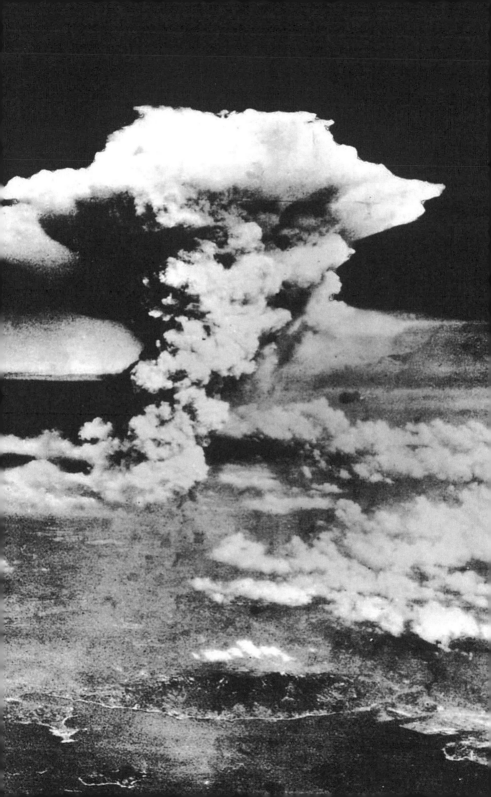

On May 8, 1945, Churchill declared victory over Germany to a throng of revelers from a balcony overlooking Whitehall. That same day, resistance forces deep in the heart of Telemark went into action. After years of fighting as an underground army, they took back Rjukan and the surrounding towns in open daylight. They occupied Vemork and other power stations in the area, seized control of communication lines and key public buildings, and took responsibility for law and order, including the arrest of Norwegian traitors and SS officers. The soldiers in the German garrisons surrendered their weapons and went where they were told. Similar scenes played out across the rest of Norway. The invaders numbered almost 400,000 in total, Milorg forces roughly 40,000. There could have been an ugly last-ditch fight, but there was none. Norway was free, and parties started in the streets of Oslo and throughout the country.

A month after the German surrender, King Haakon VII stepped onto Norwegian soil at the pier in front of Oslo's town hall. Despite the steady drizzle, 50,000 Norwegians cheered and waved flags to celebrate his return. Among those present to honor him were Colonel Wilson and over one hundred members of Kompani Linge, most of them wearing helmets or badges that named their operations. Grouse and Gunnerside were well represented.

As time went on, those who had participated in the

A celebration in Oslo.

The Skinnerlands gather at their family inn.
Einar is sixth from right in the front row.

From left to right, Haukelid, Poulsson, Rønneberg, Kayser, Kjelstrup, Haugland, Strømsheim, and Storhaug receive official honors for their service.

heavy-water sabotage were pinned with medals from many grateful nations: Norway, Great Britain, Denmark, France, and the United States. Nor was the sacrifice of the British Royal Engineers and RAF crews of the ill-fated Operation Freshman forgotten. Thirty-seven bodies were recovered and buried at grave sites in Norway. The Norwegians also erected memorials for the innocent lives lost in the American bombing raid at Vemork and in the *Hydro* sinking.

Beyond the medals and the memorials, the war marked the men of Grouse and Gunnerside in other ways, sometimes dark ones. They had all spent the rest of the war involved in various commando activities. Joachim Rønneberg destroyed German supply lines in the Romsdal Valley, including a key railway bridge. Kasper Idland operated submersible canoes in limpet-mine attacks against enemy ships in Norwegian harbors. Hans Storhaug and

Fredrik Kayser suffered great hardship while establishing resistance cells. Knut Haugland continued to set up wireless radio links with London to coordinate Milorg activities.

They had seen friends die. Some had killed. All of them had lived under the constant threat of discovery and death. At times, they woke up in the middle of the night, imagining the enemy at the door, reaching for guns that were not there. Einar Skinnarland's children knew not to approach their father suddenly.

In the years after the war, a few of the saboteurs turned to alcohol to dull memories they never asked for. Many sought solace in the Vidda, the very place they had once struggled to survive. The sense of the "smallness of being a human being in nature" was relief for Rønneberg. "You could sit down on a stone and let your thoughts fly away." Knut Haugland lived for 101 days in 1947 as the radio operator on the *Kon-Tiki*, a simple raft that crossed the Pacific Ocean with only a six-man crew. Beyond offering a great adventure, the journey helped him to heal. Only in his last years did Skinnarland revisit his war diary and the long string of telegrams he had sent from the Vidda, and only then did he allow himself some pride over what he had endured for the sake of his country — and the world. What nature and time could not mend, friendship supported them through. Until the end of their lives, the members of Kompani Linge gathered often to share experiences that few others could understand.

Sadly, Tronstad died before he could see his country free. He returned to Norway in October 1944 to oversee "Operation Sunshine," coordinating the work of 2,200 resistance fighters in Telemark and protecting "the major industrial objectives" in the area, including its power stations. Many former Kompani Linge members participated in Sunshine, including Poulsson, Helberg,

Syverstad, Poulsson, Norman Lind, and Tronstad train together for Operation Sunshine.

Kjelstrup, and Syverstad, who had come to London for training after the ferry sabotage. Einar Skinnarland served as Tronstad's radio operator. Over the next five months, they orchestrated steady drops of arms and supplies, recruited and trained resistance cells in firearms and explosives, and performed small-scale sabotages of arm dumps. Tronstad ate, slept, hunted, and skied side by side with his men. Most had thought highly of him while he was their boss in London. In the wilds of Telemark, their loyalty and respect deepened into something greater still.

By spring 1945, the time for an uprising against the Germans looked imminent. On the night of March 11, Tronstad was interrogating a Nazi sympathizer when suddenly the door to his hut burst open. The sympathizer's brother entered with a gun and started shooting. Tronstad was killed in the ambush. Jens-Anton Poulsson took over as the leader of Operation Sunshine.

Afterward, Tronstad's wife, Bassa, received a letter Tronstad had written her in case of his death. "Dearest Bassa," he wrote. "I have the honor to lead an important expedition home, which will be of great importance to Norway's future. It is in line with the course I chose on April 9, 1940, to put all my effort and abilities toward our country's welfare. . . . The war is singing its last verse, and it requires every effort from all who would call themselves men. You will understand that, won't you? We have had so many magical happy years, and my highest wish is to continue that happy life together. But should the Almighty have another course for me, know that my last thought was of you. . . . Time is short, but if all will not go well, don't feel sorry for me. I am completely happy and thankful for what I have had in life even though I very much would like to live to help Norway back to its feet." He wished the best for Sidsel and Leif and concluded that he looked forward to meeting her again. The letter was signed "Your beloved."

When Tronstad sent Gunnerside off on its mission, he spoke of their action being remembered for a hundred years. But he fought and died for a different reason than fame and renown — a different "why" — and he made that "why" plain in his letters home: for Norway, for its land, and its people.

Fredrik Kayser ruminated on the same question: "Why?" In speeches, he called on a letter written by a nineteen-year-old Norwegian to his parents and sisters before he left to fight the Germans. "I love you all, but my country first, then you . . . A poet once said that 'if a people are to live, someone must die' . . . If I do not come back, it's because someone must die."

Rønneberg, the last surviving saboteur, who was ninety-five years old in 2015, spoke eloquently about why he braved the North Sea to be trained in Britain and why he then returned, by parachute, to Norway. "You have to fight for your freedom," he said. "And for peace. You have to fight for it every day, to keep it. It's like a glass boat; it's easy to break. It's easy to lose."

The saboteurs' memorial at Vemork.

Now and again, readers ask how long it takes me to research and write a book. I ballpark it at three years, depending on the availability of sources and on narrative complexity. That amount of time sounds right to some folks, quick to others. The truth is, however, each of my books would have taken many more years if not for the community of people who contribute to the finished work. And the quality would have been far, far diminished without them.

First, I would like to applaud my research assistants who spearheaded my efforts in Norway (Windy Kester and Arne Holsen) and Germany (Almut Schoenfeld). They were tireless in helping me comb through archives and tracking down individuals to interview.

Before I began my research, all but one of the saboteurs (Joachim Rønneberg) had passed away. I had the benefit of their recollections in numerous interviews, memoirs, and diaries, but even this bounty did not provide the kind of rich portrait I hoped to paint of each of them. Fortunately, their families offered to speak with me, sharing family lore as well as a number of documents that have never before been seen. A big thanks to the Haukelids (Kirvil, Bjørgulf, Knut), Skinnarlands (Marielle, Kirvil, Ron, Inger-Berit Bakke), Hauglands (Trond, Torfinn, Torill), Tronstads (Leif Jr., Sidsel), and Finn Sørlie. In particular,

I'd like to send my appreciation to Leif Tronstad Jr., who shared many, many hours of his time and family papers with me, as well as reading the final draft of the book; to Marielle Skinnarland for her generous availability to my exhaustive list of questions; and to the Hauglands, who put me up in their cabin outside Vemork and took me on a cross-country ski tour of the area (and even offered some of their father's gear for me to use). I also appreciate the insight of former Kompani Linge member Ragnar Ulstein and a handful of Norwegians who know this story well and provided much guidance to me, including Bjørn Iversen, Svein Vetle Trae, Berit Nøkleby, Asgeir Ueland, and Tor Nicolaysen. In particular, Svein Vetle offered me a wonderful weekend at his cabin, not to mention the maps for this book.

A work of history is often only as good as the depth of primary sources available to the author. In the case of *Sabotage*, they were aplenty. One of these was the Norges Hjemmefrontmuseum (NHM). It is a gem of an archive, and its staff are first-rate experts on the Norwegian homefront resistance. My appreciation to my guides there: Frode Faerøy, Ivar Kragland, Benjamin Geissert, and Arfinn Moland (who provided me with an unpublished interview with Gunnerside leader Rønneberg that ran over a hundred pages of pure gold). Rjukan's Norsk Industriarbeidermuseum (VM) also held great treasure, and I would have been lost without its director, Kjetil Djuve, and Ingelinn Kårvand. Also a big thanks to the staff at the National Archives (UK), who fielded innumerable requests on my behalf, as well those at the Imperial War Museum, Niels Bohr Library, and Rensselaer Institute, among others. Without my translators, Carl Stoll and Mark McNaught, much of this material would have been indecipherable.

Once the research is done and the first draft complete, another community comes to my side. A shout-out to my early readers, Carl Bartoli, Henry Bartoli, John Tuohy, and Mike Faley, who clarified atomic physics as well as the intricacies of B-17 bombing runs. As always, my first-line editor, Liz O'Donnell of the Little Red Pen, shaped and shifted and refined almost every paragraph in the book. I can never sing her praises enough. Thanks to my literary agent — and consigliere in all things publishing — Eric Lupfer at William Morris Endeavor. There's no better publisher than Scholastic for my young adult work, and my editor, Cheryl Klein, is amazing. The beautiful edition in your hands is a testament to her ability to work all the levers of the publishing process. Kudos also to Els Rijper, Maya Frank-Levine, Phil Falco, and Bonnie Cutler.

And finally, thanks to Diane and our precious girls, who live through the ups, downs, and in-betweens of the life of an author. You make it all worth it.

On first blush, a bibliography often looks like a dry recounting of sources, some primary, others secondary. The list below does not do justice to the excitement that came with researching *Sabotage*, from finding the diaries of Leif Tronstad and Einar Skinnarland, to the top secret SOE files, to interviews with the families of the saboteurs, to the unpublished manuscripts of Colonel John Wilson, Rolf Sørlie, and the Skinnarland family during the war. Over the course of my research, I read through hundreds of books, some in English, some in Norwegian and German, many listed here. But the lion's share of this story was constructed from reminiscences and interviews and memoirs of the key individuals as well as correspondence, action reports, diaries, and other archival papers written at the time these events unfolded.

Archives
United States
Howard Gotlieb Archival Research Center, Boston University (Boston, MA)
National Archives (College Park, MD)
Niels Bohr Library and Archives (College Park, MD)
Rensselaer Polytechnic Institute, Archives and Special Collections (Troy, NY)

Norway
Norges Hjemmefrontmuseum (Oslo)
Norges Teknisk-Naturvitenskapelige Universitet Arkiv (Trondheim)
Norsk Industriarbeidermuseum (Vemork)

Germany
Bundesarchiv (Berlin)
Bundesarchiv (Freiburg)
Deutsches Museum Archiv (Munich)

Britain
British Online Archives (London)
Imperial War Museum (London)
National Archives (Kew)

Personal Papers

Leif Tronstad (courtesy of Leif Tronstad Junior)

Knut Haugland (courtesy of Trond, Torfinn, and Torill Haugland)

Einar Skinnarland (courtesy of Marielle Skinnarland)

Jens-Anton Poulsson (courtesy of Mia and Unni Poulsson)

Knut Haukelid (courtesy of Bjørgulf, Kirvil, and Knut Haukelid)

David Irving (courtesy of British Online Archives)

Rolf Sørlie (courtesy of Finn Sørlie)

Bjørn Iversen

Interviews

Tronstad Family

Haugland Family

Haukelid Family

Poulsson Family

Skinnarland Family

Finn Sørlie

Ragnar Ulstein

Svein Vetle Trae

Lillian Gabrielson

Norwegian- and German-Language Books and Magazines

Andersen, Ketil, *Flaggskip i Fremmed Eie: Hydro 1905–1945* (Pax Forlag, 2005)

Bagge, Erich, Kurt Diebner, and Kenneth Jay, *Von der Uranspaltung bis Calder Hall* (Rowohlt Hamburg, 1957)

Berg, John, *Soldaten Som Ikke Ville Gi Seg: Lingekaren Arne Kjelstrup, 1940–45* (Metope, 1986)

Bergfald, Odd, *Hellmuth Reinhard: Soldat eller Morder?* (Chr. Schibsteds Forlag, 1967)

Bøhn, Per, *IMI: Norsk Innsats i Kampen om Atomkraften* (F. Bruns Bokhandels Forlag, 1946)

Brauteset, Steinar, *Gestapo-offiseren Fehmer: Milorgs Farligste Fiende* (J. W. Cappelens Forlag, 1986)

Brun, Jomar, *Brennpunkt Vemork, 1940–45* (Universitetsforlaget, 1985)

Dahl, Helge, *Rjukan, Bind II fra 1920 til 1980* (Utgitt av Tinn Kommune, 1983)

Drew, Ion, Helge Sognli, Marie Smith-Solbakken, and Hans-Jorgen Weihe, *Tause Helter: Operasjon Freshman og Andre Falne* (Hertervig Akademisk, 2011)

Fjeldbu, Sigmund, *Et Lite Sted på Verdenskartet: Rjukan 1940–50* (Tiden Norsk Forlag, 1980)

Halvorsen, Odd, *Den Norske Turistforening Årbok 1947* (Den Norske Turistforening, 1947)

Halvorsen, Odd, *Den Norske Turistforening Årbok 1970* (Den Norske Turistforening, 1970)

Hedemann, Reidar, *Gestapo i Norge: Mennene, Midlene og Metodene* (Norsk Kunstforlag, 1946)

Hurum, Gerd Vold, *En Kvinne ved Navn "Truls"* (Wings, 2006)

Jensen, Erling, *Kompani Linge: Første Bind* (Gyldendal Norsk Forlag, 1949)

Karlsch, Rainer, *Hitlers Bombe: Die geheime Geschichte der deutschen Kernwaffenversuche* (Deutsche Verlags-Anstalt, 2005)

Kjelstadli, Sverre, *Hjemmestyrkene* (Bokstav & Bilde, 1959)

Larsen, Stein, Beatrice Sandberg, and Volker Dahm, eds., *Meldungen aus Norwegen* (R. Oldenbourg Verlag, 2008)

Lauritzen, Per, *Claus Helberg: Veiviser i Krig og Fred* (Den Norske Turistforening Boksenteret Forlag, 1999)

Løken, Roar, *Militær Motstand i Milorgs D. 16* (Universitetet i Oslo, 1976)

Lunde, Kjell Harald, *Sabotøren: Et Portrett av Mennesket og Krigshelten Fredrik Kayser* (Alma Mater Forlag, 1997)

Myklebust, Gunnar, *Tungtvannssabotøren: Joachim H. Rønneberg* (Aschehoug, 2011)

Nagel, Günter, *Atomversuche in Deutschland* (Heinrich-Jung-Verlagsgesellschaft, 2002)

Njølstad, Olav, *Professor Tronstads Krig* (Aschehoug, 2012)

Nøkelby, Berit, "Uforskammet opptrden mot Terboven," *Aftenposten*, February 25, 1983

Nøkleby, Berit, *Gestapo: Tysk politi I Norge, 1940–45* (Aschehoug, 2003)

Nøkleby, Berit, *Josef Terboven: Hitlers Mann i Norge* (Gyldendal, 1992)

Olsen, Kr. Anker, *Norsk Hydro: Gjennom 50 År* (Norsk Hydro, 1955)

Ording, Arne, Johnson Gudrun, and Johan Garder, *Våre Falne, 1939–1945, Annen Bok* (Grondahl, 1950)

Payton, Gary, and Trond Lepperød, *Rjukanbanen på Sporet av et Industrieventyr* (Maana Forlag, Rjukan, 1995).

Piekalkiewicz, Janusz, *Spione, Agenten, Soldaten: Geheime Kommandos im Zweiten Weltkrieg* (Schweizer Volks-Buchgemeinde, 1969)

Rostøl, Jack, and Nils Helge Amdal, *Tungtvannssabotør Kasper Idland: Fra Krig til Kamp* (Commentum Forlag, 2011)

Sæter, Svein, *Operatøren: Knut Hauglands Egen Beretning; Tungtvann, Gestapo, Kon-Tiki* (Cappelen Damm, 2008)

Schaaf, Michael, *Die Physikochemiker Paul Harteck* (Historisches Institut der Universitat Stuttgart, 1999)

Schramm, Percy, *Hitler als Militärischer Führer* (Athenäum Verlag, 1965)

Skogen, Olav, *Ensom Krig mot Gestapo* (Aschehoug Pocket, 2009)

Tranøy, Joar, *Oppvekst i Samhold og Konflikt* (Maana Forlag, 2007)

Ueland, Asgeir, *Tungtvannsaksjonen: Historien om den Største Krigsoperasjonen på Norsk Jord* (Gyldendal, 2013)

Veum, Erik, *Nådeløse Nordmenn Statspolitiet, 1941–45* (Kagge Forlag, 2012)

Werner-Hagen, Knut, "Operation Moonlight," *Truppendienst,* March 2009

English-Language Books, Magazines, and Documentary Transcripts

Adamson, Hans Christian, and Per Klem, *Blood on the Midnight Sun* (Norton, 1964)

Baden-Powell, Dorothy, *Operation Jupiter: SOE's Secret War in Norway* (Robert Hale, 1982)

Bailey, Roderick, *Forgotten Voices of the Secret War* (Ebury Press, 2008)

Bennett, John, *Letters from England* (San Antonio, 1945)

Berglyd, Jostein, *Operation Freshman: The Hunt for Hitler's Heavy Water* (Leandoer & Ekholm Publishing, 2006)

Bernstein, Jeremy, and David Cassidy, *Hitler's Uranium Club* (Springer Science & Media, 2013)

Beyerchen, Alan, *Scientists under Hitler: Politics and the Physics Community in the Third Reich* (Yale University Press, 1977)

Casimir, Hendrik, *Haphazard Reality: Half a Century of Science* (Harper & Row, 1984)

Cassidy, David, *Uncertainty: The Life and Science of Werner Heisenberg* (W. H. Freeman & Company, 1992)

Churchill, Winston, *The Churchill War Papers: The Ever-Widening War, 1941* (Norton, 2001)

Churchill, Winston, *The Hinge of Fate* (Houghton Mifflin, 1950)

Churchill, Winston, *Their Finest Hour* (Mariner Books, 1978)

Clark, Ronald, *The Birth of the Bomb* (Phoenix House, 1961)

Clark, Ronald, *Tizard* (MIT Press, 1965)

Compton, Arthur, *Atomic Quest* (Oxford University Press, 1956)

Cookridge, E. H., *Set Europe Ablaze: The Inside Story of SOE* (Thomas Crowell, 1967)

Cooper, D. F., "Operation Freshman," *The Royal Engineers Journal*, March 1946

Cruickshank, Charles, *SOE in Scandinavia* (Oxford University Press, 1986)

Dahl, Per, *Heavy Water and the Wartime Race for Nuclear Energy* (Institute of Physics Publishing, 1999)

Dalton, Hugh, *The Fateful Years: Memoirs 1931–45* (Frederick Muller, 1957)

Dank, Milton, *The Glider Gang* (J. B. Lippincott Company, 1977)

Dipple, John, *Two against Hitler: Stealing the Nazis' Best-Kept Secrets* (Praeger, 1992)

Dorril, Stephen, *MI6: Inside the Covert World of Her Majesty's Secret Intelligence Service* (Free Press, 2002)

Drummond, John, *But For These Men* (Award Books, 1962)

Ermenc, Joseph, ed., *Atomic Bomb Scientists: Memoirs, 1939–45* (Meckler, 1989)

Fen, Åke, *Nazis in Norway* (Penguin Books, 1942)

Fine, Lenore, and Jesse Remington, *The Corps of Engineers: Construction in the United States* (Office of the Chief of Military History, 1972)

Foot, M. R. D., *SOE: An Outline History of the Special Operations Executive, 1940–46* (Pimlico, 1999)

Frank, Charles, *Operation Epsilon* (University of California Press, 1993)

Freeman, Roger A., *The Mighty Eighth War Manual* (Jane's, 1985)

Gallagher, Thomas, *Assault in Norway: Sabotaging the Nazi Nuclear Program* (Lyons Press, 1975)

Gjelsvik, Tore, *Norwegian Resistance, 1940–45* (C. Hurst and Company, 1979)

Goebbels, Josef, *The Goebbels Diaries* (Hamish Hamilton, London, 1948)

Goldsmith, Maurice, *Frédéric Joliot-Curie* (Lawrence and Wisehart, 1976)

Goudsmit, Samuel, *Alsos* (Springer Science & Business, 1996)

Gowing, Margaret, *Britain and Atomic Energy, 1939–45* (Macmillan, 1982)

Grimnes, Ole, Joachim Rønneberg, and Bertrand Goldschmidt, "The Race for Norwegian Heavy Water, 1940–1945," *IFS Info*, 1995

Groves, Leslie, *Now It Can Be Told: The Story of the Manhattan Project* (Da Capo Press, 1983)

Haarr, Geirr, *The German Invasion of Norway: April 1940* (Naval Institute Press, 2009)

Hargreaves, Richard, *Blitzkrieg Unleashed: The German Invasion of Poland* (Stackpole Books, 2008)

Hauge, E. O., *Salt-Water Thief* (Duckworth & Company, 1958)

Haukelid, Knut, *Skis against the Atom* (North American Heritage Press, 1989)

Heisenberg, Werner, *Physics and Beyond: Encounters and Conversations* (Harper & Row, 1971)

Henniker, Mark, *Image of War* (Leo Cooper, 1987)

Henniker, Mark, *Memoirs of a Junior Officer* (Blackwood & Sons, 1951)

Hentschel, Klaus, ed., *Physics and National Socialism: An Anthology of Primary Sources* (Birkhäuser Verlag, 1996)

Herrington, Ian, "The Special Operations Executive in Norway 1940–45," Dissertation, De Montfort University, 2004

Hewins, Ralph, *Quisling: Prophet without Honor* (W. H. Allen, 1965)

Hinsley, F. H., *British Intelligence in the Second World War*, Volume 2 (Cambridge University Press, 1981)

Hitler's Sunken Secret, PBS Documentary Transcript, November 8, 2005

Humble, Richard, *Hitler's Generals* (Arthur Baker Limited, 1973)

Ingstad, Helge, *Land of Feast and Famine* (McGill-Queen's Press, 1992)

International Military Tribunal, *Trial of Major War Criminals*, Volume XXVII (IMT, 1947)

Irving, David, *The German Atomic Bomb: The History of Nuclear Research in Nazi Germany* (Perseus Books, 1983)

Jablonski, Edward, *Double Strike: The Epic Raids on Regensburg-Schweinfurt* (Doubleday, 1974)

Jeffery, Keith, *The Secret History of MI6* (Penguin Press, 2010)

Johnson, Amanda, *Norway: Her Invasion and Occupation* (Bowen Press, 1948)

Jones, R. V., "Thicker than Heavy Water," *Chemistry and Industry*, August 26, 1967

Jones, Reginald, *Wizard War: British Scientific Intelligence, 1939–45* (Coward, McCann & Geoghegan, 1978)

Jungk, Robert, *Brighter than a Thousand Suns* (Harcourt Brace, 1958)

Knudsen, Harald, *I Was Quisling's Secretary* (Britons Publishing, 1967)

Kramish, Arnold, *The Griffin* (Macmillan, 1986)

Kurzman, Dan, *Blood and Water: Sabotaging Hitler's Bomb* (Henry Holt, 1996)

Langworth, Richard, ed., *Churchill by Himself: The Definitive Collection of Quotations* (Public Affairs, 2008)

Lee, Sabina, ed., *Sir Rudolf Peierls: Selected Correspondence,* Volume 1 (World Scientific, 2009)

Lynch, Tim, *Silent Skies: Gliders at War 1939–1945* (Pen & Sword, 2008)

Macrakis, Kristie, *Surviving the Swastika: Scientific Research in Nazi Germany* (Oxford University Press, 1993)

Mann, Matthew, "British Policy and Strategy towards Norway, 1941–44," Dissertation, University of London, 1998

Marks, Leo, *Between Silk and Cyanide: A Codemaker's War* (Free Press, 1998)

Meacham, Jon, *Franklin and Winston: A Portrait of Friendship* (Random House, 2004)

Mears, Ray, *The Real Heroes of Telemark* (Coronet Books, 2003)

Moore, Ruth, *Niels Bohr: The Man, His Science, and the World They Changed* (Knopf, 1966)

Moran, Lord, *Winston Churchill: The Struggle for Survival, 1940–66* (Constable, 1966)

Nichols, Kenneth, *The Road to Trinity* (William Morrow, 1987)

O'Connor, Bernard, *Churchill's School for Saboteurs: Station 17* (Amberley Publishing Limited, 2013)

Palmstrøm, Finn, and Rolf Torgersen, *Preliminary Report on Germany's Crimes against Norway* (Royal Norwegian Government, 1945)

Parton, James, *Air Force Spoken Here: General Ira Eaker* (Adler & Adler, 1986)

Peierls, Rudolf, *Bird of Passage: Recollections of a Physicist* (Princeton University Press, 2014)

Perquin, Jean-Louise, *The Clandestine Radio Operators* (Histoire and Collections, 2011)

Persico, Joseph, *Roosevelt's Secret War: FDR and WWII Espionage* (Random House, 2002)

Petrow, Richard, *The Bitter Years: The Invasion and Occupation of Denmark and Norway, April 1940–May 1945* (William Morrow, 1974)

Poulsson, Jens-Anton, *The Heavy Water Raid: The Race for the Atom Bomb 1942–44* (Orion, 2009)

Powers, Thomas, *Heisenberg's War: The Secret History of the German Bomb* (Da Capo Press, 1993)

Rhodes, Richard, *The Making of the Atomic Bomb* (Simon & Schuster, 1996)

Rigden, Denis, *How to Be a Spy: World War II SOE Training Manual* (Dundurn Group, 2001)

Riste, Olav, and Berit Nøkleby, *Norway 1940–45: The Resistance Movement* (Johan Grundt Tanum Forlag, 1970)

Roane, Owen, *A Year in the Life of Cowboy Roane with the Bloody 100th* (Xulon Press, 1995)

Rose, Paul Lawrence, *Heisenberg and the Nazi Atomic Bomb Project* (University of California Press, 2002)

Sagasfos, Ole Johan, *Progress of a Different Nature* (Pax Forlag, 2006)

Sandys, Celia, *Chasing Churchill* (HarperCollins, 2004)

Seaman, Mark, ed., *Special Operations Executive: A New Instrument of War* (Routledge, 2006)

Shirer, William, *Berlin Diary: The Journal of a Foreign Correspondent* (Taylor & Francis, 2002)

Shirer, William, *The Rise and Fall of the Third Reich* (Simon & Schuster, 1990)

Smyth, H. D., *Atomic Energy for Military Purposes* (Maple Press, 1945)

Speer, Albert, *Inside the Third Reich* (Macmillan, 1981)

Stafford, David, *Secret Agent: The True Story of the Covert War against Hitler* (Overlook Press, 2001)

Suess, Hans, "Virus House: Comments and Reminiscences," *Bulletin of Atomic Scientists*, June 1968, pp. 36–39

Walker, Mark, and Rainier Karlsch, "New Light on Hitler's Bomb," *Physics World*, June 1, 2005

Walker, Mark, *German National Socialism and the Quest for Nuclear Power* (Cambridge University Press, 1989)

Walker, Mark, *Nazi Science: Myth, Truth, and the German Atomic Bomb* (Plenum Press, 1995)

Warbey, William, *Look to Norway* (Secker & Warburg, 1945)

Wiggan, Richard, *Operation Freshman: The Rjukan Heavy Water Raid, 1942* (William Kimber, 1986)

Wigner, Eugene Paul, *The Collected Works*, 8 vols., edited by Arthur Wightman and Jagdish Mehra (Springer Science and Media, 2001)

Williams, Robert, *Klaus Fuchs, Atom Spy* (Harvard University Press, 1987)

Wilson, John Skinnar, *Memoirs of a Varied Life* (Imperial War Museum, John Skinnar Wilson Collection, unpublished)

Worm-Muller, Jacob, *Norway Revolts against the Nazis* (Lindsay Drummond, 1941)

Wright, Myrtle, *Norwegian Diary: 1940–45* (Friends Peace and International Relations Committee, 1974)

NOTES

Abbreviations:

Barch-MA: Bundesarchiv-Militärarchiv, Freiburg, Germany

DIA: Papers of David Irving, German Atomic Bomb, British Online Archives

DORA: Leif Tronstad Archive, Norges Teknisk-Naturvitenskapelige Universitet, Dorabiblioteket

ESD: Diary of Einar Skinnarland, courtesy of Skinnarland Family

ESP: Papers of Einar Skinnarland, courtesy of Skinnarland Family

Haugland Report: Haugland, Knut, "Wireless Service in the Grouse Group," NHM: SOE, Box 23

IWM: Imperial War Museum, London, England

KA: Papers of Dan Kurzmann, Howard Gotlieb Archival Research Center, Boston University

LTD: Diary of Leif Tronstad, courtesy of Leif Tronstad Junior

LTP: Papers of Leif Tronstad, courtesy of Leif Tronstad Junior

NA: US National Archives, College Park, Maryland

NB: Niels Bohr Library and Archives, College Park, Maryland

NHM: Norges Hjemmefrontmuseum, Oslo, Norway

Poulsson Report: Poulsson, Jens, "General Report on Work of Advance Party by Swallow," NHM: Box 25

Rønneberg Interview, Moland: Interview with Joachim Rønneberg by Arfinn Moland, NHM

Rønneberg Report: Rønneberg, Joachim, "Operation Gunnerside Report," NHM: FOIV, Box D17

TNA: UK National Archives, Kew, England

VM: Norsk Industriarbeidermuseum, Rjukan, Norway

Prologue

In a staggered line: Draft BBC Talk by Lieutenant Rønneberg. TNA: HS 7/181; Haukelid, pp. 105–108; Rostøl and Amdal, p. 86; Rønneberg Report; Lunde, pp. 99–101; Gallagher, pp. 96–97.

Suddenly, the forest cleared: Vemork Power Station and Electrolysis Plant Report, October 30, 1942. TNA: DEFE 2/219; Adamson, p. 138; Draft BBC Talk by Lieutenant Rønneberg. TNA: HS 7/181.

The young men: Interview with Haukelid. DIA, DJ31; Berg, p. 128; Interview with Poulsson, IWM.

"to blow up a good": Interview with Poulsson. IWM; Myklebust, p. 108.

Chapter 1

In the dark early: Haarr, pp. 290–97; Fen, p. 34.

"go towards Trondheim": Haarr, p. 294.

In a large hall: Leif Tronstad Junior, Author Interview; Njølstad, pp. 15–17.

One among them: Interview with Haukelid. DIA, DJ31.

He told those: N. A. Sørensen, "Minnetale over Professor Leif Tronstad." LTP; Njølstad, pp. 15–17.

"Whatever you do": Leif Tronstad Junior, Author Interview.

"sleeping government": Njølstad, p. 15.

"we are fighting": Langworth, p. 270.

"What kind of": Leif Tronstad Junior, Author Interview.

Twenty-eight-year-old: Haukelid, pp. 16–20.

At first glance: TNA: HS 9/676/4.

"siren of the fjords": *Life magazine*, April 18, 1938.

"What are you doing": Haukelid Family, Author Interview.

Born in Brooklyn: Ibid.

One night, when: Letter to Dan Kurzman. KA.

At last, he returned: Haukelid Family, Author Interview.

"Remain true": Johnson, p. 47.

For months: Haukelid, pp. 21–25.

Reichskommissar Terboven: Fen, p. 63; Johnson, pp. 129–34, 285–87; Petrow, pp. 99–124; Ivar Kragland Interview. IWM.

In September 1941: Nøkleby, *Gestapo*, pp. 49–53, 165–69; Kjelstadli, pp. 118–24.

"He's in the": Haukelid Family, Author Interview; Haukelid, p. 31.

Three months before: N. A. Sørensen, "Minnetale over Professor Leif Tronstad." LTP; Brun, Jomar, "Leif Tronstad," *Det Kongelige Norske Videnskabers Selskab.* L-0001. DORA.

"If you like": Leif Tronstad Junior, Author Interview; Njølstad, p. 55.

After his government: Njølstad, pp. 21–30; Bjorn Rørholt Interview. NHM: Box 16; Haakon Sørbye Interview. NHM: Box 16; Einar Johansen Interview. NHM: Box 16; Reimers, Jan, "Leif Tronstad slik jeg kjente ham." NHM: Box 10B.

Chapter 2

Water ran plentifully: Norsk Hydro, Promotional Pamphlet. TNA: DEFE 2/221.

The river's flow changed: Vemork Power Station and Electrolysis Plant. NHM: FOIV, Box 78; Norsk Hydro Report, 9/14/42. TNA: HS 2/184.

The American chemist: Rhodes, p. 270; Brun, p. 9; Report by D. R. Augood, December 1954. VM: J. Brun, Box 17.

"50 tons of": Per Dahl, p. 41.

A man named Jomar Brun: P.M. fra konferanse i Trondheim, Julen 1933. VM: Box 4F-D17-99; Brun, pp. 10–13.

"Technology first, then": Leif Tronstad Junior, Author Interview.

What Tronstad and Brun: Brun, pp. 14–20; "Interrogation of G. Syverstad." TNA: HS 2/188; Per Dahl, pp. 41–48.

When the plant started: Njølstad, pp. 60–61, 77–79; Brun, p. 9.

Vemork shipped its first: Olsen, p. 399; Advertisement for "Schweres Wasser." VM: J. Brun, Box 2.

Production was shut down: Brun, p. 15.

"atoms and void": Rhodes, p. 29.

"Could a proper detonator": Ibid, p. 44.

Then, in 1932: Interview with Dr. Alan Morton. IWM; Per Dahl, p. 62; Goldschmidt, Betrand, "The supplies of Norwegian heavy water to France and the early development of atomic energy," Grimnes et al.

In December 1938, two: Rhodes, pp. 251–54.

When this happened: Ibid, pp. 256–60.

One physicist calculated: Karlsch, p. 32.

"A little bomb like": Rhodes, p. 275.

At thirty-four years: "Notes on Captured German Reports on Nuclear Physics." TNA: AB 1/356; Bagge et al., p. 157; Karlsch, p. 32.

"Malarkey": Bagge et al., p. 21.

Diebner opened the first: Powers, p. 15; Bagge et al., p. 23.

"possibility for the": Letter from Harteck to Reich Ministry of War, April 24, 1939. Papers of Paul Harteck, Rensselaer Institute.

Otto Hahn, on the other: Interview with Heisenberg. DIA, DJ31.

"If there is": Bagge et al., p. 23; Powers, p. 16.

Ten days later: Powers, p. 14.

Heisenberg made quick: G-39, Heisenberg Report, "Die Möglichkeiten der technischen Energiegewinnung aus der Uranspaltung." NB: German Reports on Atomic Energy; Cassidy, p. 422; Interview with Heisenberg. DIA, DJ31; Per Dahl, pp. 52–54.

"greater than the": G-39, Heisenberg Report, "Die Möglichkeiten der technischen Energiegewinnung aus der Uranspaltung." NB: German Reports on Atomic Energy.

In his second paper: Ibid; Cassidy, p. 422.

In recognition of: NB: Oral History, Interview with Weizsäcker; Rosbaud Report. NB: Goudsmit Papers, IV, B27, F42.

By the end of 1939: Schaaf, p. 108; Letter from Heisenberg to Harteck, 1/18/39. DIA, DJ29; Letter to Rjukan Saltpeterfabriker, January 11, 1940. VM: Box

4F-D17-98; Letter from Harteck to Heisenberg, 1/15/1940. DIA, DJ29; Walker, *German National Socialism*, pp. 18–27.

By January 1940: Olsen, pp. 399–400.

It was no matter: Letter to Aktieselskabet Rjukanfos, 6/11/40. VM: Box 4F-D17-99; Brun Report, "Some Impressions from my work with Z," 11/30/42. TNA: HS 8/955/DISR.

Chapter 3

Throughout 1940 and: Njølstad, pp. 21–30; Bjorn Rørholt Interview. NHM: Box 16; Haakon Sørbye Interview. NHM: Box 16; Einar Johansen Interview. NHM: Box 16; Reimers, Jan, "Leif Tronstad slik jeg kjente ham." NHM: Box 10B.

On the morning of: Njølstad, pp. 36–40; Reimers, Jan, "Leif Tronstad slik jeg kjente ham." NHM: Box 10B.

That evening, Tronstad: N. A. Sørensen, "Minnetale over Professor Leif Tronstad." LTP; Njølstad, pp. 15–17.

"Family, house and": September 22, 1941. LTD.

The next morning: September 23, 1941. LTD; Njølstad, p. 41.

"Take care of your": Leif Tronstad Junior, Author Interview.

In Oslo, he: September 23–24, 1941. LTD.

Weeks later in: October 19–21, 1941. LTD.

SIS arranged a room: Letter from Bjorn Rorholt to Jomar Brun, 5/3/85. VM: J. Brun, Box 17.

Tronstad knew London: October 21, 1941. LTD.

Within days of his: October 26, 1941. LTD.

"employ a weapon": Kramish, p. 59

This prompted: Clark, *Tizard*, pp. 210–14.

"destroy life in a": Ibid, pp. 214–17.

"Although personally I am": Text of Churchill's Statement. NA: Harrison-Bundy Papers.

"no time, labor, material": General Ismay to Lord President of the Council, September 4, 1941. TNA: CAB 126/330.

Two drunken German: Letter to Dr. Pye, September 11, 1941. TNA: AB 1/651.

One émigré German: NB: Oral History, Interview with Fritz Reich.

"A tale has": Telex from R. Sutton Pratt, November 10, 1941. TNA: AB 1/651

"and we're working": Powers, p. 124.

As early as: Gowing, p. 43.

On December 2: History of the Training Section SOE, pp. 14–17, 163–73. TNA: HS 8/435; Jensen, pp. 37–45; Lunde, pp. 55–57.

"Never give your": Drummond, p. 56.

"This is your": Haukelid, p. 43.

"Aim low. A bullet": Jensen, p. 41.

"Never smoke while": Ibid, p. 42.

They blew up: TNA: History of the Training Section SOE, pp. 16, 166–68. HS 8/435.

Through day after: Ibid. p. 14.

"One can go": Myklebust, p. 54.

At Meoble, an old: History of the Training Section SOE, pp. 25–27. TNA: HS 8/43; HS 2/188; Jensen, pp. 48–71; Haukelid, pp. 43–44; Foot, p. 80.

"This is war, not": Rigden, p. 362.

It was a merciless: Haukelid, p. 44–45.

The company showed: January 31–February 3, 1942. LTD; Njølstad, pp. 102–103; Kjelstadli, 176–81.

He told them: Sæter, p. 41; "Special Confidential Report." TNA: HS 9/1605/3.

Wilson had helped: Wilson, pp. 1–76.

Chapter 4

On Thursday, March 12, 1942: March 1–17, 1942. ESD; Hauge, pp. 82–83.

Skinnarland — red-haired: Marielle Skinnarland, Author Interview.

Since the invasion: Skinnarland Notes. ESP. In many of the histories on this subject, Skinnarland already had in hand intelligence on the heavy-water activities of the Germans at Vemork. This was clearly not the case, as stated by Einar Skinnarland himself. He left for England to start a wireless transmission site to provide intelligence on German activity in the area, no doubt on Norsk Hydro.

In Flekkefjord: "Cheese's Report," July 30, 1941. TNA: HS 2/150; Wilson, John, "On Resistance in Norway." NHM: Box 50a.

Two days after: "Preliminary Report on Cheese's Return Journey," March 18, 1942. TNA: HS 2/151; Hauge, pp. 90-93.

"I'm afraid I've arrived": Hauge, p. 94.

Through the night: Skinnarland Notes. ESP; Letter, May 29, 1942. NHM: SOE, Box 25; "Preliminary Report on Cheese's Return Journey," March 18, 1942. TNA: HS 2/151.

"Galtesund making for": Hauge, p. 108. For a full accounting of the Galtesund capture, an amazing story in its own right, please read Hauge's Salt-Water Thief, a biography of Starheim.

This was a: "Operation Grouse," March 28, 1942. NHM: SOE, Box 22.

Over the course: "Sergeant Einar Skinnarland," March 6, 1944. TNA: HS 9/1370/8.

On the clear: "Report on Operation Undertaken by 138 Squadron," March 29, 1942. TNA: HS 9/1370/8; Drummond, pp. 21–26.

"Feet together and": Drummond, p. 21.

At 11:44: "Report on Operation Undertaken by 138 Squadron," March 29, 1942. TNA: HS 9/1370/8.

On April 23: "Minutes of 4th Meeting of Technical Committee," April 23, 1942. TNA: CAB 126/46.

The plant had fallen: Brun Report, "Some Impressions from my work with Z," 11/30/42. TNA: HS 8/955/DISR; Brun, pp. 24–28.

"our juice": Letter from Tronstad to Brun, 5/15/1942. LTP.

On June 4: Speer, pp. 269–71; Bagge et al., pp. 29–31; Cassidy, pp. 455–57; Macrakis, pp. 173–75; Powers, pp. 142–50; Roane, pp. 48–49, 78.

Thanks to the: Irving, p. 72; Walker, *German National Socialism*, pp. 26–27.

From recent investigations: Heisenberg, Werner, "Research in Germany on the Technical Application of Atomic Energy," *Nature*, August 16, 1947; Von Weizsäcker, C. F., "A Possibility to Produce Energy from U-238," 1940. NB: Goudsmit Papers, III, B10, F95; Bothe, Walther, "Die Diffusionslänge für thermische Neutronen in Kohle," 1940–41. Deutsches Museum Archiv.

"an open road": Interview with Werner Heisenberg. DIA, DJ31.

But two months: Bagge et al., pp. 28–29; Nagel, p. 77.

"In the present": Bagge et al., pp. 29–32.

"power ships, possibly": Karlsch, pp. 87–89.

Basic research on: Walker, *German National Socialism*, p. 32.

Winston Churchill chewed: Sandys, pp. 149–51; Meacham, pp. 180–84; Moran, pp. 50–57.

"Ok": Letter to President Roosevelt from Vannevar Bush, 6/17/1942. NA: Bush-Conant Papers.

On June 20, Roosevelt: Meacham, pp. 183–84.

"What if the enemy": Churchill, *Hinge of Fate*, p. 380.

A few days: Note on Mr. Norman Brooke, Deputy Secretary of War Cabinet Office, July 3, 1942. TNA: HS 2/184; Akers Discussion with Norman Brooke, 6/30/1942. NHM: Box 16.

Chapter 5

Jens-Anton Poulsson: Poulsson, p. 76; TNA: HS 9/1205/1; Letter from Malcolm Munthe to Poulsson, June 13, 1942. TNA: HS 2/172.

"Your story will be": SOE Group B Training Syllabus. TNA: HS 7/52–54.

Norsk Hydro's top brass: Mia Poulsson, Author Interview; Unni Poulsson, Author Interview; Interview with Poulsson. IWM.

Once the proposal: TNA: HS 9/676/2; TNA: HS 9/845/2.

"fit for duty": TNA: HS 9/676/4.

The inventory list: Stores Ready to Be Packed for Swallow I. NHM: SOE, Box 22; Gallagher, p. 19.

"small independent groups": Operation Instructions for Grouse, August 31, 1942. NHM: Box 25.

That same day: August 31, 1942. LTD.

The four men: Lurgan Report, September 3, 1942. TNA: HS 2/184.

Tronstad was desperate: September 3, 1942. LTD.

After celebrating his: March 27–August 30, 1942. LTD.

Earlier in the: Nøkleby, *Josef Terboven*, pp. 197–99; Warbey, pp. 140–44.

"War makes the": August 7, 1942. LTD.

"Somewhere in England": Letters from Poulsson to Haukelid, 9/10/42. TNA: HS 2/172.

Once they connected: Letter from Munthe to Gjestland, 8/8/42. TNA: HS 2/172.

"Of course we": Letter from Poulsson/Helberg to Haukelid, 9/29/42. TNA: HS 2/172.

General Nikolaus von Falkenhorst: Freshman Report, 11/14/1942. NHM: FOIV, Box D17 (Gunnerside).

"to atone for several": Nøkleby, *Josef Terboven*, p. 213.

Terboven intensified: Kjelstadli, p. 154–56; Nøkleby, *Josef Terboven*, pp. 215–16.

"All enemy troops": German Order to Kill Captured Allied Commandos and Parachutists. Report FF-2127. TNA: WO 311/7.

When Colonel Wilson: Interview with Haugland. IWM.

"This is Piccadilly": Freshman — Appendix A, 10/17/42. NHM: Box 25.

"This mission is": Nota tang Freshman, 6/30/03. NHM: Box 25; Interview with Poulsson. IWM; Myklebust, pp. 88–89.

Chapter 6

"Number one, go!": Air Transport Operation Report, 10/18/1942. TNA: HS 2/185; Gallagher, pp. 20–21.

Below him spread: Topography of Hardangervidda Report, 10/13/1942. TNA: HS 2/184; Mcars, pp. 47–49; Adamson, pp. 141–42.

As his parachute: Poulsson Report; Gallagher, p. 22; Berg, p. 104.

For the next four: Grouse Equipment. NHM: SOE, Box 22; Myklebust, p. 86; Lauritzen, p. 32.

"There's a new": Halvorsen, 1947.

The men spent: Poulsson Report; Haugland Report; Interview with Haugland. IWM; Gallagher, pp. 24–25.

Lieutenant Colonel Mark: Minutes of Meeting in C.O.H.Q, 10/26/1942. TNA: HS 2/129; Note written by Mark Henniker, given to Peter Yeates, 1983. KA.; Report by Group Captain Tom Cooper, 1942. TNA: AIR 20/11930; Drew, pp. 87–89; Interview Notes. KA.

Combined Operations decided: Operation Freshman, Outline Plan, 10/14/1943. NHM: Box 10C; Report on 38 Wing Operation Order No. 5 – "Operation Freshman," December 8, 1942. TNA: DEFE 2/219.

On November 2: Freshman Training, 10/27/1942. TNA: DEFE 2/219; Drew, p. 92.

Leif Tronstad met: Plant Installation and Proposed Demolition, 11/16/1942. TNA: HS 2/129; Vemork Power Station and Electrolysis Plant Report, 10/30/1942. TNA: DEFE 2/219; Operation Lurgan, Preliminary Technical Report. TNA: HS 2/185.

Like all the members: Poulsson Report; Haugland Report; Interview with Poulsson. IWM; Interview with Haugland, IWM; Poulsson, pp. 91–99; Gallagher, pp. 24–27; Sæter, pp. 57–62.

Haugland had always: Haugland Family, Author Interview; Sæter, pp. 9–40; Interview with Haugland. IWM.

Now, thirteen days: Haugland Report; Interview with Haugland. IWM.

The mood in: Haukelid, pp. 97–99.

With new snowfall: Njølstad, p. 99; Berg, p. 114.

The next day: Haugland Report; Sæter, pp. 45, 62; Interview with Haugland. IWM.

In the woods by: Report from Skinnarland, 11/1/1942. NHM: SOE, Box 23; Ueland, pp. 60–61.

"Happy landing in spite": Cipher Message from Grouse Primus, 11/9/1942. TNA: HS 2/172.

Chapter 7

On November 15: Minutes of Meeting held at 154 Chiltern Court, 11/15/1942. TNA: HS 2/129; November 15–20, 1942, LTD.; Freshman — Translations of Telegrams, 11/15/1942. TNA: HS 2/184.

"super bombs": Clark, *Tizard*, p. 215.

"Good policy for": Freshman Report, 11/17/1942. TNA: DEFE 2/219.

In a dark: Interview with Haugland. IWM; Myklebust, pp. 100–101.

In the three: Poulsson Report; Helberg, Claus, "Report about Einar Skinnarland," 7/30/43. NHM: SOE, Box 23.

Some of his scheduled: Telegrams from Grouse, 11/13–19/1942. TNA: DEFE 2/219.

That afternoon, twenty-eight: Drew, pp. 93–103; Interview with Michael Douglas Green. IWM; Report by Group Captain Tom Cooper, 1942. TNA: AIR 20/11930.

"very expensive liquid": Drew, p. 93.

They wore steel: Freshman Report — Appendix A — Standard Gear. TNA: DEFE 2/219.

Most of them were: Drew, p. 103.

The floor beneath: Ibid, p. 105.

After a slight: Freshman Telegram List, 11/18–20/1942. TNA: DEFE 2/219; Report on 38 Wing Operation Order No. 5, 12/8/1942. TNA: DEFE 2/219.

"Two small birds": November 19, 1942. LTD.

When Poulsson and: Freshman — Appendix A, 10/17/42. NHM: Box 25; Interview with Haugland, IWM; Interview with Poulsson, IWM; Poulsson Report.

"I hear the": Interview with Knut Haugland. IWM; Interview with Poulsson. TNA: HS 2/190; Sæter, pp. 66–67; Poulsson Report.

Over the next: Poulsson Report.

Flying with the: Report on 38 Wing Operation Order No. 5, 12/8/1942. TNA: DEFE 2/219; Letter from Colonel Wilson to Colonel Head, January 21, 1943. TNA: HS 2/129; Drew, pp. 127–131.

Halifax B had: Report on 38 Wing Operation Order No. 5, 12/8/1942. TNA: DEFE 2/219; Eyewitness Report — The planes that were wrecked in the Egersund District, 4/6/1943. NHM: SOE, Box 23; Report from Johannes Mukejord. KA; Berglyd, pp. 59–61.

Four miles away: Report from Anne Lima, 3/13/1944. NHM: SOE, Box 23; Report to Chief of Police Rogaland from Lensmann in Helland, 11/21/1942. TNA: WO 331/18; Statement of Lensmann Trond Hovland, 1945. TNA: WO 331/18; Statement by Tellef Tellefsen, 6/1945. TNA: WO 331/18; Case No. UK-G/B. 476, United Nations War Crime Commission against Von Behrens and Probst. TNA: WO 331/387.

The ranking officer: Statement of Lensmann Trond Hovland, 1945. TNA: WO 331/18.

Walther Schrottberger: Letter from Major Rawlings, 7/2/1945. TNA: WO 331/18.

given that explosives: Berglyd, pp. 447–48.

"no quarter should": German Order to Kill Captured Allied Commandos and Parachutists. Report FF-2127. TNA: WO 311/7.

The Gestapo sent SS: Shooting by the Germans of Allied Personnel Captured in Norway, January 14, 1944. TNA: HS 2/184; Case No. UK-G/B. 476, United Nations War Crime Commission against Von Behrens and Probst. TNA: WO 331/387; Statement by Werner Siemsen, 7/6/1947. TNA: WO 331/387; Report on the Interrogation of Colonel Oberst, 9/12/1945. TNA: WO 331/387; Statement by Cid Gunner, 6/29/1945. TNA: WO 331/18; Statement by Michael Spahn, 6/29/1945. TNA: WO 331/18; Statement by Rolf Greve, 6/14/1945. TNA: WO 331/18.

Then in the late: Berglyd, pp. 50–52; Statement of Kurt Hagedorn, 8/31/1945. TNA: WO 331/387; Statement by Cid Gunner, 6/29/1945. TNA: WO 331/18; Letter from Major Rawlings, 7/2/1945. TNA: WO 331/18; Statement by Tellef Tellefsen, 6/1945. TNA: WO 331/18.

"Unfortunately, the military": Tagesmeldung, 11/20/1942. RW 39/39. Barch-MA; BDS in Oslo Berichtet, 11/21/1942. DIA, DJ31; Irving, pp. 139–42.

He ordered that: Interrogation of Wilhelm Esser, 7/10/1945. TNA: WO 331/386.

On that bleakest: November 20, 1942. LTD.

In silence, Tronstad: Drummond, pp. 51–52.

Wilson made it: Wilson, John, "On Resistance in Norway." NHM: Box 50A.

Chapter 8

"Vitally necessary": Report from Wilson (SN), 11/21/1942. TNA: HS 2/184.

Reports from London: Poulsson Report; Cipher Message from Grouse, 11/23/1942. NHM: SOE, Box 22.

On the night of: Poulsson Report.

The morning of: Poulsson, pp. 109–115; Sæter, p. 74.

"You're to be": Rønneberg, Joachim, "Operation Gunnerside," Grimnes et al; Rønneberg Interview, Moland; Interview with Rønneberg. IWM; Gallagher, p. 40.

Three days later: December 1, 1942. LTD; Minutes of Meeting Held at Norgeby House, 11/26/1942. TNA: HS 2/185; Interview with Rønneberg. KA.

Birger Strømsheim was: TNA: HS 9/1424/2; Rønneberg Interview, Moland.

Next was Fredrik: TNA: HS 9/824/2; Lunde, pp. 1–68.

Third was Kasper: TNA: HS 9/774/4; Rostøl and Amdal, pp. 1–62.

Rønneberg's fourth choice: TNA: HS 9/1420/7; Lunde, p. 88.

The fifth member: Ragnar Ulstein, Author Interview; Rønneberg Interview, Moland; Myklebust, pp. 108–11.

"vocational school for": Rønneberg Interview, Moland.

He was sure he: Ragnar Ulstein, Author Interview.

"He had a quality": Myklebust, pp. 84–85.

"Now, I do": Rostøl and Amdal, p. 75.

He then outlined: Myklebust, pp. 107–109.

Before dawn on: "Gestapo Lager Razzia og Unntagstilstand i Rjukan." NHM: FOIV, Box D17; Unpublished Memoir, Papers of Rolf Sørlie.

Rolf Sørlie: Unpublished Memoir, Papers of Rolf Sørlie.

That same day, Hans: Skinnarland, Ingeliev, *Hva Som Hendte Vår Familie i Krigsårene, 1940–45.* ESP.

Late in 1942: G-125, Bericht über einer Würfelversuch mit Uranoxyd und Paraffin. Deutsches Museum Archiv; NB: Oral History, Interview with Hartwig; Walker, *German National Socialism*, pp. 95–97.

"dreadful drudgery": Nagel, p. 73.

Earlier that summer: Irving, pp. 117–18; Walker, *German National Socialism*, p. 84.

Then, on June 23: G-135, "Bericht über zwei Unfalle beim Umgang mit Uranmetall." Deutsches Museum Archiv; Per Dahl, pp. 188–90.

The disaster did: G-125, "Bericht über einer Würfelversuch mit Uranoxyd und Paraffin." Deutsches Museum Archiv; NB: Oral History, Interview with Hartwig; Bagge et al., p. 25; Karlsch, pp. 73, 98–100; Walker, *German National Socialism,* p 97.

Chapter 9

On December 11: Rønneberg Interview, Moland.

"What the hell's": Ibid.

In the ten: Rønneberg Interview, Moland; Myklebust, pp. 110–17; Gunnerside — Operating Instructions, 12/15/1942. NHM: FOIV, Box D17; Rønneberg Report.

Rheam showed them: Orientering vedr. Gunnerside, December 11, 1942.

NHM: FOIV, Box D17; Gunnerside — Operating Instructions, 12/15/1942.

NHM: FOIV, Box D17; Myklebust, pp. 119–21; Rostøl and Amdal, pp. 74–78; Lunde, pp. 88–90; 11.

"For the sake of": Handwritten briefing notes, 12/14/42. NHM: FOIV, Box D17; Rostøl and Amdal, p. 76.

"You won't get rid of": Myklebust, p. 127.

At the Grass Valley: Poulsson Report; Sæter, pp. 74–75.

"It's full of vitamins.": Gallagher, p. 80; Sæter, p. 75.

"active part": Cipher Message to Swallow, 12/13/42. NHM: SOE, Box 22.

Misfortune hounded them: Poulsson Report; Sæter, pp. 74–75; Interview with Helberg. IWM; Mears, p. 101.

Skinnarland and a: December 10–18, 1942. ES Diary.

On December 17: Cipher Message to Swallow, 12/17/42. NHM: SOE, Box 22.

The four bearded: Poulsson, pp. 19–21; Poulsson Report.

"Just wait until": Gallagher, p. 50.

Each morning, soon: Interview with Poulsson. IWM; Gallagher, pp. 50–51.

Rønneberg and his team: Myklebust, pp. 126–28.

"Crisp and clear": Gallagher, pp. 51–52.

Over the many: Interview with Poulsson. IWM.

After zigzagging to: Poulsson, pp. 20–22; Gallagher, pp. 49–65; Svein Vetle Trae, Author Interview.

The next night: Sæter, p. 75; Poulsson, pp. 22–23.

Many miles away: Marielle Skinnarland, Author Interview; Kjell Nielsen Remembrance. NHM: Box 10B.

Only a few days: December 27, 1942. ES Diary; Marielle Skinnarland, Author Interview.

Inside, he found: Poulsson, p. 116.

Chapter 10

"Weather still bad": Cipher Message to Swallow, January 16, 1943. NHM: FOIV, Box D17.

There were petty: Report from Claus Helberg, 7/10/1943. NHM: SOE, Box 23; Interview with Poulsson. IWM; Interview with Haugland. IWM; Lauritzen, p. 63. Berg, pp. 120–22.

When they ran: Interview with Helberg. IWM.

At long last: Haukelid, pp. 15–16.

The plane zigzagged: Handwritten letter from Rønneberg to Tronstad, 1/26/43. NHM: FOIV, Box D17; Air Transport Operation Report, 1/23/1943. TNA: HS 2/131; Summary of Meeting Gunnerside Abortive Sortie, 1/26/43. TNA: HS 2/185; Letter from Flight Lieutenant Ventry to Captain Adamson, 1/25/43. TNA: HS 2/185; Lunde, pp. 92–93; Haukelid, p. 38; Rønneberg Interview, Moland.

"Do hope you": Cipher Message to Swallow, 1/28/1943. NHM: FOIV, Box D17.

As the next: Interview with Haugland. IWM.

"What was the": Poulsson, p. 127.

After the failed: Report on "Crispie." TNA: HS 2/185; Letter from Rønneberg to Tronstad, 12/29/42. NHM: FOIV, Box D17; Rønneberg Interview, Moland.

Since the Freshman: Report from Rjukan, December 1942. TNA: HS 2/186; Poulsson Report.

"Ten minutes": Haukelid, p. 81; Rostøl and Amdal, p. 45.

The team got: Rønneberg Interview, Moland; Rønneberg Report.

"I don't think": Rønneberg Interview, Moland.

A tempest enveloped: Poulsson Report; Interview with Helberg. IWM.

Rønneberg took a: Rønneberg Interview, Moland.

With no wireless set: Gallagher, pp. 70–71.

"Same weather. Storm": Rønneberg Report.

Chapter 11

As quickly as: Rønneberg Report; Gallagher, p. 73.

At 1 P.M., the: Rønneberg Interview, Moland; Myklebust, pp. 137–39; Haukelid, pp. 84–85; Rostøl and Amdal, pp. 80–81.

Kristiansen immediately proved: Rønneberg Interview, Moland.

Seven miles from: Haukelid, pp. 86–87.

The two skiers: Haukelid, p. 88.

"Stay on the": Rønneberg Interview, Moland; Rønneberg Report.

Crowded into Fetter: Interview with Poulsson. IWM.

After a night's: Orientering vedr. Gunnerside, December 11, 1942. NHM: FOIV, Box D17; Rønneberg Interview, Moland; Unpublished Memoir, Papers of Rolf Sørlie; Haukelid, pp. 97-104; Poulsson, pp. 135-41; Lunde, pp. 96-98; Berg, pp. 125-26; Halvorsen, 1947; Sæter, pp. 84-86; Interview with Poulsson. IWM; Interview with Rønneberg. IWM; Rønneberg Report; Interview with Poulsson. IWM; Interview with Helberg. IWM; February 19, 1943. ES Diary; Letters from/to Poulsson and Rønneberg. NHM: Box 25. Letters from/to Poulsson and Helberg. NHM: Box 25; Notes from Poulsson. NHM: Box 25; Interview with Haukelid. DIA, DJ31.

After a trip: Unpublished Memoir, Papers of Rolf Sørlie; Rønneberg Report; Interview with Helberg. IWM.

"If trees are": Interview with Haukelid. DIA, DJ31; Interview with Poulsson. IWM.; Poulsson Notes on *Blood and Water* manuscript. NHM: Box 25; Orientering vedr. Gunnerside, December 11, 1942. NHM: FOIV, Box D17.

An hour after: Halvorsen, 1947; Interview with Helberg. IWM.

Chapter 12

At 8 P.M.: Rønneberg Report; Rønneberg Interview, Moland; Interview with Poulsson. IWM; Draft of Rønneberg BBC Speech. TNA: HS 7/181;

Interview with Haukelid. DIA, DJ31; Interview with Helberg. IWM; Interview with Poulsson. IWM; Haukelid, pp. 102-108; Poulsson, pp. 143-46; Gallagher, pp. 96-110; Rostøl and Amdal, pp. 86-88; Lunde, pp. 99-102; Berg, pp. 127-30; Myklebust, pp. 150-57. Unless there is a direct quote or distinct piece of information needing sourcing, the author will not note any further specific references in this chapter.

"All right, let's": Gallagher, p. 100.

Rønneberg felt like: Draft of Rønneberg BBC Speech. TNA: HS 7/181.

Each man took: Gallagher, pp. 103–105.

In their cabin: February 27, 1943. ES Diary; Sæter, p. 86.

Well-trained radio: Sæter, pp. 44–45.

Leading the advance: Haukelid, p. 108; Interview with Haukelid. DIA, DJ31.

"In a few": Draft of Rønneberg BBC Speech. TNA: HS 7/181.

The trail of: Interview with Haukelid. DIA, DJ31.

"Good luck": Haukelid, p. 108.

"Good spot": Gallagher, p. 109.

"Locked": Lunde, p. 102.

Rønneberg was struck: Rønneberg Report; Rønneberg Interview, Moland; Interview with Poulsson. IWM; Draft of Rønneberg BBC Speech. TNA: HS 7/181; Interview with Haukelid. DIA, DJ31; Interview with Helberg. IWM; Haukelid, pp. 102–108; Poulsson, pp. 143–46; Gallagher, pp. 96–110; Rostøl and Amdal, pp. 86–88; Lunde, pp. 99–102; Berg, pp. 127–30; Myklebust, pp. 150–57. As previously, these references provide the lion's share of source material for this section.

At Brickendonbury Hall: Brun, pp. 71–72.

"There it is": Rønneberg Interview, Moland; Gallagher, p. 110.

"No Admittance Except": Directions Report, 11/15/1942. NHM: FOIV, Box D17.

"Put your hands": Rostøl and Amdal, pp. 102–103; Gallagher, p. 112.

"Watch out. Otherwise": Rostøl and Amdal, p. 103.

Rønneberg told Strømsheim: Extract from Report by Director Bjarne Nilssen. VM: J. Brun, Box 6a.

"Run up the": Grimnes et al.

Chapter 13

"Is that what": Interview with Poulsson. IWM.

"No": Poulsson, p. 147; Interview with Haukelid. DIA, DJ31.

"Piccadilly": Haukelid, p. 113.

Throughout, Rønneberg ran: Myklebust, pp. 162–63.

Alf Larsen, who had: Larsen, Alf, Rapport over Hendelsen i Høykoncentrering-sanlegget på Vemork 28. Febr. 1943. VM: J. Brun, Box 17; Nilssen, Bjarne. Vedr. Sabotage i tungtvannsanlegget på Vemork, March 1, 1943. NHM: Box 25.

"normal like we": Ibid.

Now Larsen stepped: Bjarne Nilssen, P.M. Sabotasje Vemork. VM: J. Brun, Box 6a; Rapport vedrörende anlegg for fremstilling av Tungt vann vad Vemork Vannstoff-fabrikk, Rjukan, 9/14/1943. NHM: FOIV, Box D17.

The saboteurs ducked: Rønneberg Interview, Moland.

After locating their supply: Haukelid, pp. 114–15; Rønneberg Interview, Moland; Rønneberg Report; Halvorsen, 1970.

The men sat: Rønneberg Interview, Moland.

After everyone was: Interview with Helberg. IWM.

The other eight: Poulsson, pp. 149–50.

"High-concentration plant": Rønneberg Report.

"Give our best": Haukelid, p. 119.

"Well, Arne": Gallagher, p. 137.

Chapter 14

On March 5: Interview with Poulsson. IWM; Poulsson, pp. 156–57; Gallagher, pp. 138–40. All quotes and descriptions in this scene from these sources.

A wireless radio: March 2–5, 1943. ES Diary.

Approaching Skårbu: Haukelid, pp. 120–21.

"Don't worry, Knut": Ibid, p. 121.

Haugland tried to: March 6–11, 1943. ES Diary; Interview with Haugland. IWM.

"Operation carried out": Message from Swallow, March 10, 1943. NHM: FOIV, Box D17.

Tronstad could not: Hurum, p. 123.

"Heartiest congratulations": Message to Swallow, March 10, 1943. NHM: FOIV, Box D17.

On March 12: SOE and Heavy Water, 3/1943. TNA: HS 2/185; Minutes of ANCC Meeting, March 12, 1943. TNA: HS 2/138; Myklebust, pp. 201–202; SOE Progress Report, 3/15/1943. TNA: HS 8/223.

"It's justified": Tronstad, Note on Heavy Water, 3/18/43. LTP.

Winston Churchill: March 15, 1943. LTD.

Rønneberg knew the: Rønneberg Interview, Moland; Myklebust, pp. 166–69; Mears, pp. 180–81.

By March 13: Rønneberg Report; Rønneberg Interview, Moland; Myklebust, pp. 173–88.

"You must all": Rostøl and Amdal, pp. 97–99.

"Guys": Myklebust, pp. 182–83.

At 8:15 P.M.: Interview with Rønneberg. IWM; Rønneberg Interview, Moland; Rønneberg Report.

Chapter 15

On March 24: Report "Angår Aksjonen på Hardangervidda," 7/17/1946. NHM: Box 10B; Report on the Interrogation of Major Ernst Lutter,

7/5/1945. NHM: Box 16; Tätigkeitsbericht AOK/Ic, April 1943. RW 39/44.
Barch-MA; Ueland, pp. 191–93; Dahl, Helge, p. 291.

In the late afternoon: Interview with Helberg. IWM; Poulsson, p. 158.

When he reached: Interview with Helberg. IWM; Report by Claus Helberg,
6/28/1943. NHM: SOE, Box 23; Interrogation of Sergeant Helberg, 7/23/1943.
TNA: HS9/689/6. The narrative of Helberg's dramatic escape between
March 25 and March 30 derives primarily from these four sources. The
author has also consulted Gallagher, pp. 149–63; Interview with Claus
Helberg. KA; Ueland, pp. 194–201, 212–16. Any quotes or other select
material will be separated out below.

"Halt! Arms up!": Interview with Helberg. IWM.

After an early: Letter from Wehrmachtsbefehlshaber in Norwegen, 5/15/1943.
RW 4/639. Barch-MA.

"You sit there": Nøkleby, "Uforskammet."

On April 17: Marielle Skinnarland, Author Interview; March 20–April 20,
1943. ES Diary.

They were ready: Haugland, Report on Wireless Service in the Grouse Group
during the period October 18, 1942 to May 1st, 1943. TNA: HS9/676/2;
Sæter, pp. 97–98.

Chapter 16

In mid-April: Bericht über Konsul Ing. E. Schöpke's Reise und Besprechungen,
3/13/1943. G-341, German Reports on Atomic Energy. NB; Rapport
vedrörende anlegg for fremstilling av Tungt vann vad Vemork Vannstoff-
fabrikk, Rjukan, 9/14/1943. NHM: FOIV, Box D17; Per Dahl, pp. 211–12;
Bericht von Konsul Schöpke über die Besprechungen am 17. und 18.6.1943.
G-341. NB.

"national Norwegian sport": Letter from Ebeling to OKH Wa Forsch,
3/2/1943. G-341, NB.

"swift decision": Ibid; Olsen, p. 417.

The German command: Andersen, pp. 400–404; Report, Gunnerside, April
15, 1943. TNA: HS 2/186.

By the time: Bericht über Konsul Ing. E. Schöpke's Reise und Besprechungen,
3/13/1943. G-341, NB.; Rapport vedrörende anlegg for fremstilling av
Tungt vann vad Vemork Vannstoff-fabrikk, Rjukan, 9/14/1943. NHM:
FOIV, Box D17; Per Dahl, pp. 211–12.

Three weeks later: Niederschrift über die Besprechung am 7.5.1943 i.d. PTR.
G-341, NB.

"Rumors abound in": Karlsch, pp. 162–63.

"uranium bombs": Osenberg, Allgemein verständliche Grundlagen zur
Kernphysik, 5/8/1943. DIA, DJ29.

His team's most: G-212, Bericht über einen Versuch mit Würfeln aus Uran-Metall und Schwerem Eis. Deutsches Museum Archiv; Irving, pp. 174–75.

"too small to": Niederschrift über die Besprechung am 7.5.1943 i.d. PTR. G-341, NB.

Diebner had his: Oral History, Interview with Harteck. NB; Oral History, Interview with Hartwig. NB.

Esau, who had: Niederschrift über die Besprechung am 7.5.1943 i.d. PTR. G-341, NB.

"Vemork reckons on": Message from Swallow, July 8, 1943. NHM: FOIV, Box D17.

Later that month: Letter to Tronstad from Wilson, July 16, 1943. Correspondence 1937-45. DORA.

Later, Selborne hosted: July 21, 1943. LTD; Myklebust, pp. 214–15; Poulsson, p. 160–63; Rønneberg Interview, Moland.

Tronstad was also: Report, "Lurgan," 7/4/1943. LTP; Letter from Brun to Thomas Powers, 10/11/88. VM: J. Brun, Box 17.

More than anything: Tronstad, "Notat vedr. X," July 19, 1943. NHM: Box 10, Folder SISB; Brun, p. 73–77.

"When we say": Letter from Tronstad to Sidsel, August 20, 1943. LTP.

"Remember: Keep your": Interrogation of Knut Haukelid, July 25, 1945. TNA: HS 9/676/4; Report by Bonzo, via Arne Kristoffersen (Kjelstrup), October 1943. NHM: SOE, Box 23.

But no matter: Berg, pp. 141, 144–47.

Soon after, Haukelid: October 13, 1943. ES Diary; Haukelid, p. 158.

Skinnarland welcomed him: Marielle Skinnarland, Notes. ESP.

He was completely: July 11–17, 1943. ES Diary; Marielle Skinnarland, Author Interview.

"The powers that": Letter from Lt. Colonel Sporborg to Brigadier Mockler-Ferryman, October 5, 1943. TNA: HS 2/218; Tube Alloys Technical Committee Meeting, September 19, 1943. TNA: CAB 126/46; Letter from L. C. Hollis to CAS, October 18, 1943. TNA: AIR 8/1767.

The order for: Letter from L. C. Hollis to Sir Charles Portal, October 18, 1943. TNA: AIR 8/1767; Letter from Sir Charles Portal to L. C. Hollis, October 20, 1943. TNA: AIR 8/1767.

"When the weather": Kurzman, p. 188; Letter from Sir Charles Portal to Brigadier Hollis, October 20, 1943. TNA: AIR 8/1767.

Chapter 17

At 3 A.M. on: Interview with Owen Roane. KA.

While Roane shaved: Freeman, pp. 7–15.

The target was: Interview with Owen Roane. KA.

"milk run": Bennett, p. 15.

Although Roane: Interview with Owen Roane. KA; Roane, pp. 1–14.

Three hundred and: Bomber Command Narrative of Operations 131st Operation, November 16, 1943. TNA: AIR 40/481.

They crossed the: Bennett, p. 17.

"Make a circle": Kurzman, p. 197.

Still, 176 Flying: Bomber Command Narrative of Operations 131st Operation, November 16, 1943. TNA: AIR 40/481.

At 11:33 A.M.: Nielsen, Kjell, "Notat angående omtalen av fergeaksjonen på Rjukan i Februar 1944." NHM: Box 10B.

"There are even": Rapport fra luftvernlederen ingeniör Fredriksen over flyangrepet på Vemork Kraftstasjon og Vemork Fabrikkompleks, November 16, 1943. VM: A-1108/Ak, Box 1.

"Run to your": Report by Unnamed Witness. KA.

At 11:43: Mears, pp. 95–101; Bomber Command Narrative of Operations 131st Operation, November 16, 1943. TNA: AIR 40/481; Quotes on Tuesday's Eighth AAF Heavy Bomber Operations, November 16, 1943. TNA: AIR 2/8002.

In total, 711: Bomber Command Narrative of Operations 131st Operation, November 16, 1943. TNA: AIR 40/481; Report, "Norway: Result of USAAF raid on Rjukan, Vemork, December 28, 1943." TNA: AIR 40/481.

Just as the: Attack on Fertilizer Works at Rjukan by USAAF, December 9, 1943. TNA: AIR 2/8002; Eighth Air Force Command Provisional Report, November 18, 1943. TNA: AIR 40/481.

"My God, what's": Kurzman, p. 202.

Rjukan, four miles: Ømkomme under bombingen, November 16, 1943. VM: A-1108/Ak, Box 1; Olsen, p. 419.

The Allies had: Notat vedrörende angrenpene på Rjukan og Vemork, November 16, 1943. NHM: Box 10, Folder SISB.

Tronstad discovered: Aide-Memoire, "The bombing of industrial targets in Norway." TNA: AIR 2/8002; Notat vedrörende angrenpene på Rjukan og Vemork, November 16, 1943. NHM: Box 10, Folder SISB; Letter from Trygve Lie, January 29, 1943. TNA: AIR 2/8002; Letter from A. W. Street, December 22, 1943. TNA: AIR 2/8002.

"filled with explosive": November 5, 1943. LTD.

Chapter 18

Through November: Walker, *German National Socialism*, pp. 100–102; Bericht über die Neutronenvermehrung einer Anordnung von Uranwürfeln und Schwerem Wasser (GIII). Deutsches Museum Archiv; Nagel, pp. 90–92; Irving, pp. 190–92.

"Given the relatively": Bericht über die Neutronenvermehrung einer Anordnung von Uranwürfeln und Schwerem Wasser (GIII). Deutsches Museum Archiv.

His success came: Letter from Göring to Esau, December 2, 1943. NB: Goudsmit Papers, IV, B27, F30; Dahl, p. 219.

Esau's replacement was: Karlsch, pp. 104–105; Nagel, pp. 94–95; Karlsch, pp. 104–105.

On December 11: Protokoll über die in Norsk Hydro Buro, Oslo, December 11, 1943. G-341, NB.

"expose the company's": Ibid.

At the same time: Walker and Karlsch; Nagel, pp. 92–93; Irving, pp. 213–17.

"It is reported": Cipher Message from London, January 29, 1943. TNA: HS 2/188.

That same day: Unpublished Memoir, Papers of Rolf Sørlie.

Neither the Hamarens: Ibid; January 30, 1943. ES Diary.

Back at Nilsbu: Marielle Skinnarland, Author Interview.

On Sunday, February: Unpublished Memoir, Papers of Rolf Sørlie.

"We will probably": Cipher Message from Swallow, February 6, 1943. NHM: SOE, Box 23

An attack still: Letter from Tronstad to Wilson, February 7, 1944. TNA: HS 2/188; February 7, 1942. LTD; Letter from Welsh to Tronstad, February 8, 1944. LTP.

"We will do": February 7, 1943. LTD.

"Einar, you awake?": Drummond, p. 156.

"We are interested": Cipher Message to Swallow, February 8, 1944. TNA: HS 2/188.

Sørlie appeared at: Haukelid, pp. 182–83; Haukelid, Report on the Sinking of the Ferry Hydro, February 20, 1944. NHM: SOE, Box 23; Account Given by Engineer Larsen of the transaction during the attack on Tinnsjø Ferry, February 20, 1944. NHM: SOE, Box 23.

"Agree to sinking": Cipher Message to Swallow, February 10, 1943. NHM: SOE, Box 23.

During Gunnerside: Haukelid Family, Author Interview; Haukelid, p. 182; Unpublished Memoir, Papers of Rolf Sørlie; Cipher Message from Swallow, February 12, 1943. NHM: SOE, Box 23; Letter to SNA, February 17, 1944. NHM: SOE, Box 23B.

"You have to": Unpublished Memoir, Papers of Rolf Sørlie.

On February 13: Ibid; February 13, 1944. ES Diary.

Two days later: "Notat angående omtalen av fergeaksjonen på Rjukan i Februar 1944." NHM: Box 10B; Interrogation of Gunnar Syverstad, April 5, 1944. TNA: HS 2/188; Haukelid, Report on the Sinking of the Ferry Hydro, February 20, 1944. TNA: HS 2/188.

"The matter has": Cipher Message to Swallow, February 16, 1943. NHM: SOE, Box 23.

"I know, it's": Drummond, p. 160.

After the meeting: Diseth, Friends Report. NHM: SOE, Box 23B; Haukelid, Report on the Sinking of the Ferry *Hydro*, February 20, 1944. TNA: HS 2/188; Gallagher, pp. 175–76.

Chapter 19

On February 18: Interview with Haukelid. DIA, DJ31.

As his timetable: Payton; Interrogation of Gunnar Syverstad, April 5, 1944. TNA: HS 2/188; Irving, p. 203.

When Haukelid boarded: Haukelid, Report on the Sinking of the Ferry *Hydro*, February 20, 1944. TNA: HS 2/188; Haukelid, pp. 187–88; Interview with Haukelid. DIA, DJ31; Interview with Haukelid. IWM.

Knut Lier-Hansen was: Interview with Knut Lier-Hansen. KA; Report by Gunlsik Skogen, December 1, 1943. TNA: HS 2/174; Knut Lier-Hansen, Friends Report. NHM: SOE, Box 23B.

That same day: February 18, 1944. LTD; Letter to Michael Perrin, February 15, 1944. TNA: HS 8/955/DISR.

When Skinnarland sent: February 10, 1944. LTD.

Nonetheless, Tronstad: Wilson, John, "On Resistance in Norway." NHM: Box 50A; Interview with Michael Perrin. DIA, DJ31.

Two pops ripped: Haukelid, p. 188.

"At least they": Drummond, p. 162.

Diseth had removed: Haukelid, Report on the Sinking of the Ferry *Hydro*, February 20, 1944. TNA: HS 2/188; Gallagher, p. 176; Interview with Haukelid. DIA, DJ31.

At Vemork on: Account given by Engineer Larsen of the transaction during the attack on Tinnsjø Ferry, February 20, 1944. NHM: SOE, Box 23.

Shortly before midnight: Haukelid, Report on the Sinking of the Ferry *Hydro*, February 20, 1944. TNA: HS 2/188; Interview with Haukelid. DIA, DJ31; Interview with Knut Lier-Hansen. KA; Haukelid, pp. 191–93; Drummond, pp. 167–70; Gallagher, pp. 179–82; Account by Engineer Larsen of the transaction during the attack on Tinnsjø Ferry, February 20, 1944. NHM: SOE, Box 23; Unpublished Memoir, Papers of Rolf Sørlie. Other than specifically noted quotes, the narrative of the placing of the explosives aboard the D/F *Hydro* is drawn from these sources collectively.

"Is that you": Gallagher, p. 181; Haukelid, Report on the Sinking of the Ferry *Hydro*, February 20, 1944. TNA: HS 2/188; Sikkerhetspoliti Rapport av John Berg, February 21, 1944. NHM: Box 10B.

"I'll be back": Drummond, p. 171.

Chapter 20

On Sunday morning: Vedr. D/F *Hydro* forlis 2/20/1944. VM: IA4FB, Box 13; Irving, p. 209.

At Kongsberg: Haukelid, p. 195.

From a hillside: Interview with Lier-Hansen. KA.

It was a cold: Raport Sørensen, February 21, 1944. VM: IA4FB, Box 13; *Aftenposten*, February 23, 1944. TNA: HS 2/188; *Fritt Folk*, February 23, 1944. TNA: HS 2/188; *Rjukan Dagblad*, February 22, 1944. TNA: HS 2/188. Interview with Eva Gulbrandsen. KA; Omkomne D/F *Hydro*, February 20, 1944. VM: IA4FB, Box 13.

"Steer toward land!": Raport Sørensen, February 21, 1944. VM: IA4FB, Box 13.

"A bomb!": Interview with Eva Gulbrandsen. KA.

Four minutes after: Haukelid, p. 197; Omkomne D/F *Hydro*, February 20, 1944. VM: IA4FB, Box 13.

"Railway Ferry *Hydro*": Haukelid, pp. 195–202; IWM; Haukelid Family, Author Interview.

On February 26: February 26–March 7, 1944. LTD.

"Very soon I": Karlsch, pp. 166–67.

Few people believed: Irving, pp. 217–19; Bericht uber die Arbeiten auf Kernphysikalischen Gebiet. NB: Goudsmit Papers, IV, B25, F13.

"Germany had no": Goudsmit, p. 71; Alsos Mission Report. DIA, DJ31.

But at the start: NB: Oral History, Interview with Hartwig; Nagel, pp. 129–30; Cassidy, p. 496.

After Germany surrendered: Powers, pp. 434–35; Bagge et al., pp. 51–55.

"shattered": Frank, p. 70.

"the greatest destructive": Bernstein and Cassidy, Appendix C.

"the obliteration": Bagge et al., p. 35.

Epilogue

On May 8: Report of Operation Sunshine. TNA: HS 2/171; Herrington, pp. 283–85; Military Homefront Survey, December 1, 1944. NHM: SOE, Box 4.

A month after: Colonel Wilson, Diary of a Scandinavian Tour. TNA: HS 9/1605/3.

They had all: TNA: HS 9/676/2; TNA: HS 9/1424/2; TNA: HS 9/824/2; TNA: HS 9/1420/7.

Einar Skinnarland's children: Marielle Skinnarland, Author Interview.

"smallness of being": Interview with Rønneberg. IWM.

Knut Haugland lived: Haugland Family, Author Interview.

Only in his last: Marielle Skinnarland, Author Interview.

"the major industrial": Appendix A, Sunshine Action Plans. NHM: Box 10C.

Many former Kompani: Report of Operation Sunshine. TNA: HS 2/171.

On the night of: Skinnarland Report on the Deaths of Major Tronstad and Sergeant Syverstad, March 16, 1945. TNA: HS 2/171; Njølstad, pp. 410–24.

"Dearest Bassa": Letter from Tronstad to Bassa, August 27, 1944. LTP.

"I love you": Lunde, p. 213.

"You have to fight": "If Hitler Had the Bomb," transcript from documentary at the Norsk Industriarbeidermuseum, Vemork.

Cover top: Norges Hjemmefrontmuseum; bottom: Norsk Hydro/Norsk Industriarbeidermuseum; xxii: Rainer Lesniewski/Shutterstock; 4: ullstein bild via Getty Images; 8: National Archives of Norway via Flickr; 10: Haukelid Family Collection; 13,14: Norges Hjemmefrontmuseum; 16: Schrøder/Sverresborg Trøndelag Folkemuseum; 18: Norges Hjemmefrontmuseum; 20: Hardanger Folkemuseum; 21: Friedrich Saurer/Science Source; 22: Norsk Hydro/Norsk Industriarbeidermuseum; 23: Norges Hjemmefrontmuseum; 25: Heinrich Pniok www.pse-mendelejew.de; 27: AIP Emilio Segre Visual Archives; 28: Peter Hermes Furian/Shutterstock; 30: US National Archives and Records Administration, courtesy AIP Emilio Segre Visual Archives; 31: Sueddeutsche Zeitung Photo/ Alamy; 37: J. A. Hampton/Topical Press Agency/Getty Images; 39: LAPI/Roger Viollet/Getty Images; 42: US National Archives and Records Administration; 44-45,47: Norges Hjemmefrontmuseum; 49: The Longum Collection/Norsk Industriarbeidermuseum; 51: Norges Hjemmefrontmuseum; 54: Skinnarland Family Collection; 57: Norges Hjemmefrontmuseum; 58: Erich Lessing/Art Resource, NY; 60: dpa/picture-alliance/AP Images; 65: Keystone-France/ Gamma-Keystone via Getty Images; 68,69,71,73,76,80,83: Norges Hjemmefrontmuseum; 86: courtesy of Tun Abdul Razak Research Centre, Brickendonbury, Hertford, UK; 92: Freia Beer/Orkla Industrimuseum; 98-99: Charles E. Brown/Royal Air Force Museum/Getty Images; 100: Signals Collection '40-'45, www.SignalsCollection.nl; 108,110,111,112: Norges Hjemmefrontmuseum; 114: Haukelid Family Collection; 115: The Longum Collection/Norsk Industriarbeidermuseum; 117: Photograph by Samuel Goudsmit, courtesy AIP Emilio Segre Visual Archives, Goudsmit Collection; 121: Lex Peverelli; 129: Eric Chretien/Gamma-Raphovia Getty Images; 134,136: Norges Hjemmefrontmuseum; 139: Haukelid Family Collection; 148-149,152: Norges Hjemmefrontmuseum; 154: Hero Film/Ronald Grant Archive/Alamy; 158,161: Norsk HYDRO/Norsk Industriarbeidermuseum; 170: Norsk Industriarbeidermuseum; 172: Norges Hjemmefrontmuseum; 186: Corbis; 198: AIP Emilio Segre Visual Archives; 200-201,204: Norges Hjemmefrontmuseum; 206,207: Courtesy of 100th Bomb Group www.100thbg.com; 208-209: Norges Hjemmefrontmuseum; 212: The Frognes collection/Norsk Industriarbeidermuseum; 214: Norges Hjemmefrontmuseum; 216: AIP Emilio Segre Visual Archives; 224: Haukelid Family Collection; 228: Norges Hjemmefrontmuseum; 230: Private collection/Norsk Industriarbeidermuseum; 237,240-241: Anders Beer Wilse, Norsk Folkemuseum; 242: Jürgen Sorges/AKG Images; 248-249: AP Photo; 251 top: Norges Hjemmefrontmuseum; 251 bottom: O. H. Skinnarland Family Photo; 252,254; Norges Hjemmefrontmuseum; 256-257: Jürgen Sorges /AKG Images.

p. x: Northern Europe, June 1940: *The Atlas of the Second World War* by John Keegan

p. 90: Grouse's Arrival in Norway; Jens-Anton Poulsson, Knut Werner Hagen

p. 104: Operation Freshman; Per Johnsen

p. 124: Grouse Hideouts; Jens-Anton Poulsson, Knut Werner Hagen

p. 146: Gunnerside's Landing; Jens-Anton Poulsson, Knut Werner Hagen

p. 174-175: Attack on Vemork; Jens-Anton Poulsson

p. 184: Gunnerside's Retreat; Joachim Rønneberg

Map p. x by Jim McMahon

Maps pp. 90, 104, 124, 146, 174-175, 184 by Svein Vetle Trae/Fossøy, redrawn for Scholastic by Jim McMahon

INDEX

Note: Page numbers in *italics* refer to illustrations.

This book was edited by Cheryl Klein and designed by Phil Falco, with photo research by Els Rijpers. The text was set in Stempel Garamond, with display type set in Bureau Agency. Maya Frank-Levine oversaw the production. This book was printed and bound by R. R. Donnelley in Crawfordsville, Indiana. The manufacturing was supervised by Angelique Browne.